Mathematics Education Atlas: Mapping the Field of Mathematics Education Research

CHRISTOPHER H. DUBBS, PH.D.

Printed in the United States of America

FIRST EDITION

ISBN PB: 978-1-952352-04-1
ISBN HC: 978-1-952352-05-8

Published by:
Crave Press
www.cravepress.com

DEDICATION

To Edward, Mom, and Dad—
I couldn't have written this book without your support.

To Tonya, Beth, Lynn, and Amy—
I wouldn't have had the courage to write this book without your encouragement.

To Molade and Missy—
I couldn't have finished this book without your company.

To the reader—
I hope that this book makes you feel *freer*, that it helps you to navigate the field of mathematics education research. May you find the bubbles you seek or breathe life into new ones.

CONTENTS

DETAILED CONTENTS

ACKNOWLEDGEMENTS

The proverb goes that "it takes a village to raise a child." I also know that it takes a village to finish a dissertation, and later, to turn that dissertation into a book. The writing that follows is my own but, without the support of the village around me, these ideas would have never made it onto paper in the form that they did. This is a thank you letter to my village.

First, I have to thank my husband, Edward. Without your support, I would have never finished. You spent late nights with me, listened to me even when I rambled about Foucault and Rancière, nodded when I just needed someone to agree, and looked at pictures when I couldn't see their beauty. You were my rock throughout this adventure, and I can never say thank you enough—I love you.

Second, I have to thank my parents, Holly and Harold. You both instilled a love of learning in me, always telling me that I was capable of anything—I love you both.

Third, I have to thank my besties Mo and Missy. Mo you've been my cohort bestie, the best officemate, and I'm so glad we experienced our first AMTE conference together. Since our grad school adventure began, I've been so very thankful for you. From practicum, comps, dissertation proposal, and dissertation writing and defense: we've had each other's back (and always will). Missy, we weren't in PriME together, but we you were in my first semester ProSem so that's close enough. Thank you for being so awesome and doing the amazing work that you do. The three of us will always live our #WildcatsPHD life: we're all in this together.

Third, I have to thank my committee:

- Tonya, as my advisor, you always cheered me on. You always supported me in the work that I do and gave me the courage to keep pushing and to keep working.
- Lynn, for giving me the language to talk about my passion for philosophy of education, the courage to submit an article to the Journal of Philosophy of Education, and for helping me to see that I'm 'freer than I think.' I am forever indebted to you for introducing me to Rancière—I hope I'll always embody the ignorant schoolmaster.
- Beth, from supporting my first paper in queer theory during ProSem, to the opportunity to work and write together on MDISC, and finally to my dissertation, you've been one of the few to see my development across all five years—thank you.
- Amy, I still vividly recall you coming to talk to my qualitative methods class about your research. You were the first person that I can remember hearing sound passionate about what they do. I always knew I needed to find that passion in my own work; you've inspired me.

Fourth, to Christina and David, my family at Crave Press. Thank you for your excitement about this work and your support getting it to publication. May we have a fruitful future together.

Fifth, the financial support of Michigan State University College of Natural Science's Dissertation Continuation Fellowship, Michigan State University College of Natural Science's Dissertation Completion Fellowship, Michigan State University Program in Mathematics Education's Lappan-Phillips-Fitzgerald Fellowship were vital in supporting the dissertation that would eventually become this book.

Last, to Ranciere, Foucault, and Sloterdijk, for giving me the language to name what I see as the sensible limits of the present, to recognize the (severable) dependence of those limits on the past, and the tools (and courage) to imagine a different future. May the field of mathematics education research continue to be as fluid as it has been. Let us not congeal into something fixed, but through the emergence of new bubbles be invigorated.

LIST OF TABLES

LIST OF FIGURES

1   INTRODUCTION

My role - and that is too emphatic a word - is to show people that they are much freer than they feel, that people accept as truth, as evidence, some themes which have been built up at a certain moment during history, and that this so-called evidence can be criticized and destroyed. (Foucault, 1988, p. 10).

I can't, says the ignorant one who wants to withdraw from the task… I can't, says the student who doesn't want to submit his improvisation to his peers' judgment. I don't understand your method, someone says; I'm incompetent; I don't understand anything about it. (Rancière, 1991, p. 79).

Whenever I feel overly constrained, as though I have no options for maneuvering in a situation, I am reminded of this quote by Foucault. I seek the loophole, the compliant—even if a bit a subversive—solution that pushes the boundaries slightly. "Leave spaces freer than when you entered," my mantra, if I can be said to have one. Then it happens, I feel a sense of freedom, a breath of fresh air, and Foucault haunts me: I can be *freer*, even when I can't imagine what freer looks like. Therein, at the can't, Rancière steps in and refuses to let me idle. "I can't imagine" is really an "I won't imagine;" incapacity masquerading as unwillingness, incapacity masquerading as modesty. Thinking against the distribution of the sensible (Rancière, 2004) within which we find ourselves, thinking against the for-granted demarcations and delimitations of the sensible—what can be seen, said, or thought in a particular social space—is tiring work. But this is not only *my* work, it is *ours*. This work of looking at, and beyond, the borders of the field of mathematics education research can be taken-up by any one, or any number of ones, but has not been to any large extent.

As an emerging scholar, I was expected to survey the field of mathematics education research and to situate my work with respect to the "ongoing conversations". The imperative to "connect to mathematics teaching and learning" is a constraint, to "connect to ongoing conversations in the field" is a constraint. More than constraints, constraints under which I don't feel particularly free, these imperatives are political proclamations (Rancière, 2000): these statements attempt to establish a dividing line along which some research can be classified as proper and, therefore, should be included while others do not, and should not, count. In this sense, then, as I eventually argue that what counts should be broadened, that what mathematics education research includes should be refigured and reconfigured across time, this book is political.

The metaphorical language of "surveying the field" suggested that there could be a "map," one that shows the conversations and what conversation groups were in conversation with others. Yet, no such map existed. The field of mathematics education research, which I have operationalized as the collection of all research articles published in the name of mathematics education research, is multi-faceted: who wrote it, when was it published, what ideas they cited, how it was later taken up, etc. But, are "mathematics education research" and "research on the teaching and learning of mathematics" synonyms? I'm not convinced they are; the former contains a larger body of work than the words teaching and learning contain. Where is the knowing? The doing? The being? Looking across one slice in the development of the North American field of mathematics education research, namely those articles published in the *Journal for Research in Mathematics Education* from 1970 to present, I provide cartographic insight into the shifting landscape of our field (Chapter 4). Supplementing the full cartography of the JRME are maps of those articles published in *For the Learning of Mathematics* (Chapter 5) and *Educational Studies in Mathematics* (Chapter 6) in the 2010s.

Drawing on algorithmic graph theory and computational network analysis (Chapter 3), I mapped over 90 years of data from these three prominent mathematics education research journals. These maps are citation networks: each published article and each of the articles, books, chapters, etc. they cite are represented with circles and two circles are connected with directed line segments ($\cdot\rightarrow\circ$) if one cites the other. The radius of the circle is proportional to the number of times it is cited (larger circles are more cited). To place these representations onto a planar map, however, is not trivial. I leverage an extant algorithm (ForceAtlas2) that interprets circles as electrons and line segments as extended springs. By simulating this physical system of electron repulsion and spring contraction, ForceAtlas2 runs until a stable state is found. The resulting map encodes the relationship between articles spatially. In the stable state, articles which are close together are strongly connected in the ideas that they use, whereas those farther apart have fewer, or no, citations in common. The resulting maps then give snapshots into the state of the field of mathematics education research across time and in different journals.

To identify the conversation groups, then, I use a well-documented community finding algorithm (i.e., Louvain Modularity) to find densely connected subsets of articles. These densely connected subsets correspond to the conversation groups within the field of mathematics education research. For example, this algorithm identifies one cluster of research where scholars are studying computers in mathematics education, and other clusters group those interested in equity, discourse, problem solving, psychology of learning, pedagogical content knowledge, international comparative assessment, and more.

My project, though much less ambitious than Foucault's, is twofold: (1) to show and name the limits of mathematics education research as a field and (2) to consider what might be possible if what *can be* mathematics education research is severed from *what is* and *has been* mathematics education research. While I have presented my project as a duality, these two threads are intertwined and my methods for addressing each are necessarily entangled. In chapter 4, in the study of the JRME, I show that what has counted as mathematics education research in that journal has shifted across time. By bringing the findings of chapters 4, 5, and 6 together in the discussion (Chapter 7), I am able to show that what currently constitutes mathematics education research is different in different spaces. These two results together, then, suggest that there is not a fixed object that constitutes the proper object of mathematics education research. Instead, each of these views constitute partages of the sensible in mathematics education research—demarcations and delimitations of what is sensible as mathematics education research—what can be seen, said, or thought as mathematics education research. Since what has been has not been constant and there is not currently a consensus on what is mathematics education research, it is easier to think of alternatives. There are several theories that orient this work, that influence my interpretation of these maps and shape the claims I make; I introduce them next (Chapter 2).

2   THEORETICAL ORIENTATIONS

I am more than a linear thinker. Linear thinking is characterized by sequential, logico-deductive, rational processing of information (Groves & Vance, 2014). Non-linear thinking, furthermore, is "greatly influenced by fundamental assumptions of reality based on reductionism and determinism" (p. 112). Contrasted with linear thinking is non-linear thinking: nonsequential, automatic, unconscious, and experiential strategies of information processing that include intuition, emotion, values, insight, creativity, and imagination (Groves & Vance, 2014). Non-linear or multidimensional thinking is a "valuable decision-making resource that complements and may extend individual capacity beyond that which is restricted to rational, linear thinking" (p. 113). In this chapter—and from this non-linear perspective—I introduce the various theories that influenced the framing, analysis, and findings of this study. The form of a book, with its numbered and ordered pages, however, requires a linear structure.

While what follows is a sequential presentation beginning with researching mathematics education research, moving to a Foucaultian perspective on history, then to Sloterdijkian concepts of bubbles and foams, before culminating with Rancièrean equality and distribution of the sensible, the process of coming to these theories was not so straightforward. Nevertheless, I hope this sequence guides you from a general orientation towards this work, to the ideas that motivated my decision to tell a history of mathematics education research, the ideas that influenced my interpretation of that history that I formed, and the ideas that outline one path forward that I have chosen to take. But I ask you, the reader, to only hold this ordering as contingent, for "I don't think an author should lay down the law about his own book... It's hard to say whether a book has been understood or misunderstood. Because, after all, perhaps the person who wrote the book is the one who misunderstood it" (Foucault, 2011, p. 385). The sections that follow might be read in a different order—to greater effect, persuasion, or cohesion—you are invited to do so. Recall, however, that you never needed my permission to stray from this order: "[people] are much freer than they feel" (Foucault, 1988, p. 10).

Researching Research and Producing Multiple Knowledges

> When a field begins to raise questions not only about its primary object of study, but also about itself and its status as a science, this is usually called reflexivity. (Bloor, 1976; Bourdieu, 2001). Such has been the case for many social sciences that, at a certain point of their development, turn back upon themselves to investigate their own ways of working. (Pais & Valero, 2012, p. 10, emphasis in original).

Pais and Valero (2012) use the phrase "researching research" to denote the mathematics education research that takes as its unit of analysis mathematics education research itself. Others have called this looking back reflexivity (e.g., Bourdieu, 2001), but I have chosen to call my own work "researching research" since "reflexivity is a central tenet of a feminist methodology whereby the researcher documents the production of knowledge and locates herself in this process" (Mauthner, 2000) and my project is less about how my own location influences the knowledges I can produce and more on interrogating the research done by the collective of researchers producing knowledges within the field of mathematics education research:

Following Foucault, the production of knowledge is an exercise of power, which makes it possible for some concepts, ideas, and theories to be thought easily and for some concepts, ideas, and theories to be impossible (or nearly so) to be thought. Ideas are not seen as located within individual minds but as truths shared through retelling in communities. (Parks & Schmeichel, 2012, p. 241)

This is not to say that I do not believe that a researcher does not influence the knowledges they produce; indeed, I believe nearly the opposite: "the knower and the known are intertwined" (Doll, 1989, p. 248). And, as queer theorist Anzaldúa says, "there is no way that I can put myselves through this sieve, and say okay, I'm only going to let the 'lesbian' part out, and everything else will stay in the sieve. All the multiple aspects of identities (as well as the sieve) are part of the 'lesbian'" (Anzaldúa, 1991, p. 252-3). Anzaldúa is responding to critics suggesting that her writing was too Chicana and not lesbian enough for her queer audience, instead arguing that there is no way to separate the various facets of her identity; as such, there is no way that I as a researcher can hold back aspects of my identity and only let out the "mathematics education researcher" when I conduct mathematics education research (Dubbs, 2016).

My identity, however, is not the only aspect of my experiences that influence the knowledges I can produce. Fendler summarizes Foucault's theory of power-knowledge thus:

In chemistry, we get different products depending on which substances are combined in what quantities under which conditions. Foucault's theory of power-knowledge is something like that. We get different products of knowledge depending on which beliefs are combined with what societies under which political conditions. Foucault studied history to learn more about how various combinations of factors and power relations produced one kind of knowledge rather than another. (Fendler, 2010, p. 53)

Then, in addition to my identity, the society in which I exist, the perspective whence I observe, the theories that I employ, and the data that I analyze each influence the conclusions I can draw, the knowledges I can produce. I have represented Foucault's theory of power-knowledge with the equation shown at the top of Figure 1. Substituting the relevant concepts from this study to this equation, yields, the equation shown at the bottom of Figure 1 (with the addition of "& perspective" as knowledge production is also influenced by the perspectives I take on research). Knowledges are produced by applying theories to observations within particular contexts. In the present analysis, then, knowledges about mathematics education research as a field are produced by applying Foucaultian, Rancièrean, and Sloterdijkian theories to citation data within this particular mathematics education context and from my particular perspective.

Figure 1. Equations showing my interpretation of Foucault's theory of power-knowledge (top) and an application of that theory to this study (bottom).

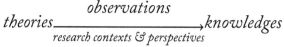

$$theories \frac{observations}{research\ contexts\ \&\ perspectives} \rightarrow knowledges$$

$$\frac{Foucault}{Rancière}\frac{citation\ data}{mathematics\ education\ research\ context} \rightarrow knowledges$$
$$Sloterdijk\ _{researcher\ context\ \&\ perpsectives}$$

The result of my researching research then, will be only one of many potential productions of knowledge. Others who have undertaken researching research have produced knowledges such as "learning has been used to make school mathematics an efficient mechanism of bio-politics and…mathematics functions as the sublime object of the field's ideology, making it difficult for researchers to conceive of its importance in terms of there than knowledge and competence" (Pais & Valero, 2012, p. 11), "as a community of researchers in mathematics education, we need to help each other increase the accuracy and integrity of our citation practices" (Leatham, 2015), "JRME and ESM are the two most cited and respected journals in our field by a substantial margin" (Williams & Leatham, 2017, p. 389), and "citation-based metrics are most appropriately interpreted as a direct measure of article impact but only an indirect measure of journal impact" (Nivens & Otten, 2017

I am indebted to the groundwork laid by these researchers yet have chosen to proceed on a different path. The method of this analysis, detailed in Chapter 2, is citation network mapping. This method draws upon computational graph theory, citation network analysis, and cartography to draw maps of articles published in three High- and Very-High-Quality journals (Williams & Leatham, 2017) in mathematics education: *The Journal for Research in Mathematics Education, Educational Studies in Mathematics*, and *For the Learning of Mathematics*. These maps will show the articles published, each of the references that those articles cite, and trace the connections from published article to cited reference, to understand which articles are highly-cited and which topics constitute research foci within the field. Inglis and Foster (2018) undertook researching research from a linguistic perspective (word co-occurrence), studying how the topics the field of mathematics education research has shifted across the past five decades. The research foci that I identify will be contrasted with those identified by the by Inglis and Foster (2018) in Chapter 7. This novel method and study will contribute to the body of works concerned with researching research.

Mirrors as Levers: Foucault on History

Objective history is meant to function like a mirror that provides us with a reflection of the past. In contrast, effective history is meant to function like a lever that disrupts our assumptions and understandings about who we think we are. Foucault's history, with its provocative and ironic stance, conveys the message that mirrors make the best levers. (Fendler, 2010, p. 42).

In the spring semester of 2017, I took a humanities-oriented research course. In one of the early weeks, before we read about Foucault's historiography, I asked a question "If history is the study of what has been, what is the study of what could be?." Lynn Fendler's response: philosophy. I share this story for two reasons. First, I share this story to show how my understanding of history has changed. Originally, I equated history writ large with objective history, with a way to look back and tell the story of what has been. Now, my own ideas about history have moved much closer to Foucault's, particularly when considering that those stories preserved in the archives, those stories told in the annals of history, are precisely those who were included, in positions of privilege, wealth, authority, or some combination of the three (Rancière, 1994): history as an objective mirror is fraught with inequality.

What at first seems to be a limitation (inequality), however, can also be history's advantage. If the official record, the image that we see when looking back, is the story of those included, instead of focusing on the visible, we can shift our gaze towards the invisible . Looking at the invisible—the gaps, the margins, the borders–to see what is missing, what is excluded, and what is outside the neat picture that we are presented, claiming to tell what was, can instead tell us what was excluded and ignored; this can tell us what we can work towards including moving forward. It is for this reason, that I believe that mirrors (looking back) make the best levers. By looking back at what has been done in the name of mathematics education research, by looking at what has been published in three prestigious mathematics education research journals (this historian's archive), and by mapping the references cited in those journals, I am able to see one story of what *has been*. Within those images of what has been, however, we can also see gaps, margins, and borders, specters of what also was, but was not deemed worthy of inclusion. These gaps indicate some (but not all) of the areas to develop moving forward.

Second, I share this story to show how chance figures into my own story; it is only because of Fendler's course that Foucault and the idea that mirrors can be levers came onto my radar. This notion of chance, that things can happen in unexpected and unpredictable ways, is another characteristic of Foucault's history:

> Foucault celebrated the role of chance in history because chance makes change easier to imagine. If we do not think of history as proceeding in some inevitable or predictable manner, then history is not so deterministic, and it is easier for us to imagine that things might be different in the future. (Fendler, 2010, p. 42.)

Thus, if I am able to look back, to see a story of what has been and show that what has been done in the name of mathematics education research has shifted across time, that what has been included, and therefore excluded, has neither been fixed nor progressive—thereby arguing that what is included (and excluded) today is not the inevitable accomplishment of directed action by a cohesive collection of researchers—I might be able to restore the role of chance in the field. In fact, my goal is to show that the research foci of our field of mathematics education research are "neither discovered truths nor preordained developments, but rather the products of conglomerations of blind forces" (Prado, 1995, p. 38). This tracing of what has been, it turns out, is precisely the lever that I unpack in the next section. This lever will enable me to use "what *has been done* in mathematics education research" as a lever to change "what *can be done* in mathematics education research."

Bubbles and Foam: Sloterdijkian Reading of Scientific Fields

> Politics is commonly viewed as the practice of power or the embodiment of collective wills and interests and the enactment of collective ideas. Now, such enactments or embodiments imply that you are taken into account as subjects sharing in a common world, making statements and not simply noise, discussing things located in a common world and not in your own fantasy. (Rancière, 2004, p. 10).

Jacques Rancière is a political philosopher and a philosopher of equality. Rancière's notion of politics, however, is not equivalent to the practice of power mentioned in the epigraph. Instead, for Rancière, politics consists of redefining who is taken into account, who has a share in the common world, whose speech is classified as statements and not noise, and whose fantasy becomes part of a

6

common world (2004, 2009). From this perspective, then, my goal is political since I wish to reconfigure what we can do, say, and think in the name of mathematics education research. My first step is to consider a different metaphor for the field of mathematics education research, a metaphor "to counter the view of the emergent as inevitable" (Prado, 1995, p. 38).

I have heard the field mathematics education research described as a cocktail party, a group of individuals mingling in a common space (we might call that salon mathematics education) and gathering into small groups, each having their own conversations (these conversations constitute different research foci). From this metaphor, our role as emerging scholars is to distinguish the conversations from the cacophony, to listen to the conversation, then slip into the ongoing conversation (cite exiting research). This perspective, however, limits what we can do. We cannot step into a group and begin talking about something new, we need to join the conversation that is already happening.

Instead of thinking of the field of mathematics education research as a cocktail party, I propose that we consider bubbles and foam (Sloterdijk 2011, 2016). By way of analogue, the conversation groups of the cocktail party correspond to the bubbles and the cocktail party itself corresponds to the foam. Sloterdijk, in his Spheres Trilogy comprised of *Bubbles* (2011), *Globes* (2014), and *Foams* (2016), offered a theorization of space and the places that people take up in space. For Sloterdijk, "humans live in spheres which give them meaning and provide them with a protective membrane" (Borch, 2010, p. 224). These spheres, the contained spaces in which people attain meaning, are bubbles and these bubbles constitute "microspherical worlds" (p. 226) each with their own rules for who is taken into account, who has a share in that micro-world, whose speech is classified as noise, and whose fantasy is valued in that common world. These bubbles correspond to the distinct research foci within the field of mathematics education research: each bubble of research has its own knowledge base, its own experts, its own expectations for research methods, types of findings, etc. The field of mathematics education research is not, however, merely an agglomeration of bubbles, it is a foam.

First, the foam metaphor is helpful since, from afar, a foam looks like a solid object. From afar, mathematics education research seems like an ontologically solid object, something that is and has been: fixed, inevitable, undeniable. Yet, from up close, we can see that the foam is comprised of many bubbles. Foams of bubbles "are fragile and protected by frail membranes, immunity maintenance is a crucial concern" (Borch, 2010, p. 232). Within the mathematics education context, these research bubbles are not fixed, they are volatile. It is necessary for those located within a particular research bubble to work towards maintaining the bubble's boundary since bubbles are cofragile: the if one bubble pops, the neighboring bubbles will be affected (Borch, 2010). Bubbles within a foam can burst, merge, and split; new bubbles can emerge.

Second, this metaphor, together with a Foucaultian reading of history, gives us an understanding of the field of mathematics education research wherein "it is easier for us to imagine that things might be different in the future" (Fendler, 2010, p. 42), since we no longer need to change the field as a whole, nor change the conversations happening with groups of people, but rather split, burst, merge, or emerge. Revisiting Rancière, our levers need not be large, we need not burst all the bubbles, we need not completely reconfigure the foam at once: "change is the result of a thousand creeping encroachments" (Rancière, 2000, para. 8).

What can be seen, said, and thought: Rancière's Distribution of the Sensible

> The distribution of the sensible refers to the implicit law governing the sensible order that parcels out places and forms of participation in a common world by first establishing the modes of perception...a system of self-evident facts of perception based on the set horizons and modalities of what is visible and audible as well as what can be said, thought, made, or done. (Rancière, 2009, p. 89.)

Rancière's distribution [*partage*] of the sensible is "the system of self-evident facts of sense perception that simultaneously discloses the existence of something in common and the delimitations that define the respective parts and positions within it" (Rancière, 2009, p. 12). In other words, a partage of the sensible is a set of implicit laws that govern what we can see, say, or do as mathematics education research (the thing in common). It further indicates what is sensible: how the ways of doing, seeing, and saying fit together (parts and positions within it). Therefore, when we look at some article, book, or dissertation and decide if it is mathematics education research, if it fits within the coordinates that we use to determine if something makes sense as mathematics education research, we are operating within a particular partage of the sensible.

Each journal that publishes mathematics education research has its own aims and scope. These journal aims outline the expectations for topic, included content, acceptable theories and analyses, types of conclusions, etc. As a result, "the distribution of the sensible reveals who can have a share in what is common to the community based on what they do and on the time and space in which this activity is performed." (Rancière, 2004, p. 12). So, within the 1970s when quantitative analyses providing statistically generalizable results were dominant (see Chapter 3), there was little room or acceptance for qualitative studies: this would outline a particular partage of the sensible. Today, however, a variety of methods, foci, theories, etc. are acceptable: this outlines another partage of the sensible. Since journals often prescribe that authors connect to the ongoing conversations within their journals (bubbles), these constitute partages of sensible research. I am interested in which ideas appear in multiple partages and which appear in fewer (or are absent completely) since "the more frequently certain ideas are produced in speech and writing, the more true they seem, and the less often certain ideas appear, the less possible they seem" (Parks & Schmeichel, 2012, p. 241)

Each of Chapter 3, Chapter 4, and Chapter 5 outline partages of mathematics education research. In Chapter 3, I outline the partage of research within the *Journal for Research in Mathematics Education*. I present the bubbles and foam of each decade from the 1970s to the 2010s to show how the bubbles and foam change across time, showing evidence of the volatility of these foams. In Chapters 4 and 5, I show the partage of research outlined by the research published within *For the Learning of Mathematics* (FLM) and *Educational Studies in Mathematics* (ESM), respectively. By naming the bubbles within the JRME 2010s foam, the FLM 2010s foam, and the ESM 2010s foam, I show the differences between what constitutes mathematics education research between different journals. Showing this variation likewise shows that what is mathematics education research is not fixed, there is variation in what can be mathematics education research. This furthermore shows the disagreement on what constitutes mathematics education research:

Disagreement is not the conflict between one who says white and another who says black. It is the conflict between one who says white and another who also says white but does not understand the same thing by it or does not understand that the other is saying the same thing in the name of whiteness. (Rancière, 1999, p. x.)

My goal in the end, however, is not to reach a consensual definition of mathematics education research. Establishing a singular and totalizing definition of what mathematics education research is and can be would necessarily lead to policing (Rancière, 1999), of ensuring compliance to the given definition and of maintaining the boundary to mitigate its fragility (Borch, 2010). Instead, my aim is to institute and maintain a politics of aesthetics of mathematics education research—of constant refiguration of what we can see, say, think, and do in the name of mathematics education research. Taking these theories together, then, indicates a primary goal of this book: to perturb the sensible. Perturb the Sensible as changing the coordinates that figure what is sensible as mathematics education research, in what we can see, say, think, and do in the name of mathematics education research.

Eschewing the Literature Review

In this chapter, and indeed book, I did not provide (and will not be providing) a literature review. One definition of the literature review is "a written document that presents a logically argued case founded on a comprehensive understanding of the current state of knowledge about a topic of study" (Machi & McEvoy, 2016, p. 5). Yet, no comprehensive understanding can be recorded, no account of the literature of the field on a given topic can be complete, "no history includes everything about everything" (Fendler, 2010, p. 41), and I will not pretend that it can be. I could list and describe the 96 articles in the ERIC database that cite Rancière. I could tell you that of the four articles in the ERIC database that cite Sloterdijk, only one cites his Spheres trilogy that I use in this study. I could refer you to any number of the literature reviews on Foucault or construct my own. But each of these moves serves a similar purpose, to locate the present work within the coordinates of a common world, to establish my inquiry as proper mathematics education research, to prove my membership within the common world of mathematics education research, to assert that what follows is not noise but speech (Rancière, 2004).

My goal, however, is not assimilation, but liberation (Dubbs, 2016). I do not wish to outline the existing coordinates by which we locate and define mathematics education research and to situate my work within them; I aim to bring those very coordinates into question, to perturb the distribution of the sensible that outlines what makes sense as mathematics education research. Part of this goal, then, takes the shape of rejecting that a review of literature that establishes how the present study is novel or necessary. Knowledges are not cumulative, they are plural: I do not build onto an existing knowledge base in a progressive way but provide but one of many possible additional knowledges in the foam of mathematics education research. Nevertheless, I hope you accompany me on the journey that follows.

The text that follows may be disorienting, it may feel like uncomfortable chaos, but critical moments are "disturbing and disorienting moments, precisely because we lose our moorings at these moments, do not always know how to locate ourselves, do not know what it is we have thought we have always known" (Butler, 2000). Through these critical moments, we can change:

Change always starts with confusion; cherished interpretations must dissolve to make way for the new. Of course, it's scary to give up what we know, but the abyss is where newness lives...I want to sit down with you and talk about all the frightening and hopeful things I observe, and listen to what frightens you and gives you hope...I need to learn to value your perspective, and I want you to value mine. I expect to be disturbed, even jarred, by what I hear from you. I expect to feel confused and displaced—my world won't feel as stable or familiar to me once we talk...As I explore my willingness to be disturbed, I'm learning that we don't have to agree with each other to think well together. There is no need for us to be joined at the head. We are joined already by our human hearts" (Wheatley, 2005, p. 213)

3   A SENSIBLE INTRODUCTION TO CITATION NETWORKS

Imagine a connect-the-dots image where a seemingly random layout of dots, numbered sequentially from 1 to 2 to 3 to some n, are placed. The rule of engagement for these dots is simple: draw a line segment from 1 to 2, then from 2 to 3, and from 3 to 4, and so on, until the final *n*th dot. Images composed of multiple sequences of dots might denote different sequences by prepending letters (e.g., a1, a2, …), by using sequences of numbers and sequences of letters (e.g., 1, 2, 3, … and a, b, c, …), or by color coding the dots. After connecting the dots and viewing the whole connected sequences of dots, an image takes form. Such an image is not unlike a citation network.

A citation network uses dots to represent articles, books, book chapters, websites, videos, and any other reference that some collection of works cites. Instead of numbers, these dots are labelled with an author and year (e.g., Fennema, 1974). Unlike a dot-to-dot image, the dots are not connected sequentially but, instead, the first dot is connected to another if it cites the work represented by the second dot. Furthermore, these dots are connected with an arrow, indicating the citation direction: in this case, an arrow beginning at the first dot and ending at the second would indicate that the first work cites the second. Consider the example shown in Figure 2 which I unpack next.

Figure 2. A sample citation network; shown is a subset of bubble 11 from the JRME in the 1970s.

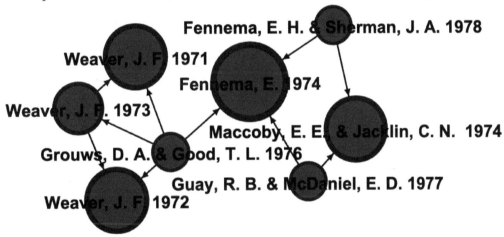

What are graphs and how might graphs be used?

In this chapter, I proceed through an introduction to mathematical graphs and their uses before introducing the computational side of graphs. These two fields, called graph theory and algorithmic graph theory, respectively, have grown in theory and application since at least the mid-1700s (cf. Euler, 1741). Graph theory, since Euler's seminal investigation, has been largely application driven and continues to have applications in sociology (Scott, 2017), computer science (Riaz & Ali, 2011), data science (Chen, 2006), and other nascent areas of data visualization (Lima, 2011).

Graphs can be described as a "diagram consisting of a set of points together with lines joining certain pairs of these points" (Bondy & Murty, 2008, p. 1). A simple graph representation is shown in Figure 3. The collection of these points is called the set of vertices, or nodes, (A, B, C, & D in Figure

3) and the collection of lines which connect pairs of points--or even a point to itself--is called the set of edges (a, b, c, d, e, & f in Figure 3). Since each edge begins and ends at a vertex, the edges encode the relationship between vertices. If a vertex is one of the endpoints of an edge, that vertex is said to be incident to that edge. The number of edges incident to a vertex is called that vertex's degree.

Figure 3. The nodes A, B, C, & D are represented with circles and the edges a, b, c, d, e, f & g are represented with lines.

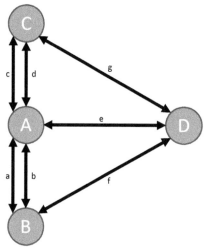

These graphs, distinct from say a graph of a curve in the Cartesian plane, show pairwise relationships between objects. A graph in which the direction of the connection is relevant, is called a directed graph. Directed graphs will serve as the foundation for the analysis of the citation relationships of the field of mathematics education research. To elaborate, in a graph of an article and the articles it cites, it is important to include which article cites which other article. If article A cites article B, it's not necessarily true, and indeed unlikely, that B also cites A. Therefore, every edge in a citation network, the name given to directed graphs showing the relationship between articles and their citations, will be directed. An edge will start at A and end at B if A *cites* B. For example, see a subset, called a subgraph, of the JRME 1970s citation network in Figure 2 (the full network is presented and unpacked in the next chapter).

The subgraph in Figure 2 includes four articles published in the JRME during the 1970s (Weaver, 1973; Grouws & Good, 1976; Guay & McDaniel, 1977; and Fennema & Sherman, 1978) and five cited articles. Since Fennema and Sherman cited Maccoby and Jacklin (1974) and one of Fennema's earlier works (1974), directed edges are drawn from Fennema and Sherman to these two articles. Extending the meaning of degree, the number of edges which end at a node is called the indegree. Indegree, then, corresponds to the number of times an article has been cited. Similarly, the outdegree is the number of edges which begin at a node; outdegree corresponds to the number of references an article cites. In this example, the indegree of Fennema 1974 is four and the outdegree of Fennema & Sherman 1978 is two.

This subgraph also illustrates an additional feature of the citation networks as I have chosen to represent them: node size is proportional to the number of times an article has been cited. For example, in Figure 2, Fennema's 1974 article is most cited within this group of works (indegree 4), which is denoted by its being the largest node.

Some History of Citation Networks

This section serves as an introduction to some relevant literature on citation networks and the study of scientific fronts, the development of software vital to this work, some algorithms for extracting and identifying patterns within citation networks, and some contemporary citation network analyses from both within and outside education. I include examples from outside education because of the limited number of education examples but, these external examples help to illustrate the uses of citation network analyses. While some of these articles establish a few significant points in the history of citation network analysis, and a glimpse into the larger field of information science, I refer the reader to Chen's *Mapping Scientific Frontiers: The Quest for Knowledge Visualization* (2013) for a more complete orientation to such endeavors.

In 1965, Derek de Solla Price published the seminal "Networks of Scientific Papers" in Nature. In that work, Price "attempt[ed] to describe in the broadest outline the nature of the total world network of scientific papers" (p. 510). By using processed data from other studies on citation patterns of published articles, Price was able to determine quantitative features in research patterns: 85% of research articles cite 25 or fewer articles apiece (p. 510), about 35% of all articles are never cited while 49% are only ever cited once (p. 511), papers are most likely to be cited when they are less than 15 years old (p. 513), etc. From his findings, Price characterizes two different patterns within research citations, either "the research front builds on recent work, and the network becomes very tight" (p. 515) or research "draw[s] upon the totality of previous work" (p. 515), expanding over time. The notion of research front, or the scope and direction that the publications in a field move, is precisely the object of study in this book.

Building upon the characterization of citations within scientific disciplines, Narin, Carpenter, and Berlt (1972) in "Interrelationships of Scientific Journals" sought to understand the ways that different scientific journals cited each other. These researchers developed citation relationship models: models where each journal is denoted with a circle and a Journal A is connected to a Journal B with an arrow if Journal B is the journal most cited by the articles published in Journal A. This citation relationship model was applied to the fields of mathematics, physics, chemistry, biochemistry, and biology to establish a hierarchy of journals within a discipline (journals were classified as Outstanding, Preferentially Cited, or Highly Cited) and, through combining these disciplinary hierarchies, a model of the flow of information across disciplines was developed. In this latter model, Narin and colleagues traced the flow of information from Mathematics to Physics to Chemistry to Biochemistry to Biology (empirical evidence for the informal spectrum of pure-to-applied science) and identified the key journals which served as disciplinary bridges. Certainly, the work of Narin and colleagues begins to signal the shift towards the citation networks I have begun to outline in this chapter, albeit at a much coarser scale.

Within this history of citation network analysis, the Institute for Scientific Information's *Atlas of Science: Biochemistry and Molecular Biology 1978-80* (1981) moves even closer to the project that this study undertakes. This Atlas rose out of Garfield's (1955) argument in Nature for the use of citation indices to trace the development of scientific research and his position as the founder of the Institute for Scientific Information (ISI). Further, the Atlas was experimental and served as a proof of concept for the technique of clustering and citation mapping. In the Atlas, Garfield and his team identified 102 research front specialties within the field of Biochemistry and Molecular Biology and provided a Global Map which situated the 102 clusters relative to each other. Each cluster, corresponding to a particular research focus (e.g., DNA Replication Proteins), is unpacked in its own chapter, providing: (1) a mini-review, a brief summary of the research within the cluster, (2) a map of the central articles, (3) a list of its core documents, those most cited articles which constitute the cluster, and (4) a list of citing documents, documents from 1978 and 1980 which cited the core documents in (3). Unfortunately, the ISI did not publish additional volumes in the Atlas of Science series and the Biochemistry and Molecular Biology volume was the only one to be published. It is clear that the Atlas is similar to the current project—indeed, I have named my project an *Atlas of Mathematics Education Research* and have chosen to unpack each bubble/research focus in turn, providing both global and cluster maps in the next chapter—I did not encounter ISI's Atlas until after drafting my dissertation.

Having now provided a sketch of the ideas that brought information science close to the aim and scope of my current project, I discuss next the software tools and algorithms that enable such an ambitious analysis. After that review, I will outline several citation network analyses, emphasizing the ways that they depart either in aim, scope, or analytic method from the project of this book. In that way, this project evidences a novel application of a novel process within one particular context. Future directions and pathways will be discussed in a later chapter.

Software for Citation Network Analysis

My goal, now, is not to provide a complete overview of all possible software choices for citation network analysis. Instead, I refer the reader to Cobo, López-Herrera, Herrera-Viedma, and Herrera's extensive review of software choices (2010) and Pan, Yan, Cui, and Hua's (2018) detailed study on the use of software by researchers for different purposes and across various disciplines. Instead, I introduce a few of the software tools that researchers have used for citation network analysis and present my own decision on whether or not it would serve the needs of the present analysis.

First, for researchers already familiar with the statistical package R, Aria and Cuccurullo (2017) developed the bibliometrix package for R, an integrated data import through visualization tool. However, the visualizations are limited in nature and cannot provide the detailed citation maps needed for the present analysis.

Next, Chen's (2006) CiteSpace is well documented (Aria & Curcurullo, 2017; Cobo et al., 2010; Pana, Yan, Cui, & Hua, 2018) and can generate detailed maps, yet is designed to work with Clarivate's Web of Knowledge (WoK) citation database which does not index *For the Learning of Mathematics* (FLM) nor does it include complete data for the *Journal for Research in Mathematics Education* (JRME; see the section Acquisition and Processing of Data for a detailed discussion on the limitations of WoK).

HistCite, developed by ISI's Garfield (2009), focuses on historical analyses, certainly showing an affinity to the present analysis, but is likewise bound to the WoK database and "HistCite has not been in active development for some time. It is no longer officially supported by Clarivate Analytics" (Clarivate, 2019).

Van Eck and Waltman's (2014, 2017) related CitNetExplorer and VOSViewer are both tools for citation network analysis with the former being primarily for analysis and the latter emphasizing the visualization of networks. Again, these tools are designed to import results from WoK. Additionally, however, these tools can import standardized Graph Markup Language (.gml) files which can be exported from other tools. Given this additional necessary step, CitNetExplorer and VOSViewer are not ideal.

Gephi (Bastian, Heymann, & Jacomy, 2009) is an open-source tool for creating, analyzing, and visualizing citation networks. Like bibliometrix, Gephi is an integrated solution for importing, analyzing, and visualizing citation networks. First, Gephi can import spreadsheets of data directly, given that it contains either a list of articles (nodes) or a list of article-to-article citations (edges). Further, it can analyze and visualize very large networks (over 20,000 nodes) and generate both static and interactive maps. Given, then, that Gephi is not dependent on the WoK database and can create both static and dynamic representations, I chose Gephi as the software of choice for the present analysis. Other researchers facing the same WoK limitation (e.g., Nylander, Österlund, & Fejes, 2018) likewise chose Gephi.

Methods for Network Analyses

Citation network analyses can take references (e.g., this present analysis; Nylander, Österlund, & Fejes, 2018), authors (e.g., ISI, 1981), or journals (e.g., Bruce et al., 2017; Wang & Bowers, 2016) as their unit of analysis. Depending on the unit of analysis, but regardless of the software package chosen, citation network analyses take one of three forms: coupling, mapping, or clustering. Coupling analyses connect two nodes whenever they share a reference (co-citation coupling), share keywords (co-classification coupling), share words within the title/abstract/body (co-word coupling), share an author (co-author), or are cited together by another article (co-citation coupling). I have chosen not to undertake a coupling analysis since it reduces the complexity of the network by approximating article content by its keywords (co-classification coupling), the words used in the title/abstract/text (co-word coupling), or its author (co-author coupling). Instead, I have chosen to perform a citation analysis directly where the data remains the complete list of every reference of every included article.

Layout analyses use mapping algorithms to calculate a placement for nodes on a map so that relative position of nodes encodes information about the relationships between them. For example, Fruchterman and Reingold's (1991) novel force-directed layout algorithm (called Fruchterman-Reingold) treats nodes as electrons, whose physical tendency is to repel each other, and the edges between nodes as springs, whose physical tendency is to contract and attract each other. As shown in Figure 4, electron repulsion is governed by Coulomb's Law and the force repelling nodes decreases as the distance between them increases. Similarly, Hooke's Law governs spring contraction and the force contracting the spring increases as the distance between the ends of the spring increases. Between any two nodes, then, there is a force that increases as the distance increases and a force that decreases as the distance increases so that there is guaranteed to be a point at which these two forces are at equilibrium. Fruchterman-Reingold calculates these spring and electron forces for every node in a system in discrete steps. After a first calculation is made, the forces between nodes and on springs, are recalculated, continuing until a stable state is found (i.e., the next step returns a result sufficiently close to the previous). Jacomy, Venturini, Heymann, and Bastian updated (2014) Fruchterman and Reingold's algorithm to a continuous model (ForceAtlas2). With this update,

Figure 4. Physical systems used in force-directed layout algorithms.

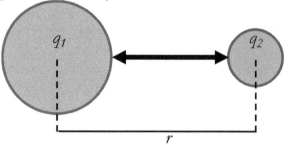 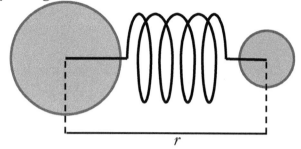

$$(1) \quad F_e = k_e \frac{q_1 q_2}{r^2} = (k_e q_1 q_2)\frac{1}{r^2}$$

$$(2) \quad F_s = k_s \cdot r$$

From Coulomb's Law: Treating two nodes as electrons, the force repelling them (F_e) is inversely proportional to the distance between their centers (r). Since $k_e, q_1, \& q_2$ are constant for any pair of nodes, as the distance between two nodes increases the force repelling each other decreases.

From Hooke's Law: Treating the edge between two nodes as a spring, the force attracting them (F_s) is proportional to the distance between their centers (r). Since k_s is the so-called spring constant, fixed for a given edge, as the distance between two nodes increases the force attracting each other increases.

ForceAtlas2, instead of presenting snapshots of the map that successively approach the final state, presents a fluid animation and transformation from the initial to final state. Fruchterman and Reingold showed that such a force-directed algorithm encodes information about the nodes: articles of a similar topic attract each other and articles with vastly different topics repel (1991). It is for this reason that I chose to use a force-directed algorithm to develop the maps of the JRME, FLM, and *Educational Studies in Mathematics* (ESM): articles of similar topic will be placed near each other. Furthermore, both Fruchterman-Reingold and ForceAtlas2 are included in Gephi.

Clustering algorithms are quantitative calculations that are independent of the layout of a citation network. While clustering algorithms do not consider the distance between two nodes, they do, however, consider the number of edges between nodes. For example, Newman (2006) discusses the use of modularity to study the relationship between nodes and returns subsets of nodes which are densely connected, or in other words, clusters of articles that are heavily cross-citing the same literature. I illustrate the basic ideas of modularity by way of an example. Consider a graph that has 4 nodes (see Figure 5).

Figure 5. An illustration of modularity on a graph with 4 nodes.

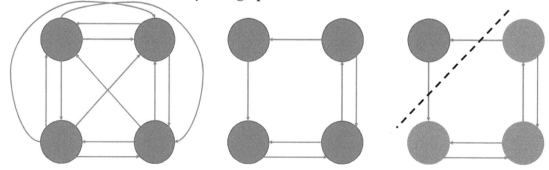

If every node was connected to every other node, there would be a total of 12 edges (Figure 5, left). Now, suppose the graph with 4 nodes only has 6 edges (e.g., Figure 5, middle). Then, if we were to divide those 4 nodes into two groups (a group might have 1, 2, or 3 nodes), we would expect half of the 6 edges to be in each group if they were randomly placed. Consider the division into orange and blue nodes shown in Figure 5 (right). The orange group has 4 edges, more than half of the total edges and the blue group does not fully contain any. From Newman's modularity algorithm, the blue node would be in one modularity group (or class) and the orange nodes would be in another modularity class. Those two modularity classes are preferable to say dividing the network into the two left nodes and two right nodes since, in that arrangement, neither modularity class would contain more than half the edges: the left class would contain one and the right class would contain two.

The time to calculate every possible division into modularity classes, since it involves considering all possible subgroups of nodes and counting the number of edges contained in each group, is not computationally feasible on a large citation network in that it would take too long to complete the computation. Blondel, Guillaume, Lambiotte, and Lefebvre (2008), researchers at the Université catholique de Louvain, addressed this computational limit and modified Newman's algorithm to quickly calculate modularity in large networks. This modified algorithm, called Louvain modularity, improves Newman's algorithm by beginning with a random subdivision of nodes and by calculating the benefit of adding or removing a given node. If the benefit is not sufficiently large, the change in layout is not made. The algorithm runs from several different starting conditions and returns the result that is most modular. The Louvain Modularity algorithm is included in Gephi and is used to identify the clusters of research in each map. As will be seen in the next chapter, and as shown by Waltman, van Eck, and Noyons (2010), the articles that ForceAtlas2 places near each other spatially are also clustered into the same modularity class by the Louvain Modularity algorithm. This successive process of dividing a network into more modularity classes until no additional benefit is achieved is shown in Figure 6. First, the JRME 1970s network is divided into two groups, then, looking across each row and across successive rows, the final result shows the network divided into 18 groups.

Example Analyses

As mentioned above, a citation network analysis can consider various units of analysis, apply different algorithms, and use different software to accomplish those goals. I present here what few education relevant analyses have been undertaken. Two articles that focused on journals as a unit of analysis were Bruce and colleagues (2017) and Wang and Bowers (2016).

Considering the topic "spatial reasoning," Bruce and colleagues (2017) created a citation network of recently published articles on spatial reasoning to understand the flow of information between Education, Psychology, Neuroscience, and Mathematics journals. They found that "although mathematics education appears to both adopt and adapt ideas from other disciplines, it was rare to find examples of other disciplines borrowing from Mathematics Education" (p. 157). Bruce and colleagues argue, then, that mathematics education is a uniquely interdisciplinary field that could facilitate the transfer of information between the other relevant fields.

Similarly studying journals, Wang and Bowers (2016) performed a citation network analysis of recent education administration publications to determine which journals were most central to the

Figure 6. The result of successive subdivisions by the Louvain modularity algorithm from the JRME 1970s.

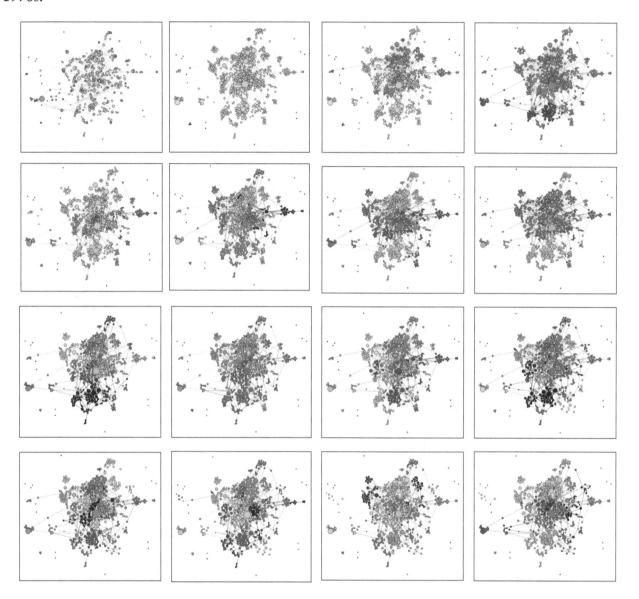

field, those that were most cited across all publications. They found that *Educational Administration Quarterly* was most cited and most central to the field of educational administration.

Shifting towards a focus on authors, Nylander, Österlund, and Fejes (2017) performed a citation network analysis on articles published on adult learning. They found that the authors most central to the study of adult learning were Wenger, Billett, and Lave: each contributing to sociocultural theories of learning.

Lastly, Özkaya (2018) published "Bibliometric analysis of the studies in the field of mathematics education" in *Educational Research and Reviews*, an open-access Turkish journal. Özkaya aimed "to review all works concerning mathematics education, published in [Web of Knowledge] database between 1980-2018, to identify the authors and journals that have performed important works in mathematics education area from past to present; and to reveal popular topics according to years" (p. 724). In this study, Özkaya used CiteSpace because of its compatibility with the WoK search results and presented the quantitative results that CiteSpace could generate: citation counts, author country counts, and keyword analysis. This study, therefore, provided interesting quantitative insight into citation counts, sources, etc. but did not consider the citation relationships between articles, nor in identifying the clusters of research, and their positions within the field. I also find this use of WoK problematic given the missing and incorrect data (elaborated in the section titled "Choice of Data"). For these reasons, the current research project takes a significantly different research focus (the development of the field across five decades and a comparison of three mathematics education journals), uses a substantially different data source (manual extraction of complete reference data from articles directly instead of the WoK database), and provides substantial new insight into the field of mathematics education research.

Cartography: Typical and extended use

Cartography is the practice/science/art of drawing maps (MacEachren & Taylor, 1994). Gerardus Mercator (1595) first used the term atlas to refer to a collection of maps in *Atlas sive cosmographicæ meditationes de fabrica mundi et fabricati figura* (*Atlas, or Cosmographic Meditations on the Fabric of the World and the Figure of the Fabrick'd*). There, Mercator aimed to document the entirety of God's Creation. My aims are less ambitious, however; in this atlas, I intend to map some parts of the field of mathematics education research in order to show how the foci of the field has changed over time, to show how new foci have emerged, old foci have burst, and different foci have morphed and merged. Other researchers have referred to such citation mapping as bibliographic cartography (Hinze, 1994) and bibliometric cartography (Ding et al., 2001; Noyons & van Raan, 1994). As discussed in the theoretical orientations section, since my interest is in discussing what can be seen, said, and thought as mathematics education research, to cartography I join the adjective sensible and call the present endeavor a *sensible cartography*.

In Visual Complexity (2011), Manuel Lima outlines five purposes of cartography: (1) in the spirit of documenting, to map something new; (2) in the spirit of clarity, to make the network more understandable in its representation; (3) in the spirit of revelation, to identify "a hidden pattern in or explicit new insight into the system" (p. 81); (4) in the spirit of abstraction, to illustrate some feature beyond the data of the network itself, and (5) in the spirit of expansion, to set the stage for more exploration. In this way, the present analysis will:

(1)   document the citation relationships between those articles published in the JRME (1970-2019), ESM (2010s), and FLM (2010s);

(2)   provide clarity regarding the patterns, quantity, and nature of citations across time and journals;

(3)   reveal the densely-connected bubbles of research within the data which correspond to research foci of the field;

(4)   provide an abstraction of these bubbles into foams of the field which present different perspectives on what constitutes the field of mathematics education research across time and journal contexts; and

(5)   generate interactive citation maps, freely available online at MathEdAtlas.org, to set the stage for more exploration.

Having, to this point, provided an overview of the relevant literature and situated this endeavor as a cartographic one, I proceed now through the practicalities of generating this atlas of mathematics education research. In turn, I discuss the source of data, the analysis of data, and the results of the analytic process.

Practicalities of this method

Since citation networks fundamentally encode the citation relationships between a publication and its references, the references comprise the data of the analysis. The citation data, then, must be located, extracted, and imported into network analysis software before the analytic process can be undertaken. Citation network software then can be used to create the citation maps which comprise the result of the analytic process.

Choice of Data

For this analysis, I chose to consider the *Journal for Research in Mathematics Education* (JRME), *Educational Studies in Mathematics* (ESM), and *For the Learning of Mathematics* (FLM). These journals were chosen given their position within the field of mathematics education research: JRME claims to be "premier research journal in mathematics education" (JRME Journal Aims) while ESM aims to "[present] new ideas and developments of major importance to those working in the field of mathematical education…[where the] emphasis is on high-level articles which are of more than local or national interest" (ESM Journal Aims). In contrast, FLM aims to "promote criticism and evaluation of ideas and procedures current in the field" (FLM Journal Aims). I chose FLM as one journal for analysis so that I might provide empirical evidence to either support or refute this claim and the intuition of researchers that qualitatively feel as though FLM is a *different sort of journal*. Furthermore, these three journals constitute three of the eight "Major Journals in Mathematics Education" identified in the *Compendium for Early Career Researchers in Mathematics Education* (Kaiser & Presmeg, 2019).

The choice of which journals were included in this analysis is not neutral. In fact, choosing any number of mathematics education journals, from the start, privileges those journals that specifically claim to be 'mathematics education' while simultaneously excluding those any articles published in journals relevant to 'education at large.' For example, articles published in the Journal of Philosophy of Education on mathematics education would likely construe a different image of what mathematics education research can be. For the sake of this project, I chose to include the citation data for five decades of the JRME (see chapter 4), one decade of ESM (chapter 5), and one decade of FLM (chapter 6). These choices enabled me to trace the development of the field across time and to compare and contrast how the field is construed by each journal (JRME vs. FLM vs. ESM; See chapter 7).

Acquisition and Processing of Data

The citation network data includes every reference from every article published in these three journals during these three time periods. There were a few options for acquiring this data: the references could be manually extracted from the published articles (either pdf or html versions depending on the journal offerings), reference information could be extracted from an article database such as JSTOR (jstor.org), or the references could be extracted from an existing database of citation relationships such as Clarivate's Web of Knowledge (webofknowledge.com). The last option seems quite attractive; however, this method is heavily dependent on the quality of the data within the WoK database. Indeed, WoK only included JRME articles as early as 1986, meaning at least 16 years of data would need to be added manually. Furthermore, 191 of the JRME articles in the WoK were attributed to anonymous authors: a pass through the articles published in the JRME shows this to be inaccurate. Additionally, many articles in WoK only included one of its references with the remainder missing. Given these inadequacies, and the fact that FLM is not indexed in the WoK database, WoK was not a suitable data source for this project.

The first option, manually extracting references from pdf or webpage versions of articles would work if a webpage version of the article existed so that the references could be copied and pasted into a spreadsheet, or if a webpage version did not exist, the pdf file would need to be selectable (some pdf files do not have the text stored as text so that it is selectable; older pdf files in particular store the text as a non-selectable image). Early JRME articles are of this non-selectable form, meaning that each reference of nearly 30 years of articles would need to be manually transcribed from a pdf to a spreadsheet.

JSTOR, it turns out, is the most convenient option for several reasons. First, while JSTOR stores the articles for each of JRME, ESM, and FLM as pdf files, JSTOR has extracted every reference from every article and lists them on a webpage. For example, going to the JSTOR listing of a JRME article (see Figure 7, left) includes article information (author, year, issue, volume, title, etc.), a link to the pdf file, and a list of the references from the article (sorted alphabetically by author and year as they appear at the end of the article; see Figure 7, right). Even with this text easily copied and pasted from the JSTOR page to a spreadsheet, manually extracting this data would be time prohibitive since the JRME published 1,090 articles between 1970 and 2019, ESM published 445 articles between 2010 and 2016, and FLM published 82 articles between 2010 and 2017. Now, these date ranges are not uniform because of the only limitation of using JSTOR: the publishers of ESM and FLM each impose an embargo of two and three years, respectively, meaning that articles cannot be added to the JSTOR database until they are two or three years old. Even with this limitation, and since my goal of mapping ESM and FLM are to contrast the foci of those journals with the foci of JRME, this missing data is not prohibitive to my goal.

Nevertheless, manually copying and pasting the data for 1,617 articles would be time prohibitive. Therefore, I chose to develop a custom software tool to automate the processing of these references. I began by downloading every article's webpage (1,617 .html files). Then, since the references were each listed in the source text of the html file (see Figure 7, right) in a uniform manner (the block of references is tagged "reference_content" and each reference is tagged "reference_data"), a simple text processing script could extract each reference's details from the html files and store them into a plaintext file that could be imported into Microsoft Excel. Then, since references, at least when written using APA guidelines, are written in a standardized order (Author(s), year, title, journal, etc.), Microsoft Excel's formulae were sufficient for splitting apart a complete reference into its component pieces (i.e., author, year, title, etc. were split into separate columns; see Figure 8). Such a spreadsheet was made for each decade slice (JRME 1970s, JRME 1980s, …, ESM 2010s, FLM 2010s). Then, the Excel spreadsheet was imported into the citation network software; the details of which are unpacked next.

Figure 7. Sample JSTOR article webpage (left), list of references (middle), and source code (right).

Figure 8. Sample Excel spreadsheet showing the extracted and split data.

Volume	Number	Author_formatted	Year	Source_Title	Source	References	Ref_author	Ref_year	Target	Ref_title
34	1	Selden, A. & Selden, J.	2003	Validations of Pro	Selden, A. & Selden, J., 2003	Baddeley, A. (1995). Working r	Baddeley, A.	1995	Baddeley, A., 1995	Working memory.
34	1	Selden, A. & Selden, J.	2003	Validations of Pro	Selden, A. & Selden, J., 2003	Bagchi, A., & Wells, C. (1998).	Bagchi, A., & Wells, C.	1998	Bagchi, A., & Wells,	Varieties of mathematical p
34	1	Selden, A. & Selden, J.	2003	Validations of Pro	Selden, A. & Selden, J., 2003	Barnes, M. (2000). 'Magical' m	Barnes, M.	2000	Barnes, M., 2000	'Magical' moments in math
34	1	Selden, A. & Selden, J.	2003	Validations of Pro	Selden, A. & Selden, J., 2003	Bogdan, D., & Straw, S. B., [Ed	Bogdan, D., & Straw, S. B., [Eds.].	1990	Bogdan, D., & Straw	Beyond communication: Re
34	1	Selden, A. & Selden, J.	2003	Validations of Pro	Selden, A. & Selden, J., 2003	Burton, L., & Morgan, C. (2000	Burton, L., & Morgan, C.	2000	Burton, L., & Morga	Mathematicians writing.
34	1	Selden, A. & Selden, J.	2003	Validations of Pro	Selden, A. & Selden, J., 2003	Chomsky, N. (1957). Syntactic s	Chomsky, N.	1957	Chomsky, N., 1957	Syntactic structures.
34	1	Selden, A. & Selden, J.	2003	Validations of Pro	Selden, A. & Selden, J., 2003	Cuoco, A. (2001). Mathematics	Cuoco, A.	2001	Cuoco, A., 2001	Mathematics for teaching.
34	1	Selden, A. & Selden, J.	2003	Validations of Pro	Selden, A. & Selden, J., 2003	De Villiers, M. (1998). To teach	De Villiers, M.	1998	De Villiers, M., 1998	To teach definitions in geor
34	1	Selden, A. & Selden, J.	2003	Validations of Pro	Selden, A. & Selden, J., 2003	Dubinsky, E., & Yiparaki, O. (20	Dubinsky, E., & Yiparaki, O.	2000	Dubinsky, E., & Yipa	On student understanding c
34	1	Selden, A. & Selden, J.	2003	Validations of Pro	Selden, A. & Selden, J., 2003	Edwards, B. (1997). An underg	Edwards, B.	1997	Edwards, B., 1997	An undergraduate student's
34	1	Selden, A. & Selden, J.	2003	Validations of Pro	Selden, A. & Selden, J., 2003	Ernest, P. (1998). Social constr	Ernest, P.	1998	Ernest, P., 1998	Social constructivism as a p
34	1	Selden, A. & Selden, J.	2003	Validations of Pro	Selden, A. & Selden, J., 2003	Fillmore, C. J. (1968). The case	Fillmore, C. J.	1968	Fillmore, C. J., 1968	The case for case.
34	1	Selden, A. & Selden, J.	2003	Validations of Pro	Selden, A. & Selden, J., 2003	Freudenthal, H. (1973). Mathe	Freudenthal, H.	1973	Freudenthal, H., 197	Mathematics as an educatic
34	1	Selden, A. & Selden, J.	2003	Validations of Pro	Selden, A. & Selden, J., 2003	Halliday, M. A. K. (1977). Explo	Halliday, M. A. K.	1977	Halliday, M. A. K., 1	Explorations in the function
34	1	Selden, A. & Selden, J.	2003	Validations of Pro	Selden, A. & Selden, J., 2003	Hanna, G. (1989). Proofs that	Hanna, G.	1989	Hanna, G., 1989	Proofs that prove and proof
34	1	Selden, A. & Selden, J.	2003	Validations of Pro	Selden, A. & Selden, J., 2003	Harel, G., & Sowder, L. (1998).	Harel, G., & Sowder, L.	1998	Harel, G., & Sowder	Students' proof schemes: R
34	1	Selden, A. & Selden, J.	2003	Validations of Pro	Selden, A. & Selden, J., 2003	Kintsch, W. (1974). The repres	Kintsch, W.	1974	Kintsch, W., 1974	The representation of mear
34	1	Selden, A. & Selden, J.	2003	Validations of Pro	Selden, A. & Selden, J., 2003	Kurtz, D.C. (1992). Foundations	Kurtz, D.C.	1992	Kurtz, D.C., 1992	Foundations of abstract ma

Map Creation: Analysis of Data

The previous section describes the process of acquiring, extracting, and formatting the necessary citation data for a citation network analysis. I begin here by discussing the various options for citation network software before providing a justification for my choice of Gephi. Then, I will describe the algorithms used in this study to layout the citation network maps and to identify the densely connected bubbles of research. Lastly, I will describe my process for naming the research focus of each bubble before turning to the final section of this chapter detailing the static and dynamic map representations that are the result of my analysis. First, however, I provide the flowchart in Figure 9 as a visual summary of the process so far and the steps to be discussed next.

The acquisition and processing of data comprised steps 1-5 of Figure 9: (1) identify the decades of interest from JRME, ESM, and FLM; (2) download the 1,617 .html files, (3) compile a list of .html filenames, (4) input the list of filename to the `JSTORrefextract` tool, extract the references for each file, and store the data as a tab-separated plaintext file, and (5) import the plaintext file into Excel. Then, as I outline next, I (6) imported the Excel file into Gephi, (7) ran the ForceAtlas2 algorithm to generate the map layout, (8) applied the Louvain Modularity algorithm to identify research bubbles, and (9) exported static and dynamic representations of the maps.

Figure 9. Process flowchart from webpage download to map generation.

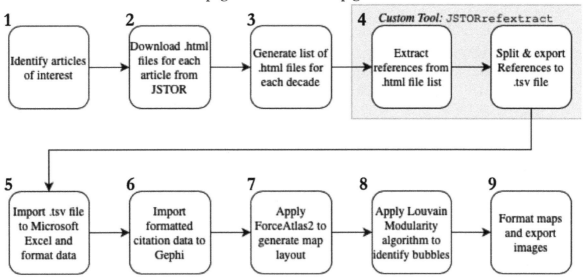

After the Louvain Modularity algorithm identifies which nodes are in which modularity class, I used a Wordle (Feinberg, 2014), a word cloud generator, on the titles of the references corresponding to each node included in each modularity class. Wordle displays the most frequently occurring words in a random layout with the size of the word proportional to the number of times it occurs. Based on this quantitative information, I use the most frequently occurring words to name each modularity class. One advantage to this approach is that it provides a visual summary of quantitative data: the more frequently a word appears in the titles, it will be larger in the word cloud. This approach, however, excludes words that are absent from the title but may be helpful for the classification of the bubble. For example, an article on students understanding of equality might take a cognitive or sociocultural approach to understanding but those words may be absent from the title. Two sample wordles are included in Figure 10.

Figure 10. Wordles for two modularity classes from the JRME 2010s: addition and subtraction (left) and problem solving (right).

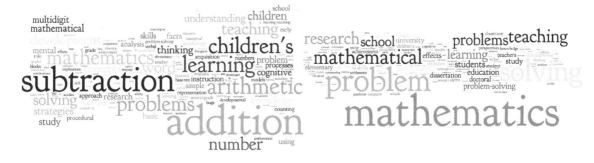

The left image is the wordle for cluster 4 of the complete JRME network (1970s-2010s): Arithmetic. The right image is the wordle for cluster 5 of the complete JRME network (1970s-2010s): Problem Solving. See Chapter 3 for a further discussion of the clusters for each decade of the JRME (1970s, 1980s, 1990s, 2000s, 2010s) and the complete JRME network (1970s-2010s).

Presentation of Maps

The results of the analysis are maps for each decade of analysis (JRME 1970s, JRME 1980s, JRME 1990s, JRME 2000s, JRME 2010s, ESM 2010s, and FLM 2010s) and the complete JRME network (JRME 1970s-2010s). Static maps are exported as images and included in the following chapters and at MathEdAtlas.org. For each decade, a map is shown that is the result of running both ForceAtlas2 (force-directed layout) and Louvain Modularity (modularity class identification). The map of the JRME 2010s is shown in Figure 11 as one example. While the entirety of this map is unpacked in the next chapter, for the interested reader, the circles indicate the general location of each bubble and the numbers correspond to the following bubble names (generated via the Wordle process described above): (1) Standards, (2) Young Children's Learning and Development, (3) (Scientific) Research Agenda, (4) Linking Research and Learning, (5) Mathematics Knowledge for Teaching, (6) Cognition, (7) Teaching, Learning, & Understanding Fraction Concepts, (8) Solving Algebraic Equations and Errors, (9) Meaning Making in Mathematics - Social and Cultural Aspects, (10) Pedagogy and Learning, (11) Social Context of Learning - International Perspectives, (12) Comparative Assessment, (13) Developing Algebraic Thinking in Schools, (14) Mathematical Proof, (15) Discourse & Language, (16) Epistemology: Knowledge and Understanding in Mathematics, (17) Equitable Achievement: Class, Race, Sex, (18) Fractions, (19) International Comparative Assessment, (20) Mathematics in the Middle School, (21) Data & Statistics, (22) Mathematics Learning Systems, (23) Multiple Mathematical Representations, (24) Solving Arithmetic & Algebraic Word Problems, (25) Standards-Based Curriculum and Achievement in Schools, (26) Geometry and Measurement, (27) Equity and Equitable Pedagogy, (28) Constructivist Teaching and Learning, (29) Calculus and Function Concepts, (30) Transfer of Mathematics, (31) Research on the Teaching and learning of Children, (32) Probability, (33) Scientific Research, (34) Gender Differences in performance, and (35) Mathematical Enculturation. These names, together with the map and labelled bubbles shows the analysis that I provide for each of the journals and each of the decades. These bubbles denote the different research foci of the field and their relative centrality/marginality to the field during that decade.

In addition to these decade maps, I create an image showing each of the modularity classes and its relative position within the map (see Figure 12). Since the circles illustrate the general location of each bubble, these detailed maps, which show only a single bubble, are generated to better show the topic's position within the field during that decade: showing only the nodes of interest in color (blue here), helps to isolate its location from the other nodes (in gray).

Since another objective of this research, aligning with objective 5 of cartography, is to enable the further exploration, these static images are not the only output. Another output is fully interactive maps. Companion to this book is the website MathEdAtlas.org. There, each decade is presented in an interactive form. The layout and coloring matches static images but mousing-over a node displays its name and highlights its adjacent nodes and clicking on a node lists the name of all adjacent nodes and its modularity class.

Figure 11. Map of the JRME 2010s showing the result of ForceAtlas2 in its layout and the colors/circles correspond to the Louvain modularity classes.

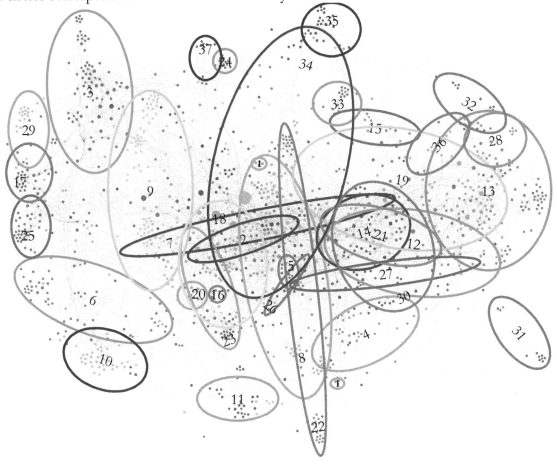

Figure 12. A bubble map of JRME 2010s bubble #9: Mathematics Knowledge for Teaching.

As the first three chapters of this text described the purpose and method of this study, I transition next to the analysis. In chapter 4, I describe the five-decade citation network analysis of the JRME. Then, in chapters 5 and 6, I describe the FLM and the ESM analyses respectively.

This chapter proceeds from an introduction to the *Journal for Research in Mathematics Education* (JRME) to an investigation into the JRME of the 1970s, 1980, 1990s, 2000s, and 2010s. For each decade, I provide a list of the bubbles that constitute the various research foci of the field during that decade, a map which shows the relative position of each bubble within the foam of that decade, a list of the most-cited articles within that bubble, and a list of a few of the JRME articles inside that bubble. In the 1970s, I will provide a detailed account of each bubble to illustrate the process of determining the research focus of each bubble and, correspondingly, its name. In contrast to the process of the JRME 1970s, for the 1980s and onward, I summarize each of the bubbles in the form of a table that includes (1) the bubble's number, (2) the bubble's name, (3) a map with the bubbles relative location within the foam, (4) a list of the most cited articles within that bubble, and (5) a list of a few JRME articles within that bubble. My reasoning for doing this is twofold.

The first is brevity; unlike the single decade analyses of FLM (14 bubbles unpacked in Chapter 5) and ESM (8 bubbles unpacked in Chapter 6), the analysis for the JRME comprises five decades for a total of 128 bubbles across those decades: 18 bubbles in the 1970s, 15 bubbles in the 1980s, 22 bubbles in the 1990s, 35 bubbles in the 2000s, and 38 bubbles in the 2010s.

The second is a shift in the purpose for each section; my detailed elaboration of the JRME 1970s provides insight into the method of naming and identifying each bubble. My goal for the remaining sections is, instead of elaborating the method of naming, to introduce each of the decades bubbles so that I can provide an analysis of the bubbles' position relative to each other and relative to the position of the foam. For the interested reader, interactive versions of each map, complete with every node of each bubble and their relative positions within the foam are available on the companion website at MathEdAtlas.org.

Recalling the Sloterdijkian notion of bubbles, these bubbles each constitute contingent groupings of related research clustered around particular research foci. The bubbles of each decade form a foam, or collection of co-fragile, codependent bubbles that together constitute a map of the foci that collectively outline the scope of mathematics education research during each decade Therefore, I will conclude by comparing and contrasting the bubbles and foams across time. First, I will show a composite foam that takes each decade together to identify the macro-foci of the field. Then, I will provide a sequential view of the foci from each decade to show those bubbles that pop, those that emerge, those that merge, etc. Finally, I will provide a discussion on how the bubbles move from marginal to central and back to the margins over time. This discussion emphasized the shifting value that mathematics education researchers have placed on particular foci across time, suggesting that the research foci within the field of mathematics education researchers are neither the necessary nor inevitable destination of the field but rather are determined by researchers shifting interests.

About the Journal

An official journal of the National Council of Teachers of Mathematics (NCTM), JRME is the premier research journal in mathematics education and is devoted to the interests of teachers and researchers at all levels--preschool through college. JRME is a forum for disciplined inquiry into the teaching and learning of mathematics. (JRME Aims).

According to the aims of the JRME, mathematics education research is 'disciplined inquiry into the teaching and learning of mathematics' which begins to suggest that the proper object of study of mathematics education research is the "teaching and learning of mathematics." According to Cai, Hwang, and Robison (2019) the most frequently published paper type in the JRME is the research report, about research reports these authors elaborate:

> Research Reports aim to move the field of mathematics education forward and include, but are not limited to, the following: various genres and designs of empirical research; philosophical, methodological, and historical studies in mathematics education; and literature reviews, syntheses, and theoretical analyses of research in mathematics education (p. 428).

Looking critically at the language of this statement, there are three kinds of research reports: (1) empirical research, (2) studies in mathematics education, and (3) analyses of research. This shift to studies and analyses suggests that while they fall under the research report umbrella for publication, those kinds of papers are qualitatively different than empirical research. This is one way that the editors of JRME begin to outline a particular partage of the sensible.

Mathematics education research *per se* makes sense to be called research when it is empirical. This stance is more restrictive than the American Education Research Association (AERA) which published its "Standards for Reporting on Humanities-Oriented Research in AERA Publications" (2009, emphasis added) to address the unsuitability of its earlier "Standards for Reporting on Empirical Social Science Research in AERA Publications" (2006) to address a "constellation of familiar education research genres used in domains such as…linguistics, literary theory, history, jurisprudence, philosophy, and religion" (2009, p. 481, emphasis added).

In what follows, I begin to identify the bubbles of research, inclusive of philosophical, historical, and other non-empirical research articles, published within the JRME. Starting with the 1970s, I detail the journal articles published by the JRME that fall into each bubble and the most-cited references by those articles. For each decade, 1980 through 2010, I summarize the bubbles of research before transitioning into a chronological analysis of the bubbles across time. This spherological analysis (Sloterdijk, 2011, 2016) considers the bubbles and foams formed by the 1,090 articles published in the JRME between 1970 and 2019. These articles together included 33,273 citations. This analysis, the primary analysis of this chapter serves to show how what counts as mathematics education research, what topics comprise the foam of each decade and the shifting position of the bubbles across time, reveals the fluidity and volatility of the field of mathematics education research.

Unlike an aims document, or the statements by Cai and colleagues, my goal from this perspective is not to establish a positive definition that encompasses all of what mathematics education research *is* or *can be*, but rather to perturb any such definition. Enacting a Rancièrean (2004) politics, my goal is to introduce a concept of mathematics education research that seeks to refigure and redistribute what is sensible as mathematics education research. As Foucault (Fendler, 2010) reminds us, sometimes mirrors into the past (looking back at these bubbles across time) can make the best levers.

JRME in the 1970s

First, I present a map of the research foam of the JRME in the 1970s (See Figure 13). After providing this orienting image, I summarize each of the 18 bubbles. After describing those bubbles, I zoom back out to provide a macroanalysis of the foam that is the JRME in the 1970s. The microanalyses serve to orient the reader towards the key research foci of the decade and the focal articles that comprise them. In contrast, the macroanalysis of the foam interprets the relative positions of the bubbles, paying particular attention to adjacent, intersecting, and disjoint bubbles to emphasize which foci are closely related and which are separate. A fully interactive map of the JRME 1970s is available for the reader at MathEdAtlas.org and I encourage the reader to explore the nodes which comprise each bubble and the overall foam to develop an intuition about the research of the JRME 1970s.

Microanalysis: Bubbles in the 1970s

I proceed now by describing each of the 18 bubbles of research in the 1970s JRME: (1) Computers and Statistical Methods in Mathematics Education, (2) Piaget's Spatial Concepts, (3) Piaget's Developmental Psychology, (4) Learning Sequences and Manipulatives, (5) Statistical Psychology of Learning, (6) International Comparative Assessment, (7) Heuristics and Processes of Problem Solving, (8) Effect of Activity-Oriented Instruction, (9) The Learning of Basic Facts, (10) Quantitative Research Methods, (11) Factors for Differences in Achievement, (12) Logic, (13) Geometry Secondary Mathematics Learning, (14) Conceptual Organizers and Assessment, (15) Attitude towards Mathematical Topics, (16) Word Problems, (17) Ability-Instruction Interaction, and (18) Attitude and Learning. For each bubble, I provide a mini map that shows the bubble's relative location within the foam of the field in the JRME in the 1970s. Then, I unpack the bubble by presenting the most cited article(s) and which JRME articles cited it. Since providing a detailed review of every article is beyond the scope of this work, I merely provide some orienting work so that the reader might come to know what is present within each bubble and how those articles constitute a particular research focus.

Bubble 1: Computers and Statistical Methods in Mathematics Education

The first bubble discussed of the JRME 1970s is named Computers and Statistical Methods in Mathematics Education. This bubble is clustered into two pieces, one very marginal to the foam and the other quite central (see Figure 14). Those marginal articles include Alspaugh's (JRME, 1971) "The relationship of grade placement to programming aptitude and FORTRAN programming achievement" and Hatfield and Kieren's (JRME, 1972) "Computer-assisted problem solving in school mathematics," both of which drew on Lindquist's (1953) "Design and analysis of experiments in psychology and education." Building on the work of Hatfield and Kieren was Robitaille, Sherrill, and Kaufman's (JRME, 1977) "The effect of computer utilization on the achievement and attitudes of ninth-grade mathematics students." The remaining articles in the marginal part of Bubble 1 are comprised solely of articles cited by both Hatfield and Kieren and Robitaille and colleagues.

Figure 13. Bubbles of research that comprise the JRME 1970s foam.

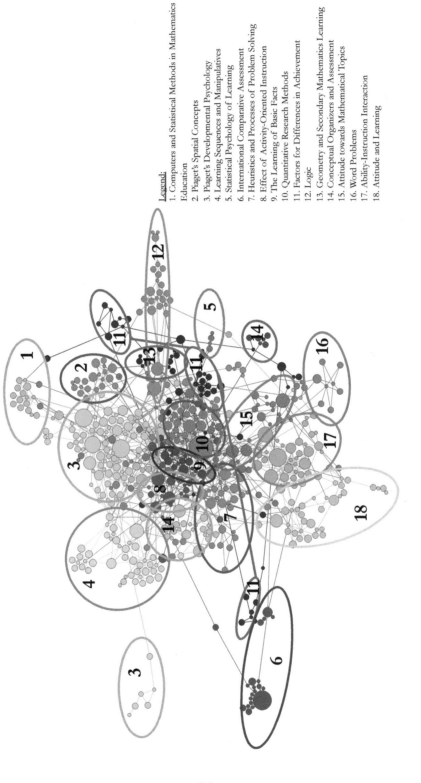

Legend:
1. Computers and Statistical Methods in Mathematics Education
2. Piaget's Spatial Concepts
3. Piaget's Developmental Psychology
4. Learning Sequences and Manipulatives
5. Statistical Psychology of Learning
6. International Comparative Assessment
7. Heuristics and Processes of Problem Solving
8. Effect of Activity-Oriented Instruction
9. The Learning of Basic Facts
10. Quantitative Research Methods
11. Logic
12. Logic
13. Geometry and Secondary Mathematics Learning
14. Conceptual Organizers and Assessment
15. Attitude towards Mathematical Topics
16. Word Problems
17. Ability-Instruction Interaction
18. Attitude and Learning

30

Figure 14. Location of the bubble "Computers and Statistical Methods in Mathematics Education" (in green) within the foam of the JRME 1970s.

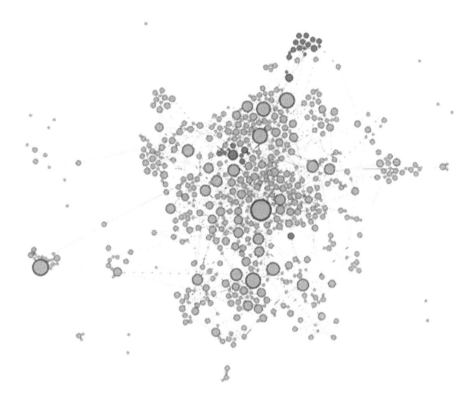

In addition to Lindquist's statistical methods for experiments, Alspaugh also cited Siegel's (1956) *Nonparametric statistics for the behavioral sciences*. Siegel's (1956) methods is the most cited article in the more central portion of Bubble 1 and serves as the bridge between the two clusters of Bubble 1. The JRME articles that cite it, in addition to Alspaugh, are Bright and Carry's "The Influence of Professional Reference Groups on Decisions of Preservice Secondary School Mathematics Teachers" (1974), Sowder's "Performance on Some Discovery Tasks, Grades 4-7" (1971), and Bright, Harvey, and Wheeler's "Incorporating Instructional Objectives into the Rules for Playing a Game" (1979). The unifying theme of these articles was their use of statistical methods. Thus, several articles focused on computers in mathematics education and the unanimous use of statistical methods account for the naming of Bubble 1 as "Computers and Statistical Methods in Mathematics Education." Further, the more central location of the statistical methods cluster foreshadows the most central Bubble: Bubble 10 – Quantitative Research Methods.

Bubble 2: Piaget's Spatial Concepts

The second bubble discussed of the JRME 1970s is named Piaget's Spatial Concepts. Tied for most cited reference within this bubble is Piaget and Inhelder's foundational *The Child's Conception of Space* (1967) and the closely related "A follow-up study of some aspects of the work of Piaget and Inhelder on the child's conception of space" by Lovell (1959). The next most cited reference, Dodwell's "Children's understanding of spatial concepts" (1963) again points towards the central idea of spatial concepts. Each of these articles are cited by Martin's (1976) JRME article titled "A Test with Selected Topological Properties of Piaget's Hypothesis concerning the Spatial Representation of the Young Child" situating Martin's article as central to this bubble together with Moyer's "The Relationship between the Mathematical Structure of Euclidean Transformations and the Spontaneously Developed Cognitive Structures of Young Children" (19758) and Davis' "A Study of the Ability of School Pupils to Perceive and Identify the Plane Sections of Selected Solid Figures" (1973) which together sought empirical evidence of and to elaborate cognitive structures for Piaget's claims on the spatial development of children. This bubble is shown in Figure 15.

Figure 15. Location of the bubble "Piaget's Spatial Concepts" (in purple) within the foam of the JRME 1970s.

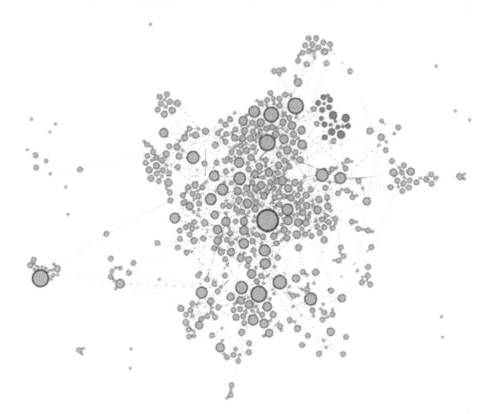

Bubble 3: Piaget's Developmental Psychology

While Bubble 2 focuses on Piaget's Spatial Concepts, Bubble 3 of the 1970s focuses more broadly on Piaget's developmental psychology. The most cited reference within this bubble is Piaget's *The child's conception of number* (1952) followed closely by Piaget and colleagues' *The child's conception of geometry* (1960) and Flavell's Piagetian overview *The developmental psychology of Jean Piaget* (1963). Carpenter's "Measurement Concepts of First-and Second-Grade Students" (1975) and Taloumis' "The Relationship of Area Conservation to Area Measurement as Affected by Sequence of Presentation of Piagetian Area Tasks to Boys and Girls in Grades One through Three" (1975) both cited each of the Piagetian references and Flavell's overview.

Related to this central focus on Piagetian developmental psychology are the child development work in Rothenberg's "Conservation of number among four- and five-year-old children: some methodological considerations" (1969) and Beilin's "Learning and operational convergence in logical thought development" (1965). Steffe & Carey's "Equivalence and Order Relations as Interrelated by Four- and Five-Year-Old Children" (1972) built on the work of both Rothenberg and Beilin.

Notice, however, that this bubble is not neatly clustered at one locus. Instead, there are a few articles to the left edge (see Figure 16) that are included in Bubble 3. These articles are comprised of a research niche by Campbell into children's understanding of image, namely, "Textbook Pictures and First-Grade Children's Perception of Mathematical Relationships" (1978) and "Artistic Motion Cues, Number of Pictures, and First-Grade Children's Interpretation of Mathematics Textbook Pictures" (1979).

Figure 16. Location of the bubble "Piaget's Developmental Psychology" (in green) within the foam of the JRME 1970s.

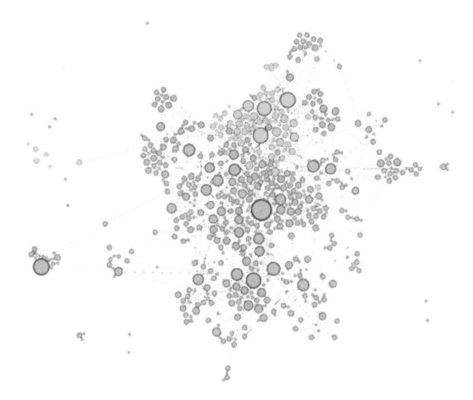

Bubble 4: Learning Sequences and Manipulatives

The fourth bubble discussed of the JRME 1970s is named Learning Sequences and Manipulatives. This bubble draws primarily on the psychological perspectives of Gagné (*The Conditions of Learning*, 1965) and Bruner ("Some Theorems on Instruction Illustrated with Reference to Mathematics," 1964). Indeed, Phillips and Kane's "Validating Learning Hierarchies for Sequencing Mathematical Tasks in Elementary School Mathematics" (1973) cited both Gagné and Bruner.

Otherwise, Eisenberg and Walbesser's "Learning Hierarchies: Numerical Considerations" (1917) and King's "On Scrambling Instructional Stimuli" (1970) both cited Gagné only, while Barnett and Eastman's "The Use of Manipulative Materials and Student Performance in the Enactive and Iconic Modes" (1978) and Williams and Mick's "Measuring the Effectiveness of Using Slide-Tape Lessons in Teaching Basic Algebra to Mathematically Disadvantaged Students" (1976) only cited Bruner. Topically, these articles are concerned with the learning of mathematics through the presentation of carefully sequenced problems or though the incorporation of manipulatives. The cluster of articles on manipulatives are at the top portion of Bubble 4 in Figure 17. The articles on learning sequences and hierarchies constitute the remainder of the bubble.

Figure 17. Location of the bubble "Learning Sequences and Manipulatives" (in blue) within the foam of the JRME 1970s.

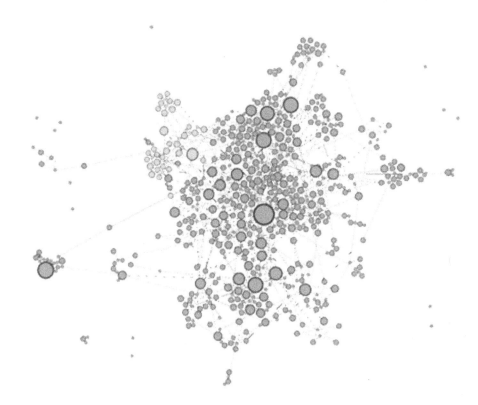

Bubble 5: Statistical Psychology of Learning

The fifth bubble discussed of the JRME 1970s is named Statistical Psychology of Learning and is relatively central to the foam (see Figure 18). The key JRME articles in this bubble are Branca and Kilpatrick's "The Consistency of Strategies in the Learning of Mathematical Structures" (1972), Van Wagenen and Flora's "The Introduction of Mathematics through Measurement or through Set Theory: A Comparison" (1976), Gawronski's "Inductive and Deductive Learning Styles in Junior High School Mathematics: An Exploratory Study" (1972), Bana and Nelson's "Distractors in Nonverbal Mathematical Problems" (1974), and Coulson and Howe's "Certain School and Pupil

34

Characteristics and Mathematics Test Results in Wisconsin" (1977). Topically, these articles drew primarily on the structural mathematical psychology of Dienes (1965, 1970) and problem-solving work of Kilpatrick (e.g., 1969). The unifying characteristic of these works, however, is their use of statistical methods, namely, Hays' *Statistics for psychologists* (1963) and Snedecor and Cochran's *Statistical methods* (1967). The sole exception to the empirical nature of this bubble is the commentary "Is the (Psychological) World Flat?" by Christopher Columbus [attributed to Larry Sowder in a footnote]. There, Sowder was critical of the sole use of linear regression in much statistical analyses, arguing instead to consider empirical or theoretical arguments for more complicated (e.g., quadratic) models.

Figure 18. Location of the bubble "Statistical Psychology of Learning" (in yellow) within the foam of the JRME 1970s.

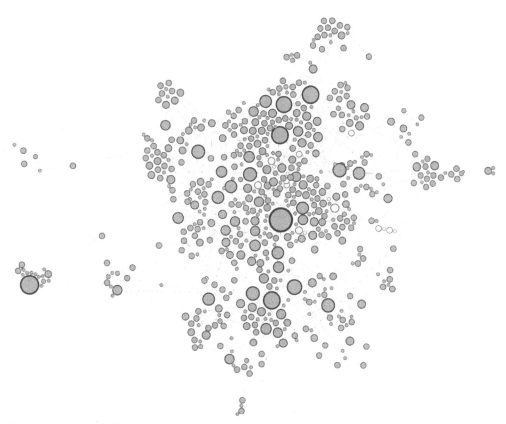

Bubble 6: International Comparative Assessment

The sixth bubble discussed of the JRME 1970s, named International Comparative Assessment, largely focuses on the results of the *International study of achievement in mathematics: A comparison of twelve countries* (Husén [ed.], 1972). Volume 2, Number 2 of the JRME was a special issue titled "International Study of Achievement in Mathematics" and each of its 14 articles cites the findings of that assessment. The other most-cited references include Fehr's "Mathematics program in Japanese secondary schools" (1966), Willoughby's "Who won the international contest?" (1968), and the National Advisory Committee on Mathematical Education's (1975) "Overview and analysis of school mathematics, grades K-12." Relative to the foam, however, these articles are quite marginal (see Figure 19): showing the (literal and figurative) distance between international comparative assessments and the majority of mathematics education research.

Figure 19. Location of the bubble "International Comparative Assessment" (in orange) within the foam of the JRME 1970s.

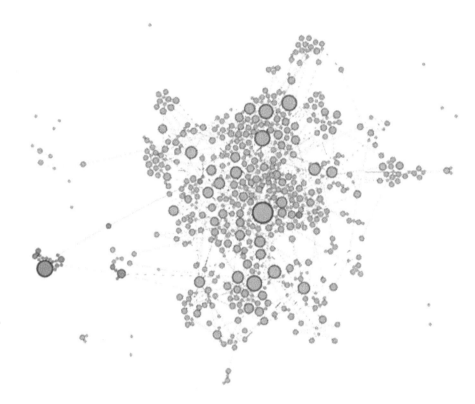

Bubble 7: Heuristics and Processes of Problem Solving

The seventh bubble discussed of the JRME 1970s is named Heuristics and Processes of problem solving. This bubble, shown in Figure 20, shows the relatively clustered nature of this bubble and its location near the center of the foam. This cluster primarily draws on three unpublished doctoral dissertations: Wilson's "Generality of heuristics as an instructional variable" and Kilpatrick's "Analyzing the solution of word problems in mathematics: An exploratory study" (both of Stanford in 1967) and Lucas' "An exploratory study on the diagnostic teaching of heuristic problem solving strategies in calculus" (Wisconsin-Madison in 1972). The JRME articles which cite this further reinforce the connection between heuristics and problem-solving: Kantowski's "Processes Involved in Mathematical Problem Solving" (1977) and Schoenfeld's "Explicit Heuristic Training as a Variable in Problem-Solving Performance" (1979).

Another two highly cited references of this bubble include a chapter by Shulman "Psychology and mathematics education" (1970) in Begle's edited collection *Mathematics education: Sixty-ninth Yearbook of the National Society for the Study of Education* and Pólya's *Mathematical discovery: On understanding, learning, and teaching problem solving* (1962). Begle was on both of Wilson's and Kilpatrick's dissertation committees and Pólya was on Kilpatrick's dissertation committee; this shows the dense connections of not only the citations, but interpersonal relations of this bubble.

Figure 20. Location of the bubble "Heuristics and Processes of Problem Solving" (in purple) within the foam of the JRME 1970s.

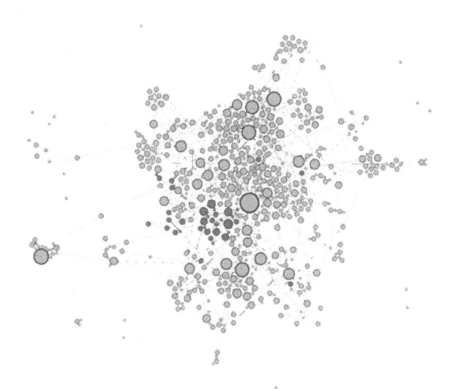

Bubble 8: Effect of Activity-Oriented Instruction

The eighth bubble discussed of the JRME 1970s is named Effect of Activity-Oriented Instruction (see Figure 21). This bubble is anchored by several JRME articles including Moody, Abell, & Bausell's "The Effect of Activity-Oriented Instruction upon Original Learning, Transfer, and Retention" (1971) and Holz's "Comments on the Effect of Activity-Oriented Instruction" (1972) which both show benefits of activity-oriented instruction for student achievement. Austin's later "An Experimental Study of the Effects of Three Instructional Methods in Basic Probability and Statistics" (1974) considered the effects of activity, pictoral, and symbolic engagement that correspond to Bruner's model of cognitive development in Toward a theory of instruction (1966). Other foundational texts that this JRME work builds upon are Kieren's review "Activity learning" (1969) and Dienes' "Some basic processes involved in mathematics learning" (1967).

Figure 21. Location of the bubble "Effect of Activity-Oriented Instruction" (in navy) within the foam of the JRME 1970s.

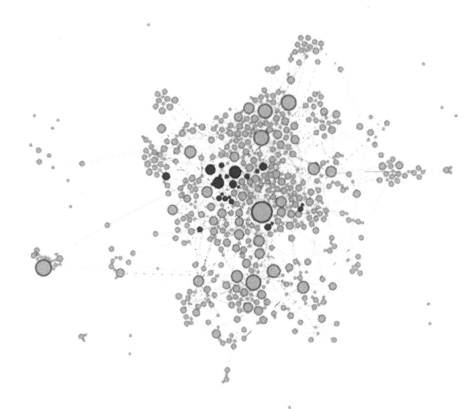

Bubble 9: The Learning of Basic Facts

The ninth bubble discussed of the JRME 1970s is named The Learning of Basic Facts (see Figure 22). This bubble draws foundationally on the early work of Brownell: "The development of children's number ideas in the primary grades" (1928) and "The effects of premature drill in third-grade arithmetic" (with Chazal, 1935). Kilpatrick & Weaver's JRME article "The Place of William A. Brownell in Mathematics Education" (1977) emphasizes the central role that Brownell's early work has within this bubble.

A later JRME article by Cifarelli & Wheatley "Formal Thinking Strategies: A Prerequisite for Learning Basic Facts?" (1979) questioned Rathmell's assumption in "Using thinking strategies to learn the basic facts" (1978) that that drill method of instruction has indeed failed and that the teaching of formal thinking strategies is a necessity. Rathmell used Brownell and Chazal's study (above) as evidence of this, which Cifarelli & Wheatley argued is an over-simplification. Indeed, Cifarelli & Wheatley cited Wheatley's earlier "A comparison of two methods of column addition" (1976) which found that "strategies stressing understanding actually decreased the computational skills of children who utilized these strategies while performing an algorithm" (Cifarelli & Wheatley, 1979, p. 369).

Steffe (1979) and Rathmell (1979) both replied to Cifarelli & Wheatley. Rathmell replied directly to their critique of his work by arguing that there are sufficient additional studies—he offered four additional citations—that supported his claim that "Teaching thinking strategies and then providing follow-up drill does facilitate learning and retention of the basic facts" (1979, p. 375) but conceded that more studies on whether "formal instruction in thinking strategies attain the goals the strategies are designed to achieve" (p. 375) are warranted.

Steffe's (1979) refutation of Cifarelli & Wheatley took a different approach, instead suggesting that:

> Brownell's (1928) classical study was predicated on an assumption that acquisition of basic facts was indeed the goal of thinking strategies. Although none would argue that the basic facts should be meaningfully habituated, I submit they should not be considered the only goal of thinking strategies, or even the one most important. (p. 373).

These later responses, together, suggested that there was sufficient evidence for the teaching of thinking strategies to support the learning of basic facts, even if that is not the only or primary goal of such instruction.

Figure 22. Location of the bubble "The Learning of Basic Facts" (in green) within the foam of the JRME 1970s.

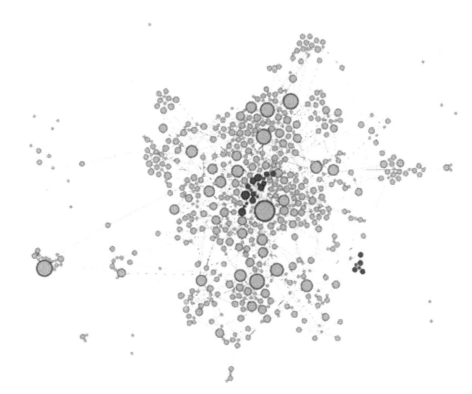

Bubble 10: Quantitative Research Methods

The tenth bubble discussed of the JRME 1970s is named Quantitative Research Methods. This bubble's most cited reference, and indeed the most cited reference across the entirety of the JRME in the 1970s is Winer's *Statistical principles in experimental design* (1962). The next most cited references are Henderson's "A model for teaching mathematical concepts" (1967), Bloom's "Taxonomy of educational objectives" (1956), and Rector and Henderson's "The relative effectiveness of four strategies for teaching mathematical concepts" (1970). Of articles published in the JRME, Gaston and Kolb's "A Comparison of Three Strategies for Teaching a Selected Mathematical Concept to Students in College Algebra" (1973) and Dossey and Henderson's "The Relative Effectiveness of Four Strategies for Teaching Disjunctive Concepts in Mathematics" (1974) both cite all four of these highly-cited references, indicating not only the centrality of their work within the foam of the 1970s but also the affinity that these methods and topics have. In other words, studies on effectiveness or comparison of teaching strategies used statistical methods. Spatially across the foam of the 1970s, this bubble is most centrally located (see Figure 23), indicating the status that statistical experiments on teaching efficacy held during the 1970s.

Figure 23. Location of the bubble "Quantitative Research Methods" (in green) within the foam of the JRME 1970s.

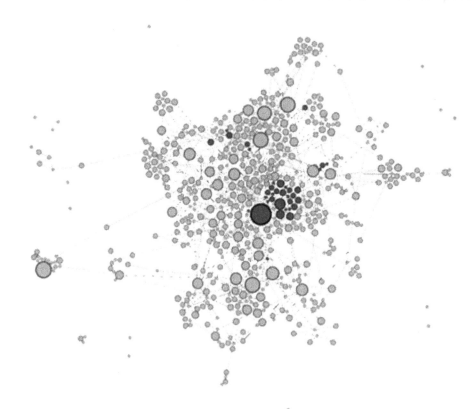

Bubble 11: Factors for Differences in Achievement.

The eleventh bubble discussed of the JRME 1970s is named Factors for Differences in Achievement. This bubble is comprised five clusters that are spread across the foam of the 1970s (see Figure 24). Given this complex structure, I provide the following outline of the clusters and connections across the clusters before I unpack them:

Figure 24. Location of the bubble "Factors for Differences in Achievement" (in brown) within the foam of the JRME 1970s.

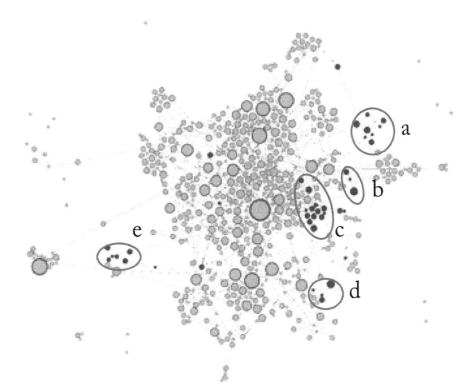

- a is anchored by Fennema & Sherman's "Sex-Related Differences in Mathematics Achievement and Related Factors: A Further Study" (JRME, 1978) which interrogated sex as a related factor to mathematics achievement, and found that when they exist, differences between boys' and girls' achievement are not large;
- b is anchored by Diedrich & Glennon's "The Effects of Studying Decimal and Nondecimal Numeration Systems on Mathematical Understanding, Retention, and Transfer" (JRME, 1970) which studied student differences based on two measures: IQ and MACH both based on prior standardized assessment;
- c is anchored by Fennema's "Mathematics Learning and the Sexes: A Review" (JRME, 1974) and Cathcart's "The Correlation of Selected Nonmathematical Measures with Mathematics Achievement" (1974)
- d is anchored by Harris & Romberg's "An Analysis of Content and Task Dimensions of Mathematics Items Designed to Measure Level of Concept Attainment" (JRME, 1974) which showed that their assessment of 30 mathematical concepts yielded similar results for both boys and girls;

- e is anchored by Smith & Edmonds' "Teacher Vagueness and Pupil Participation in Mathematics Learning" (JRME, 1978) which showed that high levels of teacher vagueness negatively impacted student achievement;
- a is connected to c by two shared citations in Fennema & Sherman (11a; 1978) and Fennema (11c; 1974): Aiken (11c; 1971) and Glennon & Callahan (11b; 1968);
- b contains Glennon & Callahan (1968) which bridges a to b and b to c;
- b is connected to d via Reys & Rea (1970) which cites both Glennon & Callahan (11b; 1968) and Kaiser, H. F. (11d); and
- c is connected to e via Zahn (11e, 1966) which is cited by both Fennema (11c, 1974) and Smith & Edmond (11e, 1978).

As outlined in the preceding list, each cluster within this bubble is concerned with factors that influence achievement, whether it be gender (11a & 11c), intelligence or previous mathematical achievement (11b), the tasks of the assessment itself (11d), or teacher vagueness (11e). Clusters 11a and 11c are separated, despite their common focus, since Fennema & Sherman's study (11a; 1978) is building on Weaver's (1971, 1972) studies on grade level as a factor on achievement and Grouws & Good's (1976) study on sex-differences on achievement which actually showed that girls performed better than boys when problems included sentences rather than purely symbolic representations whereas Fennema's review (11c, 1974) discusses a swath of research on gender as a factor for achievement explicitly. Within this latter cluster (11c), relevant articles include Wozencraft's "Are boys better than girls in arithmetic?" (1963), Jarvis' "Boy-girl ability differences in elementary school arithmetic" (1964), and Unkel's "A study of the interaction of socioeconomic groups and sex factors with the discrepancy between anticipated achievement and actual achievement in elementary school mathematics" (1966).

Bubble 12: Logic

The twelfth bubble discussed of the JRME 1970s is named Logic (see Figure 25). This bubble generally uses statistical methods (Winer's *Statistical principles in experimental design*, 1971) to build upon Inhelder & Piaget's *The growth in logical thinking from childhood to adolescence* (1958), Hill's "A study of logical abilities of children" (1961), and Suppes & Binford's "Experimental teaching of mathematical logic in the elementary school" (1965). Those JRME articles within this bubble largely consider the development of logic (e.g., Eisenberg & McGinty's "On Comparing Error Patterns and the Effect of Maturation in a Unit on Sentential Logic," 1974, and Lester's "Developmental Aspects of Children's Ability to Understand Mathematical Proof," 1975), pre-service teacher's interpretation of logical statements (e.g., Damarin's "The Interpretation of Statements in Standard Logical Form by Preservice Elementary Teachers," 1977), or particular logical constructs such as negation (e.g., Shumway's "Negative Instances and Mathematical Concept Formation: A Preliminary Study," 1974) and conjunctions (e.g., Damarin's "Conjunctive Interpretations of Logical Connectives: Replication of Results," 1977).

Figure 25. Location of the bubble "Logic" (in orange) within the foam of the JRME 1970s.

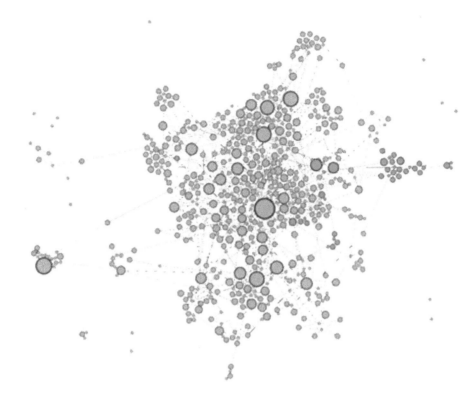

Bubble 13: Geometry and Secondary Mathematics Learning.

The thirteenth bubble discussed of the JRME 1970s is named Geometry and Secondary Mathematics Learning (see Figure 26). This articles in this bubble generally drew on Butler, Wren, & Banks' *The teaching of secondary mathematics* (1970) and conduct analyses from a statistical perspective (Ostle's *Statistics in research*, 1963). Three articles that do so are Hater & Kane's "The Cloze Procedure as a Measure of Mathematical English," Carroll's "The Relative Effectiveness of Three Geometric Proof Construction Strategies" (1977), and Austin's "High School Calculus and First-Quarter College Calculus Grades" (1979). Hater and Kane's article, at first glance, may not seem focused on secondary learning, in their study, the authors used Cloze assessments on mathematical passages to assess lower-secondary (grades 7-10) students' understanding of mathematical language and concepts. These assessments are mathematical passages with key words removed, the students then fill-in-the-blank with the 'missing' word.

Bubble 14: Conceptual Organizers and Assessment

The fourteenth bubble discussed of the JRME 1970s is named Conceptual Organizers and Assessment. The work in this bubble (see Figure 27) centers primarily around the use of advance organizers to facilitate student learning: Romberg and Wilson's "The Effect of an Advance Organizer, Cognitive Set, and Post Organizer on the Learning and Retention of Written Materials" (1973), Scandura and Wells' "Advance organizers in learning abstract mathematics" (1967), Peterson and

Figure 26. Location of the bubble "Geometry and Secondary Mathematics Learning" (in brown) within the foam of the JRME 1970s.

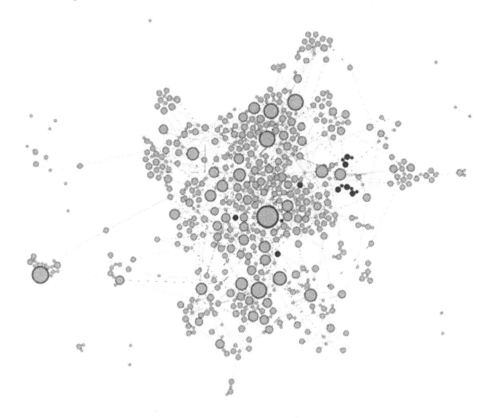

colleagues' "The effect of organizers and knowledge of behavioral objectives on learning a mathematical concept" (1973), and Bright's "Use and Recall of Advance Organizers in Mathematics Instruction" (1976).

Advance organizers (Ausubel, 1960) are teacher presented high-level outlines of the technical material that is to follow, into which students assimilate the detailed explanations they hear through lecture. For example, a lesson on quadrilaterals might begin with an advance organizer that names squares, rhombuses, rectangles, trapezoids, quadrilaterals, and kites. The details and definitions of these objects are excluded until later in the lecture when they are introduced and contrasted with each other. This outline-like cognitive structure serves as the foundation upon which student learning develops.

Romberg and Wilson's "The Development of Tests" (1969), however, is the most cited reference within this bubble; indicating part of this research focus is on the measurement of learning. Together with Ausubel's *The psychology of meaningful verbal learning* (1963), the second most cited, these articles paint a particular picture in which student learning is organized by the teacher, presented verbally to the students to receive, and assessed via testing. This picture is further colored-in by Sowder's "The Influence of Verbalization of Discovered Numerical- or Sorting-Task Generalizations on Short-Term Retention in Connection with the Hendrix Hypothesis" (1974) and Eisenberg's

Figure 27. Location of the bubble "Conceptual Organizers and Assessment" (in blue) within the foam of the JRME 1970s.

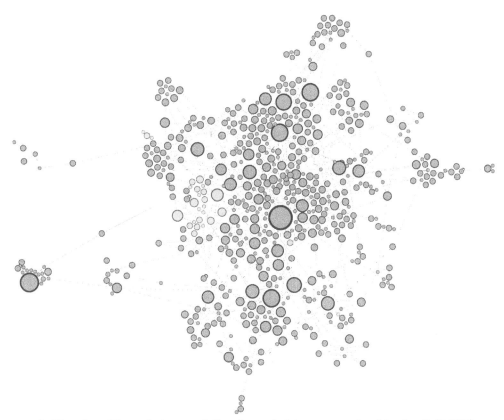

"Begle Revisited: Teacher Knowledge and Student Achievement in Algebra" (1977); as these both indicate the roles of teacher and student.

Bubble 15: Attitude towards Mathematical Topics

The fifteenth bubble discussed of the JRME 1970s is named Attitude towards Mathematical Topics (see Figure 28). This bubble builds on Dutton & Blum's "The measurement of attitudes toward arithmetic with a Likert-type test" (1968) and Aiken's review "Attitudes toward mathematics" (1970), largely via statistical methods (e.g., Cambell & Stanley's Experimental and quasi-experimental designs for research, 1963). Core JRME articles of this bubble include Hogan's "Students' Interests in Particular Mathematics Topics" (1977) and Shann's "Children's Discrimination between Enjoyment and Value of Arithmetic" (1979).

Bubble 16: Word Problems

The sixteenth bubble discussed of the JRME 1970s is named Word Problems. Caldwell & Goldin's "Variables Affecting Word Problem Difficulty in Elementary School Mathematics" (JRME, 1979) sets the tone for this bubble which primarily focuses on children's ability to solve word problems, with a particular emphasis on their difficulties. The three articles near the very center of the foam (see Figure 29) focus on work by Olton on "A self-instructional program for developing productive

Figure 28. Location of the bubble "Attitude towards Mathematical Topics" (in salmon) within the foam of the JRME 1970s.

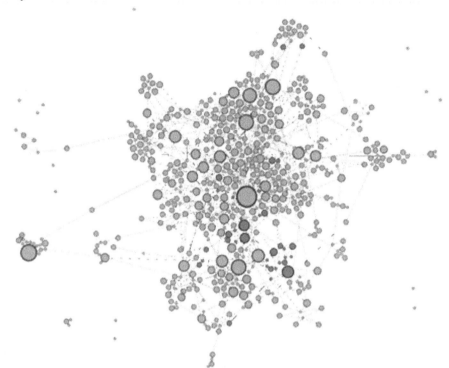

Figure 29. Location of the bubble "Word Problems" (in orange) within the foam of the JRME 1970s.

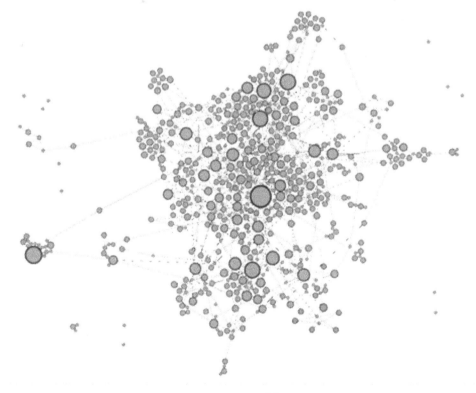

thinking skills in fifth- and sixth-grade children" (1969) and by Jerman on "Individualized instruction in problem solving in elementary school mathematics" (1973). Included is a critique by Callahan titled "Some General Questions about Jerman's Study of Problem Solving" (1974) in which he challenges Jerman's use of the term "individualized instruction" arguing it is more properly called "self-instruction" as Olton names it.

Other researchers consider reading difficulties by Knifong & Holtan "An Analysis of Children's Written Solutions to Word Problems" (1976) and "A Search for Reading Difficulties among Erred Word Problems" (1977), which builds upon earlier work including Martin's "Reading comprehension, abstract verbal reasoning, and computation as factors in arithmetic problem solving" (1963), Balow's "Reading and computation ability as determinants of problem solving" (1964), and Lyda & Duncan's "Quantitative vocabulary and problem solving" (1967).

Bubble 17: Ability-Instruction Interaction

The seventeenth bubble discussed of the JRME 1970s is named Ability-Instruction Interaction (see Figure 30). This bubble primarily considers the interaction between student ability and the presentation of concepts by teachers. The articles within this bubble build on earlier work in scientific psychology such as Cronbach's "The two disciplines of scientific psychology" (1957), which heralded experimental and correlational psychology as two streams within scientific psychology, and French, Ekstrom, & Price's "Kit of reference tests for cognitive factors" and accompanying "Manual for kit of reference tests for cognitive factors" (1963).

Figure 30. Location of the bubble "Ability-Instruction Interaction" (in blue) within the foam of the JRME 1970s.

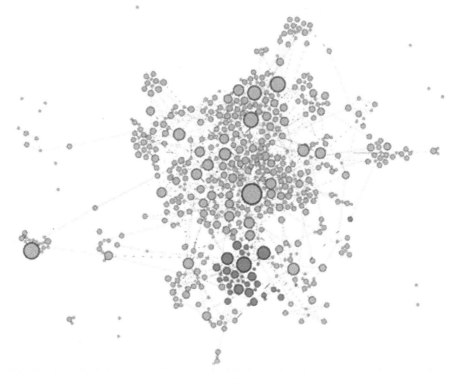

Other highly cited articles consider, more generally, the interaction between ability and instruction (Cronbach & Snow's "Individual differences in learning ability as a function of instructional variables," 1969), or, more specifically, the interaction between visualization and reasoning ability and algebra instruction (Carry's "Interaction of visualization and general reasoning abilities with instructional treatment in algebra," 1968) and the interaction between intellect and modular arithmetic instruction (Behr's "Interactions between structure-of-intellect factors and two methods of presenting concepts of modular arithmetic-a summary paper," 1970).

Much of the work done within this bubble that was published in JRME is associated with one of Behr, Eastman, or Carry. Topically, the studies on the interaction with ability and instruction consider (1) modular arithmetic (Behr & Eastman's "Interactions between Structure-of-Intellect Factors and Two Methods of Presenting Concepts of Modulus Seven Arithmetic: A Follow-up and Refinement Study," 1975), (2) logic (Eastman & Behr's "Interaction between Structure of Intellect Factors and Two Methods of Presenting Concepts of Logic," 1977), and (3) spatial visualization (Eastman & Carry's "Interaction of Spatial Visualization and General Reasoning Abilities with Instructional Treatment in Quadratic Inequalities: A Further Investigation," 1975; Webb & Carry's "Interaction of Spatial Visualization and General Reasoning Abilities with Instructional Treatment in Quadratic Inequalities: A Follow-up Study," 1975; Eastman & Salhab's "The Interaction of Spatial Visualization and General Reasoning Abilities with Instructional Treatment on Absolute Value Equations," 1978). Other researchers, however, went beyond studying the interaction between ability and instruction and instead proceeded from aptitude to design instructional methods: Becker & Young's "Designing Instructional Methods in Mathematics to Accommodate Different Patterns of Aptitude" (1978). Nevertheless, these articles are unified in their consideration of ability and instruction together.

Bubble 18: Attitude and Learning

The eighteenth, and last, bubble discussed of the JRME 1970s is named Attitude and Learning (Figure 31). The National Longitudinal Study of Mathematical Abilities (NLSMA) was a multiyear study that followed three student populations, the X-population (4th graders), the Y-population (7th graders), and the Z-population (10th graders), and measured multidimensional mathematical achievement (content area crossed with level of behavior) together with "attitude towards mathematics, anxiety, motivation, and self-concept" (Amit & Fried, 2008, p. 399). The descriptive and statistical properties of each population, tracking mathematics courses, aptitude, etc. across the length of the study was published in 1968 by the investigators (Wilson, J. W., Cahen, L. S., & Begle, E. G., 1968) and is the most cited reference within this bubble. Other frequently cited references within this bubble include Aiken's "Research on attitudes toward mathematics" (1972) and Cronbach & Snow's *Aptitudes and instructional methods* (1977).

The JRME articles which cite some combination of these references take up the measurement of some aspect of the factors studied in the NLSMA: attitude, anxiety, aptitude, and mathematical exposure. These articles include Aiken's "Two Scales of Attitude toward Mathematics" (1974), Ohlson & Mein's "The Difference in Level of Anxiety in Undergraduate Mathematics and Nonmathematics Majors" (1977), Threadgill's "The Interaction of Learner Aptitude with Types of Questions Accompanying a Written Lesson on Logical Implications" (1979), and Adams & McLeod's "The

Figure 31. Location of the bubble "Attitude and Learning" (in blue) within the foam of the JRME 1970s.

Interaction of Field Dependence/Independence and the Level of Guidance of Mathematics Instruction" (1979).

Macroanalysis: Foam in the 1970s

Having unpacked each of the 18 bubbles in turn, I now transition to the macroanalysis. Here, I shift my gaze from the bubbles as individual research foci towards their relative position within the foam and relative to each other to better understand the landscape of the field in the 1970s as presented within the JRME.

The ForceAtlas2 algorithm encodes meaning in the spatial layout of the nodes; those highly connected nodes have more edges pulling them towards the center. For those less connected, the repulsion force from the other nodes exceeds the contraction force and they settle towards the margins. Given the spatial significance from the algorithm, then, the location of the bubble corresponds to that bubble's centrality/marginality within the foam and to that bubble's research focus' centrality/marginality within the field. Since my focus shifts now to the positions of the bubbles within the foam, to assist the reader in seeing their positions I refer them to Figure 32 which shows the collection of bubbles from the foam but does not include the dots that correspond to the articles within each bubble. In the following subsections I proceed through an analysis that first considers the

Figure 32. Location of the bubbles within the foam of the JRME 1970s.

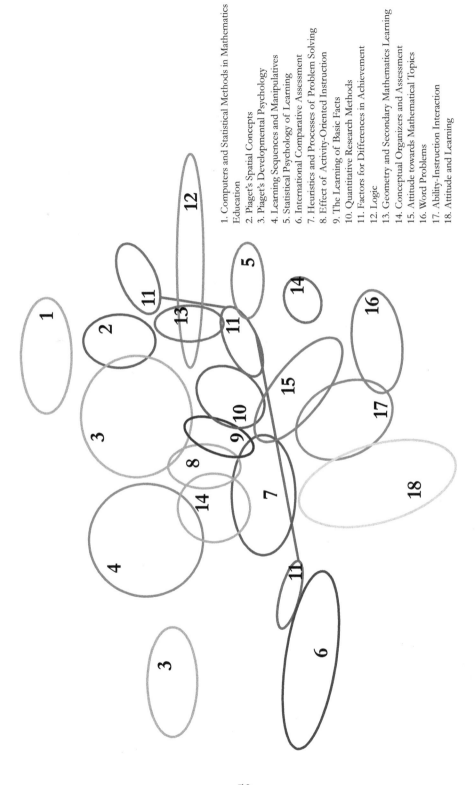

1. Computers and Statistical Methods in Mathematics Education
2. Piaget's Spatial Concepts
3. Piaget's Developmental Psychology
4. Learning Sequences and Manipulatives
5. Statistical Psychology of Learning
6. International Comparative Assessment
7. Heuristics and Processes of Problem Solving
8. Effect of Activity-Oriented Instruction
9. The Learning of Basic Facts
10. Quantitative Research Methods
11. Factors for Differences in Achievement
12. Logic
13. Geometry and Secondary Mathematics Learning
14. Conceptual Organizers and Assessment
15. Attitude towards Mathematical Topics
16. Word Problems
17. Ability-Instruction Interaction
18. Attitude and Learning

centrality of the position of bubbles within the overall foam and second that considers the adjacency and overlap of various bubbles.

Central/Marginal Analysis

The most cited article of the 1970s, Winer's *Statistical principles in experimental design* (1962), in this case (though is not *necessarily* the case), corresponds to the center of the 1970s JRME foam. Then, very central to the field's focus in the 1970s was Quantitative Research Methods (Bubble 10), The Learning of Basic Facts (Bubble 9), Attitude towards Mathematical Topics (Bubble 15), and Heuristics and Processes of Problem Solving (Bubble 7). Similarly emphasized were Effect of Activity-Oriented Instruction (Bubble 8), Conceptual Organizers and Assessment (Bubble 14), and parts of Factors for Differences in Achievement (Bubble 11). In contrast, research focusing on Computers in Mathematics Education (Bubble 1), Piaget's Developmental Psychology (Bubble 3), Learning Sequences, and Manipulatives (Bubble 4), International Comparative Assessment (Bubble 6), Conceptual Organizers and Assessment (Bubble 14) and Attitude and Learning (Bubble 16) are more marginal during the 1970s.

Nearness/Overlap Analysis

Beyond describing the location of the bubbles within the foam, we can glean meaning from the position of one bubble relative to the position of other bubbles. Since there are 153 pairwise comparisons that can be made with 18 bubbles (18 choose 2) and 816 ways to make three-way comparisons from 14 bubbles, I will not exhaustively make all comparisons. I offer a few comparisons that are striking to me, for one reason or another, but invite the reader, in an enactment of Rancièrean equality, to make their own noticings and draw their own comparisons. This act also goes back to the fifth purpose of cartography, the spirit of expansion, and I offer this as one path for further exploration.

Bubbles 2 & 3: Piaget. The reason for the nearness of some pairs of bubbles is clear. For example, there is little surprise that Bubble 2 (Piaget's Spatial Concepts) and Bubble 3 (Piaget's Developmental Psychology) are adjacent. Rather, the fact that these bubbles are distinct is noteworthy. Bubble 2 includes Piaget's *The Child's Conception of Number*, *The Child's Conception of Geometry*, and the secondary *The developmental psychology of Jean Piaget* (Flavell, 1963) while Bubble 3 includes Piaget's *Mental Imagery in the Child*. This division suggests a broader focus on child development within Bubble 2 whereas Bubble 3 is more focused on spatiality and mental imagery.

Bubbles 6 & 11: International Assessment & Factors for Differences in Achievement. Bubble 6 (International Comparative Assessment) primarily focuses on differences in student achievement on a standardized assessment of mathematics in twelve countries but is augmented by comparative research on, for example, US and Japanese schools. This focus on differences is likewise echoed in Bubble 11 (Factors for Differences in Achievement) which similarly emphasized differences in achievement between groups of students on the basis of sex, IQ, grade, teacher quality, etc. Particularly, the cluster of Bubble 11 that is adjacent to Bubble 7 (see Figure 32) is the cluster focusing on teacher influences on achievement. The bridging between these bubbles is via Price, Kelley and Kelley's "'New Math' Implementation: A Look inside the Classroom" (Bubble 6, 1977) and Smith's "Aspects of Teacher Discourse and Student Achievement in Mathematics" (Bubble 11, 1977) both of which drew on Flanders' studies on classroom and teacher behavior (*Analyzing teaching behavior*, 1970 and *Analyzing classroom behavior*, 1970).

Bubbles 12 & 13: Logic and Geometry and Secondary Mathematics Learning. Logic (Bubble 12) and Geometry and Secondary Mathematics Learning (Bubble 13) intersect towards the right of the foam (see Figure 32). Bridging these two bubbles are four articles (two in each bubble) that cite Winer's 1971 version of *Statistical principles in experimental design*. Within the Logic bubble, the citing articles are Lester's "Developmental Aspects of Children's Ability to Understand Mathematical Proof" (1975) and Adi's "Intellectual Development and Reversibility of Thought in Equation Solving" (1978). On the other hand, within the Geometry and Secondary Mathematics Learning, the citing articles are Austin's "High School Calculus and First-Quarter College Calculus Grades" (1979) and Prigge's "The Differential Effects of the Use of Manipulative Aids on the Learning of Geometric Concepts by Elementary School Children" (1978). Even though these articles share only their methods, the algorithm situates them nearby given that both bubbles consistently draw on articles on logic, proof, and secondary topics (even Prigge's article cites a dissertation on teaching geometric proof to secondary students).

Bubbles 16 & 17: Word Problems & Ability-Instruction Interaction. Aiken's literature review "Verbal Factors and Mathematics Learning: A Review of Research" (1971) published in the JRME serves as the bridge between Word Problems (Bubble 16) and Ability-Instruction Interaction (Bubble 17). Aiken's article is contained in Bubble 17 (Ability-Instruction Interaction) but cites two articles in Bubble 16: Balow's "Reading and computation ability as determinants of problem solving" (1964) and Johnson's "On the nature of problem-solving in arithmetic" (1949). These articles in Bubble 16 focused on reading ability and its relationship to ability in solving written word problems, so while Bubble 17 focus on the Ability-Instruction interaction these Bubble 16 considers the Ability-Achievement interaction.

Bubbles 17 & 18: Ability & Attitude. Bubbles 17 (Ability-Instruction Interaction) and 18 (Attitude and Learning) are adjacent (see Figure 32) and have eight edges between them (see Figure 33; Bubble 18 is on the left and Bubble 17 is on the right). Each of the articles on the left (Bubble 17),

Figure 33. Figure showing the edges and nodes that connect Bubbles 17 (right) and 18 (left).

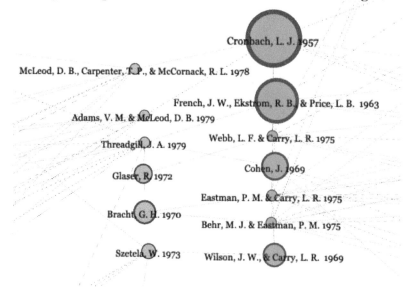

52

with the exception of Bracht, 1970, are JRME articles that cite nodes contained in Bubble 18 suggesting that Attitude and Learning draws on the Ability literature. In contrast, only three of the articles on the right (Webb & Carry, Eastman & Carry, and Behr & Eastman) are JRME articles that cite articles on the left. Those citations that serve as bridges include: Bracht's "Experimental factors related to aptitude-treatment interaction," Cronbach's "The two disciplines of scientific psychology," French and colleagues' "Kit of reference tests for cognitive factors" and its accompany manual, Cohen's "Statistical power analysis for the behavioral sciences," and Wilson & Carry's "Homogeneity of regression-its rationale, computation and use." This overlap further emphasizes the ubiquity of statistical methods across foci and common adoption of psychologistic perspectives on ability.

As I stated above, these are but a few of the comparisons and noticings that could be drawn from these bubbles and their position within the foam of the JRME 1970s. Furthermore, this section provided an overview to the foam of research of the JRME1970s. This foam constitutes one particular partage of mathematics education research, or one outline by which we as mathematics education researchers can make sense of what we can see, say, or do in the name of mathematics education research. My task was (and is) not to establish a law on the proper names of each bubble nor the common threads across bubbles. Rather, the names of each bubble and common threads that I have chosen to emphasize are knowledges produced from this analysis and my context and perspectives, theoretical lenses, and rhetorical purpose (see Chapter 2).

Moving now from the 1970s, I proceed through the 1980s, 1990s, 2000s, and 2010s. Since I illustrated my method of naming and analyzing the bubbles with this decade, I instead present the naming of the bubbles for the following decades in table form. I present those tables to move beyond the descriptive project of naming the bubbles to focus on the marginal/central analysis and bubble adjacency/overlap analysis. Giving the bubble names, however, is necessary since I will conclude this chapter by tracing the shifting nature of these bubbles over time and doing so will facilitate these analyses.

JRME in the 1980s

In this section, I unpack the research published in the JRME in the 1980s. First, I present a map of the research foam of the JRME in the 1980s. Then, I summarize each of the bubbles in the form of a table that includes (1) the bubble's number, (2) the bubble's name, (3) a map with the bubbles relative location within the foam, (4) a list of the most cited articles within that bubble, and (5) a list of a few JRME articles within bubble. My goal for this section is, instead of elaborating the method of naming, to introduce each of the decades bubbles so that I can provide an analysis of the bubbles' position relative to each other and relative to the position of the foam. For the interested reader, interactive versions of each map, complete with every node of each bubble and their relative positions within the foam are available on the companion website at MathEdAtlas.org. I encourage the reader to explore the nodes which comprise each bubble and the overall foam to develop an intuition about the research of the JRME 1980s.

Microanalysis: Bubbles

I proceed now by summarizing the 15 bubbles of research in the JRME 1980s (see Figure 34): (1) Piagetian Cognitive Development of the Child, (2) Child's use of structure, (3) Sex Differences,

Figure 34. Bubbles of research that comprise the IRME 1980s foam.

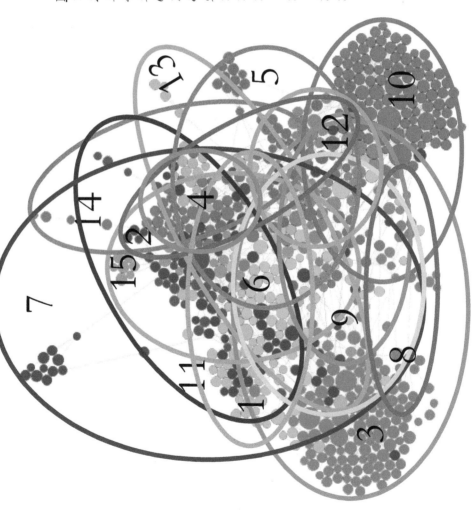

(4) Estimation and Mental Arithmetic, (5) Children's Geometry (van Hiele), (6) Psychology of Mathematics for Instruction, (7) Mathematical Thinking, (8) Teaching Effect on Mathematics Learning, (9) Developmental Mathematics, (10) Arithmetic, (11) Agenda for Action – Problem-Solving, (12) Models/Processes of Addition and Subtraction, (13) Proportional Reasoning – Multiplication and Division Processes & Structure, (14) International Policy and Responses, and (15) Algebraic Learning, Understanding, and Problem Solving. For each bubble (see Table 1), I provide the number used to indicate it on the foam of the 1980s, its name, a mini map that shows the bubble's relative location within the foam of the field, the two most cited articles within that bubble, and two sample JRME articles that are located within that bubble. To easily distinguish JRME articles from the research they cite, all JRME citations are underlined.

Bubble 1 of the JRME 1980s focuses on Piagetian cognitive development. Many articles within this bubble cite Piaget & Inhelder's *The growth of logical thinking from childhood to adolescence* (1958) and discuss topics such as the influence of aptitude (Cronbach & Snow, 1977) and experience on proportional reasoning and differences between males and females during adolescence (Linn & Pulos, 1983) and cognition and achievement (Roberge & Flexer, 1983).

Similarly, Bubble 2 focuses on children but instead draws on research into children's use of mathematical and mathematical cognitive structures (Baroody, Ginsberg, & Waxman, 1983; Geeslin & Shavelson, 1975) in such research as cognitive development and mathematical structures (Branca, 1980) and the communication of mathematical structure's relationship to achievement (McDonald, 1989).

Bubble 3, in contrast, focuses explicitly on sex-differences: drawing on research on the psychology of sex-differences (Maccoby & Jacklin, 1974) and sex-differences in mathematics achievement, learning, and participation (Fennema & Sherman, 1977). JRME articles in this bubble consider sex-differences in first-year algebra (Swafford, 1980) and in spatial visualization (Fennema & Tartre, 1985).

Bubble 4 focuses on a specific mathematical content area: estimation and computation. In the wake of an NCTM position statement on estimation (1977) and Carpenter, Coburn, Reys, & Wilson's "Notes from National Assessment: Estimation" (1976), researchers sought to understand the processes of estimators (Reys, Rybolt, Bestgen, & Wyatt, 1982) and related mathematical skills (Rubenstein, 1985).

Continuing this focus on particular mathematical streams, Bubble 5 is focused on children's geometry, particularly the Van Hiele levels (Van Hiele-Geldorf, 1957). Research in this bubble considered topics such as Van Hiele Levels together with achievement in proof writing (Senk, 1989) and the learning of geometry with LOGO (Clements & Battista, 1989), but not at the sake of excluding other mathematical understandings of children such as number (Gelman & Gallistel, 1978).

Bubble 6 zooms back out from specific mathematical concepts to consider *The Psychology of Mathematics for Instruction* (Resnick & Ford, 1981) and building on cognitive processes, for example, in problem solving (Paige & Simon, 1966). Some JRME articles in this bubble defend the approach of joining psychology to mathematics instruction (Wachsmuth, 1983) or broaden cognition to encompass other tools (e.g., calculators; Wheatley, 1980).

Table 1. The 15 Bubbles of the JRME 1980s Foam. Each includes the bubble name, its location within the foam, the most cited articles, and JRME citing articles.

Bubble Number	Bubble Name	Location within the Foam (colored nodes)	Most Cited Article(s)	JRME Citing Article(s)
1	Piagetian Cognitive Development of the Child		Inhelder & Piaget, 1958 Cronbach & Snow, 1977	Linn & Pulos, 1983 Roberge & Flexer, 1983
2	Child's use of structure		Baroody, Ginsberg, & Waxman, 1983 Geeslin & Shavelson, 1975	Branca, 1980 McDonald, 1989
3	Sex Differences		Maccoby & Jacklin, 1974 Fennema & Sherman, 1977	Swafford, 1980 Fennema & Tartre, 1985
4	Estimation and Mental Arithmetic		Carpenter, Coburn, Reys, & Wilson, 1976 NCTM, 1977 & 1978	Reys, Rybolt, Bestgen, & Wyatt, 1982 Rubenstein, 1985

Table 1 (cont.)

Bubble Number	Bubble Name	Location within the Foam (colored nodes)	Most Cited Article(s)	JRME Citing Article(s)
5	Children's Geometry (van Hiele)		Gelman & Gallistel, 1978 Van Hiele-Geldorf, 1957	Senk, 1989 Clements & Battista, 1989
6	Psychology of Mathematics for Instruction		Resnick & Ford, 1981 Paige & Simon, 1966	Wheatley, 1980 Wachsmuth, 1983
7	Mathematical Thinking		Pólya, 1957 Schoenfeld, 1983	Garofalo & Lester, 1985 Burton, 1984
8	Teaching Effect on Mathematics Learning		Good, Grouws, & Ebmeier, 1983 Romberg & Carpenter, 1986	Leinhardt, 1985 Carpenter, Fennema, Peterson, & Carey, 1988

Table 1 (cont.)

Bubble Number	Bubble Name	Location within the Foam (colored nodes)	Most Cited Article(s)	JRME Citing Article(s)
9	Developmental Mathematics		Steffe, Spikes, & Hirstein, 1976 Case, 1975	Hiebert, 1981 Moyer, Moyer, & Sowder, 1984
10	Arithmetic		Carpenter & Moser, 1984 Riley, Greeno, & Heller, 1983	Baroody, 1985 Fuson, 1984
11	Agenda for Action – Problem-Solving		NCTM, 1980 Kantowski, 1977	Cobb & Steffe, 1983 Schoenfeld, 1982
12	Models/ Processes of Addition and Subtraction		Ginsburg, 1977 Brown & Burton, 1978	Clements, 1982 Lindvall & Ibarra, 1980

Table 1 (cont.)

Bubble Number	Bubble Name	Location within the Foam (colored nodes)	Most Cited Article(s)	JRME Citing Article(s)
13	Proportional Reasoning – Multiplication and Division Processes & Structure		Vergnaud, 1983 Fischbein, Deri, Nello, & Marino, 1985	Ferrandez-Reinisch, 1985 Pothier & Sawada, 1983
14	International Policy and Responses		Piaget & Inhelder, 1956 Committee of Inquiry into the Teaching of Mathematics in Schools, 1982	Hart, 1983 Hope & Sherrill, 1987
15	Algebraic Learning, Understanding, and Problem Solving		Papert, 1980 Clement, 1982	Wagner, 1981 Clement, 1982

Continuing with this broader focus, Bubble 7 considers mathematical thinking broadly such as Pólya's *How to solve it* (1957) and Schoenfeld's push beyond purely cognitive factors of performance such as beliefs, social, and metacognition (1983). JRME articles building upon this work include Burton's "Mathematical Thinking: The Struggle for Meaning" (1984) and explicit uptake of Schoenfeld's work (e.g., Garofalo & Lester's work on metacognition and performance, 1985).

Bubble 8 likewise considers a broader scope: teaching's effect on mathematical learning. Building on research on teaching and learning (Romberg & Carpenter, 1986) such as active teaching (Good, Grouws, & Ebmeier, 1983), JRME articles in this bubble consider teacher's pedagogical content knowledge (Carpenter, Fennema, Peterson, & Carey, 1988) or the difference between novice and experienced teachers (Leinhardt, 1985).

Research within Bubble 9 focuses on developmental mathematics or the development of particular mathematical concepts. Building on early work on developmental readiness (Steffe, Spikes, & Hirstein, 1976) or tailoring instruction to developmental capacities (Case, 1975), researchers publishing in the JRME considered, among other topics, the development of linear measurement (Hiebert, 1981) or problem-solving abilities (Moyer, Moyer, & Sowder, 1984).

Bubble 10 considers children's arithmetical abilities from the foundational acquisition of addition and subtraction (Carpenter & Moser, 1984) to the application of arithmetic to problem-solving (Riley, Greeno, & Heller, 1983). JRME research that builds upon this base elaborated the distinction between a mathematical process and a particular mathematical understanding (Baroody, 1985) or unpacks complexities in subtraction (Fuson, 1984).

Bubble 11 is largely a response to NCTM's *An Agenda for Action* (1980) with particular attention to the role of the teacher (Cobb & Steffe, 1983). With the Agenda's emphasis on problem-solving, other research draws on extant research (e.g., Kantowski, 1977), to elaborate measures of problem-solving performance and the teaching of problem-solving (Schoenfeld, 1982).

Bubble 12 is related to Bubble 10 in its focus on arithmetic, but Bubble 12 focuses explicitly on models of (Brown & Burton, 1978) and the learning processes of (Ginsburg, 1977) addition and subtraction. Research published in the JRME that builds upon this research base considers not only incorrect procedures used by children when learning addition and subtraction (Lindvall & Ibarra, 1980) but also careless errors made by older children (Clements, 1982).

Bubble 13 moves beyond addition and subtraction to consider multiplicative structures (Vergnaud, 1983) and models (Fischbein, Deri, Nello, & Marino, 1985) for multiplication and division. Research that builds on this considers a range of topics from partitioning to introduce rational numbers (Pothier & Sawada, 1983) to inverse proportionality (Ferrandez-Reinisch, 1985).

Research in Bubble 14 is largely a response to the so-called Cockcroft Report titled *Mathematics Counts* (Committee of Inquiry into the Teaching of Mathematics in Schools, 1982) and the pragmatic needs of students (Hope & Sherrill, 1987). Hart (1983), in particular, argues against a deficit perspective on the child and argues that it is important to meet the child where they are in understanding (e.g., Piaget & Inhelder's developmental approach to the child and their conception of space, 1956) and a one-size-fits-all approach is not a necessary step forward in mathematics education.

Bubble 15 largely focuses on algebra. Some foundational literature includes Papert's *Mindstorms: Children, computers and powerful ideas* (1980) which draws a parallel between the computer and use of variables in algebra. Unlike other bubbles, Clements' "Algebra word problem solutions: Thought processes underlying a common misconception" (1982) was both published in the JRME and among the most cited references within this bubble. Other JRME research within this bubble considered algebraic concepts such as transformation of variables, equality, and functions (Wagner, 1981).

Macroanalysis: Foam

Having introduced each of the 15 bubbles, I now transition to the macroanalysis. Here, I shift my gaze from the bubbles as individual research foci towards their position relative within the foam and relative to each other to better understand the landscape of the field in the 1980s as presented within the JRME. Since my focus shifts now to the positions of the bubbles within the foam, to assist the reader in seeing their positions I refer them to Figure 35 which shows the collection of bubbles from the foam but does not include the dots that correspond to the articles within each bubble. In the following subsections I proceed through an analysis that first considers the centrality of the position of bubbles within the overall foam and second that considers the adjacency and overlap of various bubbles.

Central/Marginal Analysis

Unlike the 1970s, the foam of the JRME 1980s does not have a clear center. The most cited article is NCTM's *Agenda for Action* which is contained in Bubble 11 towards the top of the foam. There are two large clusters of research which separate from the center of the foam towards the lower left (Bubble 3) and lower right (Bubble 10). Also unlike the 1970s, there are no bubbles which are clearly marginal and clearly central relative to the foam. Bubble 10 (arithmetic) is the most marginal to the foam suggesting that arithmetic is not central to the field during the 1980s, or at least not in the research method that those studies adopt. To elaborate, Bubble 12, which are cognitive models and studies of addition and subtraction processes of arithmetic, are more central than Bubble 10. This suggests that if the topic is not central, the use of particular approaches, namely psychologistic perspectives (e.g., Bubble 6), bring that research more central to the field as a whole.

Nearness/Overlap Analysis

For the 1980s, there are three relative positionings of bubbles that I have chosen to unpack: the bridging of Bubble 8 between Bubbles 3 and 10, the Bubbles 9, 10, and 12 overlap, and the distance between Bubbles 4 and 10.

The Connection between Bubbles 3 and 10: Bubble 8. As discussed above, Bubbles 3 and 10 primarily focus on sex-differences in mathematical achievement and arithmetic, respectively. Bubble 3 moves beyond a presumed difference in ability, however, and considers the effect of socialization, experience, and learning opportunities. Bubble 8, then, as the teaching effect on learning, serves as a bridge between the content focus of Bubble 10 and the achievement focus of Bubble 3.

The Overlap between Bubbles 9, 10, and 12. Topically, Bubbles 9, 10, and 12 are closely related: developmental mathematics, arithmetic, and processes of addition and subtraction. Furthermore, at least one article from each bubble cites Case's "A developmentally based theory and technology of instruction" (1978) suggesting that, at least orientationally, researchers within the arithmetic bubble and processes of addition and subtraction bubble are cognizant of developmental implications in the learning of arithmetic.

The Distance between Bubbles 4 and 10. Bubble 4 (Estimation) and Bubble 10 (Arithmetic) share no overlap. This suggests that these bubbles are disjoint in the literature bases from which they draw, yet estimation is applicable across all operations (addition, subtraction, multiplication, and division) and content divisions (such as estimating length, area, volume in geometry). Therefore, it seems interesting that research into estimation in the 1980s neglects the literature on addition and subtraction since today, estimation is taught as a strategy for checking calculations, for approximating sum, differences, products, quotients, etc., and together with the operations.

As with the 1970s, these are but a few of the comparisons and noticing that could be drawn from the bubbles of the 1980s and their position within the foam of the JRME 1980s. This foam

Figure 35. The bubbles of the 1980s JRME foam.

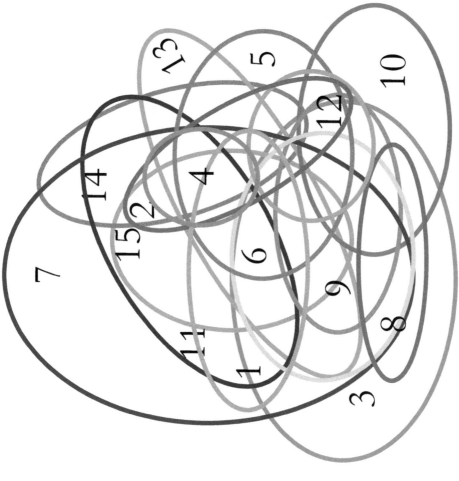

constitutes one particular partage of mathematics education research, or one outline by which we as mathematics education researchers can make sense of what we can see, say, or do in the name of mathematics education research. My task was (and is) not to establish a law on the proper names of each bubble nor the common threads across bubbles. Rather, the names of each bubble and common threads that I have chosen to emphasize are knowledges produced from this analysis and my context and perspectives, theoretical lenses, and rhetorical purpose (see Chapter 2).

JRME in the 1990s

In this section, I unpack the research published in the JRME in the 1990s. First, I present a map of the research foam of the JRME in the 1990s (see Figure 36). Then, I summarize each of the bubbles in the form of a table that includes (1) the bubble's number, (2) the bubble's name, (3) a map with the bubbles relative location within the foam, (4) a list of the most cited articles within that bubble, and (5) a list of a few JRME articles within that bubble. My goal for this section is, instead of elaborating the method of naming, to introduce each of the decades bubbles so that I can provide an analysis of the bubbles' positions relative to each other and relative to the position of the foam. For the interested reader, interactive versions of each map, complete with every node of each bubble and their relative positions within the foam are available on the companion website at MathEdAtlas.org. I encourage the reader to explore the nodes which comprise each bubble and the overall foam to develop an intuition about the research of the JRME 1990s.

Microanalysis: Bubbles

I proceed now by summarizing the 22 bubbles of research in the JRME 1990s: (1) van Hiele Understanding and Development of Geometry, (2) Equity and Politics of Mathematics Education, (3) Number Sense, (4) Children's Place-Value Addition and Subtraction, (5) Mathematics Knowledge for Teaching, (6) Case Studies of Teachers, (7) Word Problems and Problem-Solving, (8) Probability, (9) Children's Learning in Classrooms, (10) Second International Mathematics Study, (11) Constructivist Research on Teaching and Learning, (12) Problem Solving, (13) Teachers of Mathematics, (14) Mathematics Anxiety & Sex Differences, (15) Cognitively Guided Instruction, (16) Language and the Construction of Meaning, (17) Multiplicative Reasoning, (18) NCTM Standards & Culturally-Relevant Mathematics, (19) Mathematics Achievement, (20) Multicultural and Critical Mathematics Education, (21) Critical Responses to Theories of Learning, and (22) Experience of Learning Mathematics. For each bubble (see Table 2), I provide the number used to indicate it on the foam of the 1990s, its name, a mini map that shows the bubble's relative location within the foam of the field, the two most cited articles within that bubble, and two sample JRME articles that are located within that bubble.

Bubble 1, like the corresponding bubble of the 1970s, builds on Van Hiele's *Structure and insight: A theory of mathematics education* (1986). JRME research articles on young children's concept of shape (Clements, Swaminath, & Hannibal, 1999) and the use of computers to support children's geometry learning (Clements & Battista, 1990) also build on the growing secondary literature of the 1980s: Fuys, Geddes, & Tischler's "The van Hiele model of thinking in geometry among adolescents" (1988).

Figure 36. Bubbles of research that comprise the JRME 1990s foam.

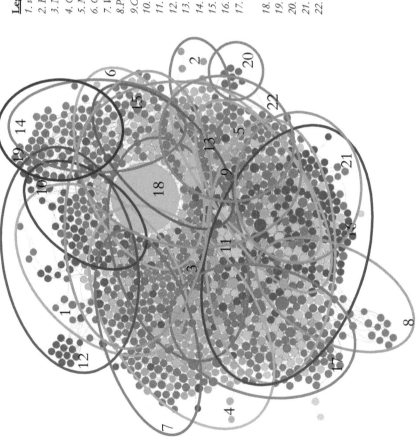

Legend:
1. *van Hiele Understanding and Development of Geometry*
2. *Equity and Politics of Mathematics Education*
3. *Number Sense (Concepts and Computation)*
4. *Children's Place-Value Addition and Subtraction*
5. *Mathematics Knowledge for Teaching*
6. *Case Studies of Teachers*
7. *Word Problems and Problem-Solving*
8. *Probability*
9. *Children's Learning in Classrooms*
10. *Second International Mathematics Study*
11. *Constructivist Research on Teaching and Learning*
12. *Problem Solving*
13. *Teachers of Mathematics*
14. *Mathematics Anxiety & Sex Differences*
15. *Cognitively Guided Instruction*
16. *Language and the Construction of Meaning*
17. *Multiplicative Reasoning – Understanding Rational Numbers, Multiplication, and Division*
18. *NCTM Standards & Culturally-Relevant Mathematics*
19. *Mathematics Achievement*
20. *Multicultural and Critical Mathematics Education*
21. *Critical Responses to Theories of Learning*
22. *Experience of Learning Mathematics (Curriculum and Writing)*

Table 2. The 22 Bubbles of the JRME 1990s Foam. Each includes the bubble name, its location within the foam, the most cited articles, and JRME citing articles.

Bubble Number	Bubble Name	Location within the Foam (colored nodes)	Most Cited Article(s)	JRME Citing Article(s)
1	van Hiele Understanding and Development of Geometry		Fuys, Geddes, & Tischler, 1988 Van Hiele, 1986	Clements, Swaminath, & Hannibal 1999 Clements & Battista, 1990
2	Equity and Politics of Mathematics Education		Apple, 1992 Secada, 1989	Peressini, 1998 Burrill, 1998
3	Number Sense		Greeno 1991 Sowder, 1992a	Greeno 1991 Reys, Reys, Nohda, & Emori, 1995
4	Children's Place-Value Addition and Subtraction		Kamii 1985 Fuson 1986 & 1988	Gray & Tall, 1994 Pepper & Hunting, 1998

Table 2 (cont.)

Bubble Number	Bubble Name	Location within the Foam (colored nodes)	Most Cited Article(s)	JRME Citing Article(s)
5	Mathematics Knowledge for Teaching		Ball 1990 Thompson 1984	Smith, 1996 Eisenhart, Borko, Underhill, Brown, Jones, & Agard, 1993
6	Case Studies of Teachers		Küchemann, 1981 Merriam, 1988	MacGregor & Stacey, 1993 Haimes, 1996
7	Word Problems and Problem-Solving		Riley, Greeno, & Heller, 1983 Fuson 1992a	Carpenter, Ansell, Franke, Fennema, & Weisbeck, 1993 Verschaffel, DeCorte, & Vierstraete, 1999
8	Probability		Fischbein, 1987 Piaget & Inhelder, 1951/75	Konold, Pollatsek, Well, Lohmeier, & Lipson, 1993 Fischbein & Schnarch, 1997

Table 2 (cont.)

Bubble Number	Bubble Name	Location within the Foam (colored nodes)	Most Cited Article(s)	JRME Citing Article(s)
9	Children's Learning in Classrooms		Rombeg & Carpenter, 1986 Glaser & Strauss, 1967	Lo, Wheatley, & Smith, 1994 Leikin & Zaslavsky, 1997
10	Second International Mathematics Study		Crosswhite, Dossey, Swafford, McKnight, Cooney, Downs, Grouws, & Weinzweig, 1986 McKnight, Crosswhite, Dossey, Kifer, Swafford, Travers, & Cooney, 1987	Flanders, 1994 Ethington, 1990
11	Constructivist Research on Teaching and Learning		Simon, 1995 Cobb, Yackel, & Wood, 1992	Simon, 1995 Steffe & Kieren, 1994
12	Problem Solving		Schoenfeld 1985 Pólya 1945	Hembree 1992 Lester 1994

Table 2 (cont.)

Bubble Number	Bubble Name	Location within the Foam (colored nodes)	Most Cited Article(s)	JRME Citing Article(s)
13	Teachers of Mathematics		Shulman 1986 Thompson 1992	Cooney, 1994 Lloyd & Wilson, 1998
14	Mathematics Anxiety & Sex Differences		Fennema & Sherman, 1976, 1977, 1978 Fennema, Peterson, Carpenter, & Lubinski, 1990	McLeod, 1994 Fennema & Hart, 1994 Ma, 1999
15	Cognitively Guided Instruction		Dossey, Mullis, Lindquist, & Chambers, 1988 Fennema, Franke, Carpenter, & Carey, 1993	Fennema, Carpenter, Franke, Levi, Jacobs, & Empson, 1996 Knapp & Peterson, 1995
16	Language and the Construction of Meaning		Lampert, 1990 Vygotsky, 1962	Wood, 1999 Cobb, Yackel, & Wood, 1992

Table 2 (cont.)

Bubble Number	Bubble Name	Location within the Foam (colored nodes)	Most Cited Article(s)	JRME Citing Article(s)
17	Multiplicative Reasoning		Steffe, Cobb, & von Glasersfeld, 1988 Steffe, von Glasersfeld, Richards, & Cobb, 1983	Hunting & Davis, 1996 Clark & Kamii 1996
18	NCTM Standards & Culturally Relevant Mathematics		NCTM, 1989, 1991 Ladson-Billings, 1997	Henningsen & Stein, 1997 Silver, Mamona-Downs, & Leung, 1996 Gutstein, Lipman, Hernandez, & de los Reyes, 1997
19	Mathematics Achievement		Hyde, Fennema, & Lamon, 1990 Friedman, 1989	Ma & Kishor, 1997 Seegers & Boekaerts, 1996
20	Multicultural and Critical Mathematics Education		Frankenstein 1989, 1990	Sleeter, 1997 Murtadha-Watts & D'Ambrosio, 1997

Table 2 (cont.)

Bubble Number	Bubble Name	Location within the Foam (colored nodes)	Most Cited Article(s)	JRME Citing Article(s)
21	Critical Responses to Theories of Learning		Walkerdine, 1988	Lerman, 1996
			Von Glasersfeld, 1990	Davis, 1997
22	Experience of Learning Mathematics		Erickson, 1986	Siegel, Borasi & Fonzi, 1998
			Eisenhart, 1988	Borasi, 1994

New in the 1990s is a bubble on the Equity and Politics of Mathematics Education: Bubble 2. Within this bubble is a literature base responding to the issue of equity and the NCTM (1989) *Standards*. Secada (1989) questions the self-interested, agenda-setting of the Standards while Apple (1992) pushes against it as a slogan system that does not go far enough to address issues of inequity. Building on this work was research on the position and portrayal of parents when discussing school reform (Peressini, 1998) and an address by then-president of NCTM's on the changing mathematics classroom (Burrill, 1998).

Bubble 3, Number Sense, includes Greeno's "Number sense as situated knowing in a conceptual domain" (1991) which is both a JRME article and one of the most cited articles within that bubble. In addition to Greeno's work, researchers such as in this bubble build on work on the relationship between number sense and estimation (Sowder, 1992a) in an investigation of Japanese students' mental computation (Reys, Reys, Nohda, & Emori, 1995).

Related to Bubble 3 is Bubble 4 on Children's Place-Value Addition and Subtraction. Serving as foundational to the research within this bubble is Kamii's work on children's reinvention of arithmetic (1985) and Fuson's studies on children's concept of number (1986) and place-value addition and subtraction (1988). The research published in the JRME included extending the study of children's number understanding to preschoolers (Pepper & Hunting, 1998) and the blended 'proceptual' view of arithmetic (Gray & Tall, 1994).

Bubble 5 of the 1990s includes articles and research on Mathematics Knowledge for Teaching. Among the literature cited in this bubble are studies on teacher knowledge (Ball, 1990) and the relationship between teachers' knowledge of teaching and their teaching practice (Thompson 1984). Building on the relationship between a teacher's knowledge of teaching and their practice, Smith (1996) indicates the challenge that 'teaching by telling' has for reform while others signal the problematic tradeoff between processes and conceptual understanding (Eisenhart, Borko, Underhill, Brown, Jones, & Agard, 1993).

The articles of Bubble 6 are united by both a methodological thread (case study research, Merriam, 1988) and content thread (e.g., Küchemann's algebra text, 1981). Some researchers consider cases of teachers in the teaching of introducing functions in an algebra class (MacGregor & Stacey, 1993) while others contribute by studying students' understandings of linear functions (Haimes, 1996).

Within Bubble 7, researchers build on literature on whole number addition and subtraction (Fuson 1992a) and its application to solving word problems (Riley, Greeno, & Heller, 1983). The research published in the JRME considers not only children's initial development of these skills in lower elementary (Carpenter, Ansell, Franke, Fennema, & Weisbeck, 1993) but also their continued development in upper elementary (Verschaffel, DeCorte, & Vierstraete, 1999).

Bubble 8 distinguishes itself through its particular focus on probability. Building from Piaget & Inhelder's *The origin of the idea of chance in children* (1951/1975) and related work on the role of intuition in science (Fischbein, 1987), researchers publishing within this bubble considered misconceptions of probability arising from misleading intuitions (Fischbein & Schnarch, 1997) and inconsistencies in children's reasoning about probabilities (Konold, Pollatsek, Well, Lohmeier, & Lipson, 1993).

Bubble 9, often from a grounded theory approach (Glaser & Strauss, 1967), focuses on teachers' teaching and children's learning in the classroom (Romberg & Carpenter, 1986). This research includes studies on participation and the construction of meaning within classrooms (Lo, Wheatley, & Smith, 1994) and the role of the teacher in facilitating discussions that support students in their learning (Leikin & Zaslavsky, 1997).

In contrast to the bubbles discussed thus far in the 1990s, Bubble 10 takes an international perspective, particularly in the discussion of the results of the Second International Mathematics Study (SIMS; Crosswhite et al., 1986) and the perception that the US was lagging behind internationally (McKnight et al., 1987). Some researchers took up the results of the SIMS to compare gendered achievement gaps, or the lack thereof, internationally (Ethington, 1990) while others compared and contrasted curriculum and teacher characteristics (Flanders, 1994).

Bubble 11 is another bubble where one of the JRME published articles is among the most cited within that bubble: Simon's "Reconstructing mathematics pedagogy from a constructivist perspective." (1995). Other orienting literature within this bubble is a constructivist view on the mathematical mind (Cobb, Yackel, & Wood, 1992) which was later elaborated together with Simon's contribution towards a unified constructivist perspective on mathematics education and mathematics education research (Steffe & Kieren, 1994).

In Bubble 12, Pólya's *How to Solve It* (1945) and Schoenfeld's work on problem solving (1985) retain their position from the 1980s (see Bubble 7 of the 1980s) as highly cited articles within their bubble. Unlike the bubble of the 1980s which considered mathematical thinking more broadly, this bubble focuses more explicitly on mathematical problem solving. Researchers within this bubble, among other efforts, offer a recap of the shifting research in mathematical problem solving since the

1970s (Lester, 1994) and defend the meta-analytic method of cross-research analyses (Hembree, 1992).

Research in Bubble 13, like Bubble 6, focuses on teachers of mathematics. Here, the most cited literature focuses on teacher knowledge (Shulman, 1986) and beliefs and conceptions (Thompson, 1992). Research published in the JRME builds on this literature by interpreting teacher conceptions in light of the ongoing education reform (Lloyd & Wilson, 1998) and making explicit attempts in bringing research and teacher education together (Cooney, 1994).

Unifying the research in Bubble 14 is research on mathematics anxiety and sex-difference. The common thread across these two bubbles is a researcher: Fennema. The Fennema-Sherman Mathematics Attitude Scales were designed to understand sex-differences in attitude towards mathematics (Fennema & Sherman, 1976, 1977, 1978), offering a more textured image than other studies that considered sex-differences in achievement alone (Fennema et al., 1990). This dual focus was taken up by some researchers as a focus on affect and mathematics learning (McLeod, 1994) and by others as a focus on gender and sex-differences (Fennema & Hart, 1994). These two threads, however, remained intertwined by additional research that offered a meta-analysis of anxiety and mathematics achievement (Ma, 1999).

Within the legacy of *The Mathematics Report Card: Are We Measuring Up?* (Dossey et al., 1988), research into cognitively guided instruction in Bubble 15, teaching that is responsive to the mathematical knowledge and brilliance of children came forth (Fennema et al., 1993). Research published in the JRME that continued to study cognitively guided instruction included a longitudinal study on teachers learning to use children's mathematical thinking (Fennema et al., 1996) and teachers understanding of cognitively guided instruction and what it means for their practice (Knapp & Peterson, 1995).

Research within Bubble 16 draws on Vygotsky's *Thought and Language* (1962) and specific studies on the role of language in supporting student constructions of meaning in mathematics classrooms (e.g., Vygotsky, 1962) to support a social constructivist ethos in the classroom. Some JRME researchers have focused on the difference between social constructivism and cognitive constructivism (Cobb, Yackel, & Wood, 1992) while others have focused on the language and context in which students can make meaning (Wood, 1999).

Building upon the constructivist paradigm of Bubble 16, but taking up radical constructivist research within the context of mathematics education itself (Steffe, Cobb, & von Glasersfeld, 1988; Steffe, von Glasersfeld, Richards, & Cobb, 1983), researchers within Bubble 17 elaborated a constructivist perspective that builds from counting, arithmetic, and strategies towards rational numbers (Hunting, Davis, & Pearn, 1996) and multiplicative reasoning (Clark & Kamii, 1996).

Bubble 18 is largely clustered around the NCTM *Standards* (1989, 1991) and researcher responses to mathematics education reform. Some authors focused on the mathematical content of reform: classroom factors that help and hinder high-level mathematical thinking (Henningsen & Stein, 1997) or mathematical problem posing (Silver, Mamona-Downs, Leung, & Kenney, 1996). Other researchers, similar to those in Bubble 2, and connecting to Apple's (1992) concerns about equity, elaborated specific applications of a culturally relevant approach (Ladson-Billings, 1997) to mathematics education research (Gutstein, Lipman, Hernandez, & de los Reyes, 1997). These show at least two ways that researchers have taken up the Standards, the first focusing on mathematical excellence and the second on equity concerns.

While Bubble 14 focused on the connection between mathematics anxiety and sex-differences in achievement, Bubble 19 focuses more exclusively on gender differences in mathematics performance and the 'gender-gap' (Friedman, 1989; Hyde, Fennema, & Lamon, 1990). Research in the JRME that builds upon this literature base departed from the presumption of anxiety and has studied gender differences in attitudes towards mathematics more broadly (Ma & Kishor, 1997; Seegers & Boekaerts, 1996).

Bubble 20 is another equity-related bubble, here focusing on multicultural and critical mathematics education (Frankenstein 1989, 1990). In 1997, the JRME had a special issue on "Equity, Mathematics Reform, and Research: Crossing Boundaries in Search of Understanding" and the articles from this issue appear here and include studies on teacher professional development in multicultural education (Sleeter, 1997) and bringing transformative multicultural education and mathematics education together (Murtadha-Watts & D'Ambrosio, 1997).

Bubble 21 takes on the constructivist perspectives discussed in Bubbles 11 and 16 (e.g., Von Glasersfeld, 1990) and offers a critique on theories of learning. Some authors situate this work in the legacy of critique (e.g., Walkerdine's *The Mastery of Reason*, 1988) to challenge the radical constructivist paradigm (Lerman, 1996) and to reimagine mathematics education (Davis, 1997).
Unlike, for example, the constructivist bubbles that begin with theory and apply it to the classroom, research within the last bubble of the 1990s, Bubble 22, takes a qualitative (Erickson, 1986) and ethnographic (Eisenhart, 1988) perspective on mathematics teaching and learning to describe the experience of learning in classrooms. Research in this bubble has described, among other topics, being responsive to unpredictable student errors as 'springboards of inquiry' (Borasi, 1994) or applications of reading to support mathematics learning (Siegel & Borasi, 1998).

Macroanalysis: Foam

Having introduced each of the 22 bubbles of the 1990s, I now transition to the macroanalysis. Here, I shift my gaze from the bubbles as individual research foci towards their position relative within the foam and relative to each other to better understand the landscape of the field in the 1990s as presented within the JRME. Since my focus shifts now to the positions of the bubbles within the foam, to assist the reader in seeing their positions I refer them to Figure 37 which shows the collection of bubbles from the foam but does not include the dots that correspond to the articles within each bubble. In the following subsections I proceed through an analysis that first considers the centrality of the position of bubbles within the overall foam and second that considers the adjacency and overlap of various bubbles.

Central/Marginal Analysis

Within the foam of the 1990s, a central topic, and indeed the most cited reference within the foam, is the NCTM Standards. The bubble containing the Standards, Bubble 18 (green), intersects with other central bubbles such as Bubble 3 (Number Sense), Bubble 5 (Mathematics Knowledge for Teaching), Bubble 6 (Case Studies of Teachers), and Bubble 11 (Constructivist Research on Teaching and Learning).

Figure 37. The bubbles of the 1990s JRME foam.

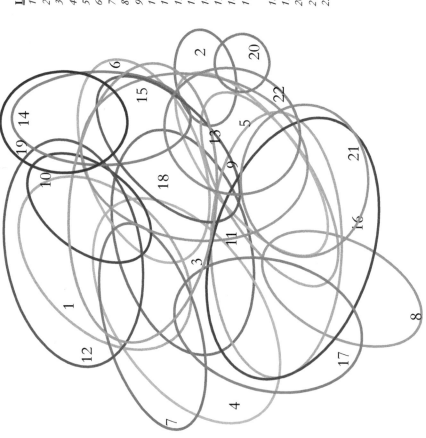

Legend:

1. *van Hiele Understanding and Development of Geometry*
2. *Equity and Politics of Mathematics Education*
3. *Number Sense (Concepts and Computation)*
4. *Children's Place-Value Addition and Subtraction*
5. *Mathematics Knowledge for Teaching*
6. *Case Studies of Teachers*
7. *Word Problems and Problem-Solving*
8. *Probability*
9. *Children's Learning in Classrooms*
10. *Second International Mathematics Study*
11. *Constructivist Research on Teaching and Learning*
12. *Problem Solving*
13. *Teachers of Mathematics*
14. *Mathematics Anxiety & Sex Differences*
15. *Cognitively Guided Instruction*
16. *Language and the Construction of Meaning*
17. *Multiplicative Reasoning – Understanding Rational Numbers, Multiplication, and Division*
18. *NCTM Standards & Culturally-Relevant Mathematics*
19. *Mathematics Achievement*
20. *Multicultural and Critical Mathematics Education*
21. *Critical Responses to Theories of Learning*
22. *Experience of Learning Mathematics (Curriculum and Writing)*

In contrast to these central topics in the field, other topics are more marginal. As was the case with International Comparative Assessment in the 1970s (Bubble 6 of the 1970s), Bubble 10 on the Second International Mathematics Study is marginal to the foam of the 1980s. Similarly, Bubble 8 on Probability is at the bottom margin of the foam. Emerging in the foam in this decade were Bubbles 2 (Equity and Politics) and 20 (Multicultural and Critical Mathematics Education).

As discussed above, part of this emergence can be traced as a critical response to the *Standards* document and another part can be attributed to the JRME special issue on equity and multiculturalism. These topics, however, are more marginal than the related Culturally Relevant Mathematics portion of Bubble 18 which explicitly connected to the mathematics content of the Standards. This suggests that the topics most central to the field, at least through the 1990s, are studies on mathematics understanding, teaching, and learning; even when considering issues of equity, the social context is marginal to the mathematics content.

Nearness/Overlap Analysis

For the 1990s, there are three relative positionings of bubbles that I have chosen to unpack: the overlap of Bubbles 2 and 20, the overlap of Bubbles 5 and 13, and the overlap of Bubbles 14 and 19.

The Overlap of Bubbles 2 and 20. Bubbles 2 (Equity and Politics in Mathematics Education) and 20 (Multicultural and Critical Mathematics Education) are both located at the right margin of the JRME 1990s foam. Recalling that part of the title of the special issue that comprises Bubble 20 is equity, it is clear that there is a common thread between these two bubbles. Yet, based on their citation patterns, an indicator of the literature base that each draws on, these bubbles are distinct. Bubble 20 draws on Frankenstein's (1983) adaptation of Freire (1973) while Bubble 2 proceeds from critical theory (e.g., Apple, 1992). Foreshadowing to the analyses of the 2000s and 2010s, this distance between critical theory and what will become teaching mathematics for social justice (Gutstein via Frankenstein) persists.

The Overlap of Bubbles 5 and 13. Bubbles 5 (Mathematics Knowledge for Teaching) and 13 (Teachers of Mathematics), while both focusing on teachers, have an overlap but there are also areas of each that are not contained within the other. This suggests that while mathematics knowledge for teaching is an important aspect of teaching mathematics, teachers of mathematics also possess other knowledges and traits: these include pedagogical knowledge, beliefs about teaching and students, etc. Similarly, Bubble 5 includes area that does not intersect with teachers of mathematics, suggesting that there are aspects of mathematics knowledge for teaching that are not about the teachers themselves. For example, research on the nature of this knowledge (whether it is cognitively constructed, socially constructed, etc.) and the relationship between mathematical knowledge and mathematics knowledge for teaching exceed the mathematics teachers themselves.

The Overlap of Bubbles 14 and 19. Sex-differences and Anxiety (Bubble 14) and Mathematics Achievement (Bubble 19) share a considerable overlap. In fact, Bubble 19 is nearly completely contained by Bubble 14. This suggests that the focus of mathematics achievement studies of the 1990s were preoccupied with sex-differences in achievement. Conversely, that Bubble 14 exceeds Bubble 19 suggests that studies on sex-differences and anxiety were not purely about achievement. Recalling the discussion on Bubble 14 above, the studies on sex-differences in attitude, beliefs, and participation did not foreground the resulting difference in achievement. Nevertheless, in both cases, the focus is on differences between groups.

JRME in the 2000s

In this section, I unpack the research published in the JRME in the 2000s. First, I present a map of the research foam of the JRME in the 2000s (see Figure 38). Then, I summarize each of the bubbles in the form of a table that includes (1) the bubble's number, (2) the bubble's name, (3) a map with the bubbles' relative location within the foam, (4) a list of the most cited articles within that bubble, and (5) a list of a few JRME articles within that bubble. My goal for this section is to introduce each of the decade's bubbles so that I can provide an analysis of the bubbles' position relative to each other and relative to the position of the foam. For the interested reader, interactive versions of each map, complete with every node of each bubble and their relative positions within the foam, are available on the companion website at MathEdAtlas.org. I encourage the reader to explore the nodes which comprise each bubble and the overall foam to develop an intuition about the research of the JRME 2000s.

Microanalysis: Bubbles

I proceed now by summarizing the 35 bubbles of research in the JRME 2000s: (1) Standards, (2) Young Children's Learning and Development, (3) (Scientific) Research Agenda, (4) Linking Research and Learning, (5) Mathematics Knowledge for Teaching, (6) Cognition, (7) Teaching, Learning, & Understanding Fraction Concepts, (8) Solving Algebraic Equations and Errors, (9) Meaning Making in Mathematics - Social and Cultural Aspects, (10) Pedagogy and Learning, (11) Social Context of Learning - International Perspectives, (12) Comparative Assessment, (13) Developing Algebraic Thinking in Schools, (14) Mathematical Proof, (15) Discourse & Language, (16) Epistemology: Knowledge and Understanding in Mathematics, (17) Equitable Achievement: Class, Race, Sex, (18) Fractions, (19) International Comparative Assessment, (20) Mathematics in the Middle School, (21) Data & Statistics, (22) Mathematics Learning Systems, (23) Multiple Mathematical Representations, (24) Solving Arithmetic & Algebraic Word Problems, (25) Standards-Based Curriculum and Achievement in Schools, (26) Geometry and Measurement, (27) Equity and Equitable Pedagogy, (28) Constructivist Teaching and Learning, (29) Calculus and Function Concepts, (30) Transfer of Mathematics, (31) Research on the Teaching and learning of Children, (32) Probability, (33) Scientific Research, (34) Gender Differences in performance, and (35) Mathematical Enculturation. For each bubble (see Table 3), I provide the number used to indicate it on the map of the foam of the 2000s, its name, a mini map that shows the bubble's relative location within the foam of the field, the two to three most cited article within that bubble, and two to three sample JRME articles that are located within that bubble.

Across the previous three decades I have unpacked 18 bubbles in detail and I have unpacked 37 bubbles more briefly. Since the 2000s is the fourth decade that I describe, I will again modify my approach to assist the reader's reading of this analysis. When a bubble is similar to a bubble previously unpacked in the 1970s, 1980s, or 1990s, I will draw those connections here and remind the reader of

Figure 38. Bubbles of research that comprise the JRME 2000s foam.

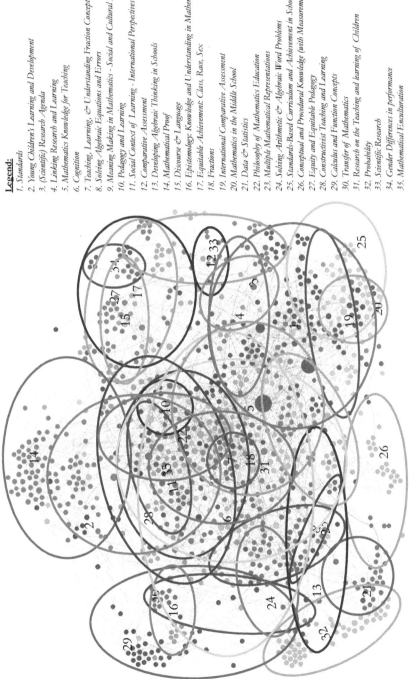

Table 3. The 34 Bubbles of the JRME 2000s Foam. Each includes the bubble name, its location within the foam, the most cited articles, and JRME citing articles.

Bubble Number	Bubble Name	Location within the Foam (colored nodes)	Most Cited Article(s)	JRME Citing Article(s)
1	Standards		NCTM 1989, 2000	Remillard & Bryans, 2004 Lloyd 2008
2	Young Children's Learning and Development		Cobb, Boufi, McClain, & Whitenack, 1997 Hiebert & Carpenter, 1992	Pesek & Kirschner, 2000 Sfard 2000 McClain & Cobb 2001
3	(Scientific) Research Agenda		Kilpatrick, Swafford, & Findell, 2001 Reys, Reys, Lapan, Holliday, & Wasman, 2003	NCTM RAC 2004 McCaffrey, Hamilton, Stecher, Klein, Bugliari, & Robyn, 2001
4	Linking Research and Learning		Simon, 2004 NRC, 2002	Simon, 2004 Smith, 2004

Table 3 (cont.)

Bubble Number	Bubble Name	Location within the Foam (colored nodes)	Most Cited Article(s)	JRME Citing Article(s)
5	Mathematics Knowledge for Teaching		Shulman, 1986 Begle, 1979	Thanheiser, 2009 Hill, Ball, & Schilling, 2008
6	Cognition		Ball, 1993 Cobb & Yackel, 1996	Lobato, Clarke, & Ellis, 2005 Fuson, Carroll, & Drueck, 2000
7	Teaching, Learning, & Understanding Fraction Concepts		Hiebert & Wearne, 1993 Mack, 1990	Empson, 2003 Saxe, Taylor, McIntosh, & Gearhart, 2005
8	Solving Algebraic Equations and Errors		Booth, 1984 Mason, 1996	Carraher, Schliemann, & Brizuela, 2006 Swafford & Langrall, 2000

Table 3 (cont.)

Bubble Number	Bubble Name	Location within the Foam (colored nodes)	Most Cited Article(s)	JRME Citing Article(s)
9	Meaning Making in Mathematics – Social and Cultural Aspects		Scribner, 1984 Chazan, 2000	Yerushalmy, 2006 Hoyles, Noss, & Pozzi, 2001 Noss & Hoyles, 2002
10	Pedagogy and Learning		Bernstein, 1996 Ensor, 2001	Adler & Davis, 2006 Ensor, 2001
11	Social Context of Learning – International Perspectives		Fuson & Kwon, 1992 Wertsch, 1985	Guberman, 2004 Murata & Fuson, 2006
12	Comparative Assessment		Lord, 1980 Campbell, Hombo, & Mazzeo, 2000	Ma & Wilkins, 2007 Griffin, & Callingham, 2006

Table 3 (cont.)

Bubble Number	Bubble Name	Location within the Foam (colored nodes)	Most Cited Article(s)	JRME Citing Article(s)
13	Developing Algebraic Thinking in Schools		Little, 2004 Kaput, 1998	Jacobs, Franke, Carpenter, Levi, & Battey, 2007 Knuth, Stephens, McNeil, & Alibali, 2006
14	Mathematical Proof		Harel & Sowder, 1998 Stylianides, 2007	Weber, 2008 Herbst, 2006
15	Discourse & Language		Morgan, 1996 Hodge & Kress, 1993	Herbel-Eisenmann, 2007 Burton & Morgan, 2000
16	Knowledge and Understanding in Mathematics		Dubinsky, 1991 Piaget, 1985	Cooley, Trigueros, & Baker, 2007 Simon, Tzur, & Heinz, 2004

Table 3 (cont.)

Bubble Number	Bubble Name	Location within the Foam (colored nodes)	Most Cited Article(s)	JRME Citing Article(s)
17	Equitable Achievement: Class, Race, Sex		Boaler, 2002 Lubienski, 2000	Boaler, 2002 Franco, Sztajn, & Ortigão, 2007
18	Fractions		NCTM, 1991 Greer, 1992	Tirosh, 2000 McGraw, Lubienski, & Strutchens, 2006
19	International Comparative Assessment		Mullis, Martin, Gonzalez, Gregory, Garden, O'Connor, et al., 2000 Beaton, Mullis, I. Martin, Gonzalez, Kelly, & Smith, 1996	Ferrini-Mundy & Schmidt, 2005 Balfanz, Mac Iver, & Byrnes, 2006
20	Mathematics in the Middle School		Billstein & Williamson, 1998/2003 Hedges & Olkin, 1985	Post, Harwell, Davis, Maeda, Cutler, Andersen, Kahan, & Norman 2008 Ellington, 2003

Table 3 (cont.)

Bubble Number	Bubble Name	Location within the Foam (colored nodes)	Most Cited Article(s)	JRME Citing Article(s)
21	Data & Statistics		Mokros & Russell, 1995 Hancock, Kaput, & Goldsmith, 1992	Konold & Pollatsek, 2002 Doerr & English, 2003 Groth, 2007
22	Mathematics Learning Systems		Sfard & Kieran, 2001 Blumer, 1969	Davis & Simmt, 2003 Rasmussen & Marrongelle, 2006
23	Multiple Mathematical Representations		Janvier, 1987 Meira, 1998	Noble, Nemirovsky, Wright, & Tierney, 2001 Zazkis & Liljedahl, 2004
24	Solving Arithmetic & Algebraic Word Problems		De Corte, Greer, & Verschaffel, 1996 Kieran, 1981	Nathan & Koedinger, 2000 Van Dooren, Verschaffel, & Onghena, 2002 Pyke, 2003

Table 3 (cont.)

Bubble Number	Bubble Name	Location within the Foam (colored nodes)	Most Cited Article(s)	JRME Citing Article(s)
25	Standards-Based Curriculum and Achievement in Schools		Riordan & Noyce, 2001 Senk & Thompson, 2003	Smith & Star, 2007 Schoen, Cebulla, Finn, & Fi, 2003
26	Geometry and Measurement		Hiebert, 1981, 1984	Barrett, Clements, Klanderman, Pennisi, & Polaki, 2006 Joram, Gabriele, Bertheau, Gelman, & Subrahmanyam, 2005
27	Equity and Equitable Pedagogy		Gutstein, 2003 Gutierrez, 2002 Boaler, 1997	Gutstein, Fey, Heid, DeLoach-Johnson, Middleton, et al., 2005 Setati, 2005 Gutstein, 2003
28	Constructivist Teaching and Learning		Lampert, 1990 Von Glasersfeld, 1995	Kirschner, 2002 Norton, 2008

Table 3 (cont.)

Bubble Number	Bubble Name	Location within the Foam (colored nodes)	Most Cited Article(s)	JRME Citing Article(s)
29	Calculus and Function Concepts		Cottrill, Dubinsky, Nichols, Schwingendorf, Thomas, & Vidakovic, 1996 Williams, 1991	Szydlik, 2000 Oehrtman, 2009
30	Transfer of Mathematics		Jones, 2009 Fuchs, Fuchs, Prentice, Burch, Hamlett, Owen, et al., 2003	Jones, 2009 Xin, 2008
31	Research on the Teaching and Learning of Children		Fuson ,1992 Clark & Kamii, 1996	Sherin & Fuson, 2005 Henry & Brown, 2008
32	Probability		Kahneman, & Tversky, 1972 Fischbein, & Gazit, 1984	Rubel, 2007 Van Dooren, De Bock, Janssens, & Verschaffel, 2008

Table 3 (cont.)

Bubble Number	Bubble Name	Location within the Foam (colored nodes)	Most Cited Article(s)	JRME Citing Article(s)
33	Scientific Research		Shavelson & Towne, 2002 Battista, Clements, Arnoff, Battista, & Borrow, 1998	Hill & Shih, 2009 Outhred, & Mitchelmore, 2000
34	Gender Differences in performance		Eccles, & Jacobs, 1986 Hyde, Fennema, & Lamon, 1990	Casey, Nuttall, & Pezaris, 2001 Ho, Senturk, Lam, Zimmer, Hong, Okamoto, Chiu, Nakazawa & Wang, 2000
35	Mathematical Enculturation		Lerman, 1996 Wenger, 1998	Nardi, Jaworski, & Hegedus, 2005 Boaler, 2000

the literature base that it draws on instead of repeating the most cited articles or mentioning the new research that build on that base; that information is presented in Table 3.

I also make this transition again to zoom out from the minutiae of the bubbles to reiterate that my focus moving forward is the macroanalysis: the location of the bubbles within the foam and the location of the bubbles relative to each other. This shift towards explicitly linking the bubbles across time will also serve as preparation for the final section of this chapter, which is a chronological analysis across the five decades. I do not adopt this approach because I feel as though the details are unimportant or irrelevant, in fact, I refer back to the fifth objective of cartography: to enable further exploration. I hope the interested reader will spend the time unpacking those bubbles interesting to them in detail, in tracing the minutiae across the decades to see the shifting and emergence within a particular bubble or group of bubbles. In this way, the interested reader could constitute their own analyses to outline partages of what is sensible as equity research, as what is sensible as number sense research, etc.

In brief, the 2000s bubbles and the connections they make across time are:

- Bubble 1 (Standards) builds on the Standards bubbles of the 1980s (Bubble 11) and 1990s (Bubble 18).
- Bubble 2 (Young Children's Learning and Development) builds upon the Piagetian bubbles of the 1970s (2 & 3), the Piagetian and Van Hiele bubbles of the 1980s (1, 2, & 5), and the Children's Place-Value and Cognitively Guided Instruction bubbles of the 1990s (4 & 15).
- Bubble 5 (Mathematics Knowledge for Teaching) builds on the bubble of the same name of the 1990s (also #5).
- Bubble 6 (Cognition) builds upon bubbles on Mathematical Thinking and Mental Models bubbles of the 1980s (7 & 12) and the Cognitively Guided Instruction bubble of the 1990s (15).
- Bubble 7 (Teaching, Learning, & Understanding Fraction Conceptions) builds upon the Proportional Reasoning and Rational Understanding bubbles of the 1980s (13) and 1990s (17).
- Bubble 8 (Solving Algebraic Equations and Errors) builds upon the Algebraic Learning, Understanding, and Problem-Solving bubble of the 1980s (15).
- Bubble 9 (Meaning Making in Mathematics—Social and Cultural Aspects) builds upon the Cognitive and Social Constructivist bubbles of the 1990s (11 & 16).
- Bubble 10 (Pedagogy and Learning) builds upon the Learning Sequences and Activity-Oriented Instruction bubbles of the 1980s (4 & 8) and the Teaching Effect on Learning bubble of the 1990s (8).
- Bubble 11 (Social Context of Learning—International Perspectives) builds up the International Policy and Responses bubble of the 1980s (14) and the Equity and Politics bubble of the 1990s (2).
- Bubble 12 (Comparative Assessment) builds upon the International Comparative Assessment of the 1970s (11) and the Second International Mathematics Study bubble of the 1990s (19).
- Bubble 13 (Developing Algebraic Thinking in Schools) builds upon the Algebraic Learning and Understanding bubble of the 1980s (15).
- Bubble 14 (Mathematical Proof) builds upon the Logic bubble of the 1970s (12).
- Bubble 17 (Equitable Achievement: Class, Race, Sex) builds upon Sex-differences and Achievement bubbles of the 1980s (3) and 1990s (19).
- Bubble 18 (Fractions) builds upon the Multiplicative and Proportional Reasoning bubble of the 1990s (17).
- Bubble 19 (International Comparative Assessment) builds upon the International Comparative Assessment of the 1970s (6) and the Second International Mathematics Study bubble of the 1980s (10).
- Bubble 21 (Data & Statistics) builds upon the Probability bubble of the 2000s (8).
- Bubble 24 (Solving Arithmetic & Algebraic Word Problems) builds upon the Word Problems bubble of the 1970 (16), the Algebraic Problem-Solving bubble of the 1980s (15), and the Word Problems and Problem-Solving bubble of the 1990s (7).

- Bubble 25 (Standards-Based Curriculum and Achievement in Schools) builds upon the NCTM Standards bubble of the 1990s (18).
- Bubble 26 (Geometry and Measurement) builds upon the Geometry bubbles of the 1970s (13), 1980s (5), and 1990s (1).
- Bubble 27 (Equity and Equitable Pedagogy) builds upon the Culturally Relevant Mathematics and Critical Mathematics Education bubbles of the 1990s (18 & 20).
- Bubble 28 (Constructivist Teaching and Learning) builds upon the Constructivist Research on Teaching and Learning bubble of the 1990s (11).
- Bubble 31 (Research on the Teaching and Learning of Children) builds upon the Teaching Effect on Mathematics Learning bubble of the 1980s (8) and the Cognitively Guided Instruction bubble of the 1990s (11).
- Bubble 32 (Probability) builds upon the Probability bubble of the 2000s (8).
- Bubble 34 (Gender Differences in Performance) builds upon the Sex-differences and Achievement bubbles of the 1990s (14 & 19).
- Bubble 35 (Mathematical Enculturation) builds upon the Social Construction of Mathematics and Meaning bubble of the 1990s (16).

The remaining ten bubbles that constitute new research foci that emerged in the 2000s include: (3) (Scientific) Research Agenda, (4) Linking Research and Learning, (15) Discourse & Language, (16) Knowledge and Understanding in Mathematics, (20) Mathematics in the Middle School, (22) Philosophy of Mathematics Education, (23) Multiple Mathematical Representations, (29) Calculus and Function Concepts, (30) Transfer of Mathematics, and (33) Scientific Research.

Bubble 3 (Scientific Research Agenda) emerged in response to *Adding It Up* (Kilpatrick, Swafford, & Findell, 2001) and assessments on the impact of reform-based curriculum on student learning (Reys, Reys, Lapan, Holliday, & Wasman, 2003). Articles in this bubble that were published in the JRME included the NCTM Research Advisory Council's research agenda setting with "An Agenda for Research Action in Mathematics Education: Beginning the Discussion" (2004). Additionally, researchers continued to research the interaction between instruction, reform-based curriculum, and achievement (McCaffrey, Hamilton, Stecher, Klein, Bugliari, & Robyn, 2001).

Relatedly, Bubble 4 focused on linking research and learning. Simon's "Raising issues of quality in mathematics education research" (2004) was both (1) published in the JRME and (2) among the most cited articles in this bubble—arguing for quality and useful research that advanced the knowledge of the field.

Bubble 15 build on works such as *Language as Ideology* (Hodge & Kress, 1993) and early critical analyses of mathematics texts (Morgan, 1996). Researchers publishing in the JRME considered, among other things, the language of mathematicians (Burton & Morgan, 2000) and the 'voice' of mathematics textbooks (Herbel-Eisenmann, 2007).

Bubble 16 focuses on Knowledge and Understanding in Mathematics, in the cognitive structures (Piaget, 1985) involved in knowing mathematics and the role of abstraction in 'advanced mathematical thinking' (Dubinsky, 1991). New research in the JRME included elaborations of schema (Cooley & Trigueros, 2007) and of the role of reflective abstraction in learning (Simon, Tzur, & Heinz, 2004).

Emerging in Bubble 20 was a focus on mathematics in the middle school, on the influence of standards-based curriculum (e.g., *Middle Grades MathThematics*; Billstein & Williamson, 1998) on students standardized assessment achievement (Post, Harwell, Davis, Maeda, Cutler, & Andersen, 2008). Other researchers used statistical meta-analyses (Hedges & Olkin, 1985) to understand the impact of calculators on achievement and attitude (Ellington, 2003).

Bubble 22 considers mathematics education from the perspective of a learning system, wherein thinking and communication (Sfard & Kieran, 2001) and learning and the social world within it occurs (Blumer, 1969) are all inextricable. Some research published in the JRME in this bubble considers complexity science as a tool to understand the mathematics education learning system (Davis & Simmt, 2003) while others focused on the ways that thinking, communication of reasoning, and mathematics can be integrated during teaching (Rasmussen & Marrongelle, 2006).

Related to Bubble 3, Bubble 33 focuses on scientific research in mathematics education, on high-quality (Hill & Shih, 2009), evidence-based research (Shavelson & Towne, 2002). Examples of such 'scientific research' include Outhred & Mitchelmore's study on young children's understanding of rectangular area (2000) in which the authors identify five developmental levels of children's understanding of finding area. This research built on earlier work on children's work with 2D arrays of squares (Battista et al., 1998).

Unlike the newly introduced bubbles discussed so far, Bubbles 23, 29, and 30 each focus specifically on mathematics content. Bubble 23 focuses on multiple mathematical representations, the translation between representations (Janvier, 1987), and the impact that particular representations have on understanding (e.g., transparencies; Meira, 1998). Some researchers in this bubble considered how change was represented in different contexts (Noble, Nemirovsky, & Wright, 2001) while others considered the representation of prime numbers (Zazkis & Liljedahl, 2004).

Research in Bubble 29, in contrast, focused on calculus and function concepts building primarily on earlier work on limits and student models of limits (Cottrill, et al., 1996; Williams, 1991). Researchers continuing this thread of research considered, among other topics, beliefs about and conceptual understanding of limits (Szydlik, 2000) and the metaphors that students use to make sense of limits (Oehrtman, 2009).

Research in Bubble 30 focused on the transfer of mathematical concepts to novel contexts (Fuchs, et al., 2003). Jones' "Transfer, abstraction, and context" (2009) was both published in the JRME and among the most cited articles in this bubble. Other researchers studying the mathematical transfer included some research on the transfer of multiplicative relations to solving novel word problems (Xin, 2008).

Macroanalysis: Foam

Now that I have unpacked the ten research foci that emerged in the JRME 2000s foam, I now transition to the macroanalysis. Here, I shift my gaze from the bubbles as individual research foci towards their positions within the foam and relative to each other to better understand the landscape of the field in the 2010s as presented within the JRME. Since my focus shifts now to the positions of the bubbles within the foam, to assist the reader in seeing their positions I refer them to Figure 39 which shows the collection of bubbles from the foam but does not include the dots that correspond to the articles within each bubble. In the following subsections I proceed through an analysis that first

Figure 39. The bubbles of the 2000s JRME foam.

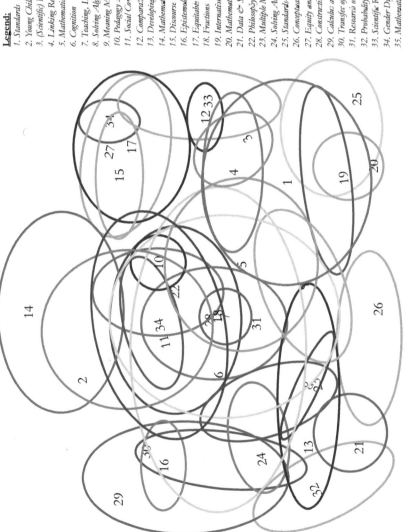

considers the centrality of the position of bubbles within the overall foam and second that considers the adjacency and overlap of various bubbles.

Central/Marginal Analysis

Among the topics that are central to the JRME 2000s foam (see Figure 40, left) are Mathematics Knowledge for Teaching (Bubble 5), Teaching, Learning, & Understanding Fraction Concepts (Bubble 7), Pedagogy and Learning (Bubble 10), Fractions (Bubble 18), and Constructivist Teaching and Learning (Bubble 28). On the other hand, among the topics that are marginal to the JRME 2000s foam (see Figure 40, right) are Scientific Research Agenda (Bubble 3), Linking Research and Learning (Bubble 4), Comparative Assessment (Bubble 12), Mathematical Proof (Bubble 14), Discourse & Language (Bubble 15), Equitable Achievement: Class, Race, Sex (Bubble 17), International Comparative Assessment (Bubble 19), Mathematics in the Middle School (Bubble 20), Data & Statistics (Bubble 21), Standards-Based Curriculum and Achievement in Schools (Bubble 25), Geometry and Measurement (Bubble 26), Equity and Equitable Pedagogy (Bubble 27), Calculus and Function Concepts (Bubble 29), Transfer of Mathematics (Bubble 30), Probability (Bubble 32), Scientific Research (Bubble 33), and Gender Differences in Performance (Bubble 34).

Figure 40. The central (left) and marginal (right) bubbles of the JRME 2000s foam.

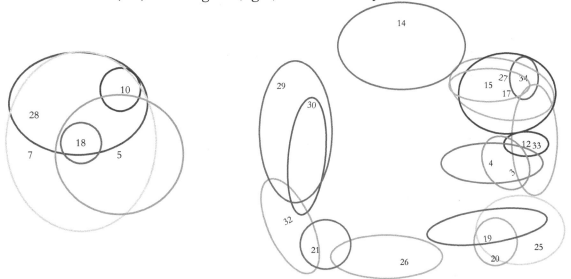

Nearness/Overlap Analysis

In contrast to previous decades, here I organize the overlap analysis into two parts. First, I discuss three sets of overlapping bubbles that are central to the foam. Second, I discuss three sets of overlapping bubbles that are marginal in the 2000s foam. The findings of each analysis are not necessarily novel in every case: when findings corroborate intuitions or 'obvious' facts, these serve as evidence to the validity of the method and the relationships between bubbles that it identifies, even when these findings are less intuitive.

Overlapping Central Bubbles. Within the central bubbles, there are three sets of overlapping bubbles that I discuss: Bubbles 10 and 28 (Constructivist Pedagogy and Learning), Bubbles 5 and 18 (Fractions and Mathematics Knowledge for Teaching), and Bubbles 7 and 18 (Fraction Content

Knowledge and Fraction Teaching and Learning). These relationships provide insight into a hierarchical relationship between the scopes of each bubble: constructivist teaching and learning is the larger dark blue bubble within which the smaller brown bubble of Pedagogy and Learning is contained. This suggests that the scope of pedagogy learning makes sense within the context of constructivism. Further, the location of fractional content knowledge (Bubble 18) within the bubble of Mathematics Knowledge for Teaching (Bubble 5) suggests that fractional content knowledge is a part of mathematics knowledge for teaching. The inclusion of fractional content knowledge within mathematics knowledge for teaching is not remarkable, however this relationship helps to tease apart the distinction between Bubble 18 and Bubble 7 (Teaching, Learning, and Understanding Fraction Concepts). This suggests that fractional content knowledge is part of the teaching, learning, and understanding of fraction concepts but there is pedagogical knowledge, research on fraction cognition, etc. that are part of teaching and learning but exceed the content knowledge itself.

Overlapping Marginal Bubbles. Within the marginal bubbles, there are five relationships of bubbles that I discuss next. The first is the achievement gap and equity overlap (Bubbles 15, 17, 27, and 34). Second, I elaborate the overlap between linking research and learning and scientific research agenda (Bubbles 3 and 4). Third, and last, I discuss the connection between international comparative assessment, mathematics in the middle school, and standards-based curriculum and achievement (Bubbles 19, 20, and 25).

The first overlap includes bubbles 15 (Discourse & Language), 27 (Equity and Equitable Pedagogy), 17 (Equitable Achievement), and 34 (Gender Differences in Performance). Those scholars within bubbles 17 and 34 classify their work as equity research (e.g., Lubienski, 2008) while other scholars have dubbed this achievement gap research "gap gazing" (Gutiérrez, 2008). Achievement gap scholars see their role as scholars as finding disparities in achievement and improving mathematics pedagogy, etc. to eliminate these gaps. Critics, however, argue that the act of gap gazing positions one group as 'normal' and another group as the 'deficit' group. In the case of racial achievement gaps, this positions the students of colors as deficient; in gender research, this positions women as deficient. To continue this critique, a gap constructed between two groups, eliminates those that fall outside of those two groups. To wit, gendered achievement gap research erases non-binary and transgender students.

Therefore, the critique is not that gap gazing is not fundamentally about achieving equity, but rather that it frames the goal as elevating the 'deficient' group's achievement to that of the 'normal' group. What is missing, therefore, is the lack of discussion of what sociocultural differences account for those differences, since there is no natural or inherent difference in ability that accounts for the gap. Further, then, it is not that achievement gap research is not about equity but rather is problematic in its approach. The very close overlap between those groups, and the common move among equity scholars to position their work as a counterpoint to achievement gap work, account for these bubbles coinciding. Unpacking these relationships via the map and overlap of bubbles identifies two distinct relationships:

- Bubble 34 (Gender Differences) is contained within Bubble 17 (Equitable Achievement: Class, Race, Sex), and
- Bubble 15 (Discourse and Language) is contained within Bubble 27 (Equity and Equitable Pedagogy).

The first relationship is discussed above while the second suggests that the discourse and language bubble that focuses on the needs of English-language learners or equitable participation in classroom discourse is an issue of equitable pedagogy.

The second overlap includes Bubbles 3 (scientific research agenda) and 4 (linking research and learning). In Bubble 4 is Simon's "Raising issues of quality in mathematics education research" (2004). In that piece, Simon argued for quality and useful research that advanced the knowledge of the field. This second thrust of the argument, that research should be useful to the field, a field thus far clustered around teaching and learning (see the central articles of this decade and the preceding decades), provides the connection to the scientific research agenda of Bubble 3. Recall that many of these articles arose in response to *Adding It Up* (Kilpatrick, Swafford, & Findell, 2001) and among those articles was NCTM Research Advisory Council's "An Agenda for Research Action in Mathematics Education: Beginning the Discussion" (2004). Among the agenda items was "clarifying ways in which research can contribute to efforts to improve mathematics education" (p. 74), further emphasizing the affinity between these two bubbles. Therefore, even with relatively few references between these two bubbles, these closely related goals are emphasized by their layout within the foam.

The last of the overlaps that I discuss here is the overlap between bubbles 19 (international comparative assessment), 20 (mathematics in the middle school), and 25 (standards-based curriculum and achievement in schools). While the titles at first seem disconnected, there are a few connections that clarify their position within the foam. First, some articles within mathematics in the middle school considered the influence of standards-based curriculum (e.g., *Middle Grades MathThematics*; Billstein & Williamson, 1998) on students standardized assessment achievement (Post, Harwell, Davis, Maeda, Cutler, & Andersen, 2008); giving the connection to bubble 25. Furthermore, across the three bubbles, a constant is standardized assessment. Particularly when the *Standards* are framed as a response to the US lagging behind in international comparative assessment (see the discussion in the 1990s bubble), the connection between 25 and 19 becomes even more explicit.

JRME in the 2010s

In this section, I unpack the research published in the JRME in the 2010s. First, I present a map of the research foam of the JRME in the 2010s (see Figure 41). Then, I summarize each of the bubbles in the form of a table that includes (1) the bubble's number, (2) the bubble's name, (3) a map with the bubbles' relative location within the foam, (4) a list of the most cited articles within that bubble, and (5) a list of a few JRME articles within that bubble. My goal for this section is to introduce each of the decade's bubbles so that I can provide an analysis of the bubbles' position relative to each other and relative to the position of the foam.

Similar to my presentation in the discussion of the 2000s, I emphasize which bubbles build upon those already discussed in previous decades and only elaborate those which represent research foci that emerged in the 2010s. When a bubble is similar to a bubble previously unpacked in the 1970s, 1980s, 1990s, or 2000s, I will draw those connections here to remind the reader of the literature base that it draws on instead of repeating the most cited articles or mentioning the new research that build on that base; that information is presented in Table 4. For the interested reader, interactive versions of each map, complete with every node of each bubble and their relative positions within the foam are available on the companion website at MathEdAtlas.org. I encourage the reader to explore the nodes

Figure 41. Bubbles of research that comprise the JRME 2010s foam.

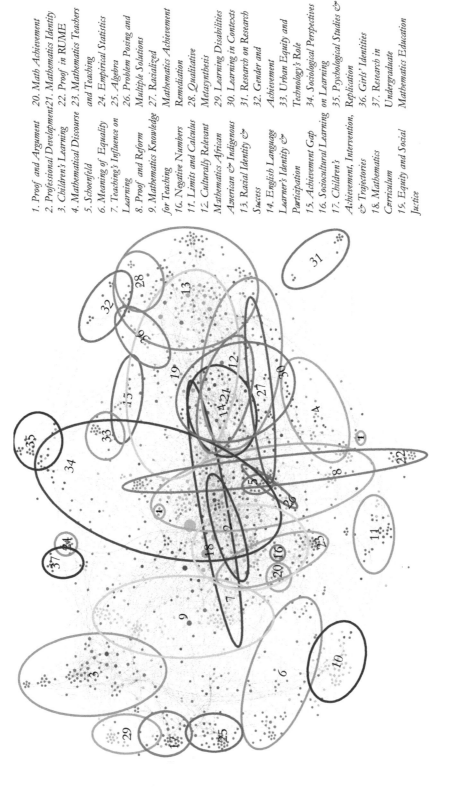

1. Proof and Argument
2. Professional Development
3. Children's Learning
4. Mathematical Discourse
5. Schoenfeld
6. Meaning of Equality
7. Teaching's Influence on Learning
8. Proof and Reform
9. Mathematics Knowledge for Teaching
10. Negative Numbers
11. Limits and Calculus
12. Culturally Relevant Mathematics African American & Indigenous
13. Racial Identity & Success
14. English Language Learner's Identity & Participation
15. Achievement Gap
16. Sociocultural Learning
17. Children's Achievement, Intervention, & Trajectories
18. Mathematics Curriculum
19. Equity and Social Justice
20. Math Achievement
21. Mathematics Identity
22. Proof in RUME
23. Mathematics Teachers and Teaching
24. Empirical Statistics
25. Algebra
26. Problem Posing and Multiple Solutions
27. Racialized Mathematics Achievement Remediation
28. Qualitative Metasynthesis
29. Learning Disabilities
30. Learning in Contexts
31. Research on Research
32. Gender and Achievement
33. Urban Equity and Technology's Role
34. Sociological Perspectives on Learning
35. Psychological Studies & Replication
36. Girls' Identities
37. Research in Undergraduate Mathematics Education

Table 4. The 38 Bubbles of the JRME 2010s Foam. Each includes the bubble name, its location within the foam, the most cited articles, and JRME citing articles.

Bubble Number	Bubble Name	Location within the Foam (colored nodes)	Most Cited Article(s)	JRME Citing Article(s)
1	Proof and Argument		Hadas, Hershkowitz, & Schwarz, 2000 Inglis, Mejia-Ramos, & Simpson, 2007	Hollebrands & Conner, 2010 Widder & Berman, 2019
2	Professional Development		Ball, Thames, & Phelps, 2008 Fennema, Carpenter, Franke, Levi, Jacobs, & Empson, 1996	Bell, Wilson, & Higgins, 2010 Gresalfi, & Cobb, 2011
3	Children's Learning		Hackenberg, 2010 Steffe & Olive, 2010	Hackenberg, 2010 Wilkins & Norton, 2011
4	Mathematical Discourse		Pimm 1987 Ryve 2011	Herbel-Eisenmann, & Otten, 2011 Lew & Mejía-Ramos, 2019

Table 4 (cont.)

Bubble Number	Bubble Name	Location within the Foam (colored nodes)	Most Cited Article(s)	JRME Citing Article(s)
5	Schoenfeld		Schoenfeld, 1992 Schoenfeld, 2002	Schoenfeld, 2010 Magiera & Zawojewski, 2011
6	Meaning of Equality		Kieran, 1992 Carpenter, Franke, & Levi, 2003	Boerst, Confrey, Heck, Knuth, Lambdin, & White, 2010 Jones & Pratt, 2012
7	Teaching's Influence on Learning		Murata, 2010 NRC, 2001	Murata, Bofferding, Pothen, & Taylor, 2012 Corey, Peterson, & Lewis, 2010
8	Proof and Reform		NCTM, 2000 Stein, Engle, Smith, & Hughes, 2008	Thompson & Senk, 2012 Munter, 2014

Table 4 (cont.)

Bubble Number	Bubble Name	Location within the Foam (colored nodes)	Most Cited Article(s)	JRME Citing Article(s)
9	Mathematics Knowledge for Teaching		Hill, 2007 Hill, Sleep, Lewis, & Ball, 2007	Hill, 2010 Izsák, Jacobson, & de Araujo, 2012
10	Negative Numbers		Vlassis, 2008 Peled, Mukhopadhyay, & Resnick, 1989	Lamb, Bishop, Philipp, & Whitacre, 2018 Stephan & Akyuz, 2012
11	Limits (and Calculus)		Gravemeijer, Cobb, Bowers, & Whitenack, 2000 Cornu, 1991	Swinyard & Larsen, 2012 Ely, 2010
12	Culturally Relevant Mathematics (African American & Indigenous)		Lubienski, 2007 Brenner, 1998	Meaney, Trinick, & Fairhall, 2013 Kisker, Lipka, Adams, Rickard, & Andrew-Ihrke,, 2012

Table 4 (cont.)

Bubble Number	Bubble Name	Location within the Foam (colored nodes)	Most Cited Article(s)	JRME Citing Article(s)
13	Race, identity, and Success (Black Student Success)		Solórzano & Yosso, 2002 McGee, & Martin, 2011	Jett, 2019 Adiredja, 2019
14	English Language Learner's Identity & Participation		Turner, Dominguez, Maldonado, & Empson, 2013 Yamakawa, Forman, & Ansell, 2009	Turner, Dominguez, Maldonado, & Empson, 2013 Shein, 2012
15	Achievement Gap		Adelman, 1999 Flores, 2007 Reys, 2006	Faulkner, Stiff, Marshall, & Nietfeld, 2014 NCTM Research Committee, 2013
16	Sociocultural Learning		Barsalou, 2008 Bowen, 2006	Krause, 2019 Graham, 2010

Table 4 (cont.)

Bubble Number	Bubble Name	Location within the Foam (colored nodes)	Most Cited Article(s)	JRME Citing Article(s)
17	Children's Achievement, Intervention, and Trajectories		Clements & Sarama, 2007, 2011	Cullen, Eames, Cullen, Barrett, Sarama, et al., 2018 Clements & Fuson, 2019
18	Mathematics Curriculum		Stein, Remillard, & Smith, 2007 CCSSM	Tarr, Grouws, & Chávez, 2013 Taylor, 2016
19	Equity and Social Justice		Gutierrez, 2008 Martin, 2009	Wilson, Nazemi, & Jackson, 2019 Bartell, Wager, Edwards, & Battey, 2017
20	Math Achievement		Ding & Davison, 2005 Tarr, Reys, Reys, Chávez, Shih, & Osterlind, 2008	Post, Medhanie, Harwell, et al., 2010 Harwell, Post, Medhanie, & Dupuis, 2013

Table 4 (cont.)

Bubble Number	Bubble Name	Location within the Foam (colored nodes)	Most Cited Article(s)	JRME Citing Article(s)
21	Mathematics Identities		Langer-Osuna, 2011 Johnstone, 2002	Wood, 2013 Esmonde, & Langer-Osuna, 2013 Bishop, 2012
22	Proof in RUME		Weber, 2004 Inglis & Alcock, 2012	Hodds & Alcock, 2014 Fukawa-Connelly & Weber, 2017
23	Mathematics Teachers and Teaching		Ball, Lubienski, & Mewborn, 2001 Hill, Rowan, & Ball, 2005	McRory, Floden, Ferrini-Mundy, & Reckase, 2012 Campbell, Nishio, Smith, Clark, et al., 2014
24	Empirical Statistics		Wild & Pfannkuch, 1999 Greer, Verschaffel, & Mukhopadhyay, 2007	Groth, 2015 English, 2016

Table 4 (cont.)

Bubble Number	Bubble Name	Location within the Foam (colored nodes)	Most Cited Article(s)	JRME Citing Article(s)
25	Algebra		Carraher & Schliemann, 2007 Lins & Kaput, 2004	Blanton, Stephens, Knuth, & Gardiner, 2015 Papic & Mulligan, 2011
26	Problem Posing and Multiple Solutions		Hiebert, Gallimore, Garnier, Givvin, Hollingsworth, Jacobs, … Stigler, 2003	Trenholm Alcock, & Robinson, 2016 Schukajlow, & Krug, 2014
27	Racialiazed Mathematics Achievement Remediation		Attewell, Lavin, Domina, & Levey, 2006 Bahr, 2008	Larnell, 2016 Mesa & Wladis, 2014
28	Qualitative Meta-synthesis		Berry & Thunder, 2012 Paterson, Thorne, Canam, & Jillings, 2001	Harper, 2019 Thunder & Berry, 2016

Table 4 (cont.)

Bubble Number	Bubble Name	Location within the Foam (colored nodes)	Most Cited Article(s)	JRME Citing Article(s)
29	Learning Disabilities		Gersten, Jordan, & Flojo, 2005 Swanson, 2007	Dyson, Jordan, Beliakoff, & Hassinger-Das, 2015 Lewis & Fisher, 2016
30	Learning in Contexts		Boaler & Staples, 2008 Boaler, 2002	Boaler & Selling, 2017 Sun, 2018
31	Research on Research and Journals		Toerner & Arzarello, 2012 Hirsch, 2005	Leatham, 2015 Nivens & Otten, 2017
32	Gender and Achievement		McGraw, Lubienski, & Strutchens, 2006 Penner & Paret, 2008	Lubienski, Robinson, & Crane, 2013 Leyva, 2017

Table 4 (cont.)

Bubble Number	Bubble Name	Location within the Foam (colored nodes)	Most Cited Article(s)	JRME Citing Article(s)
33	Urban Equity (and Technology's Role)		DiME 2007 Leonard & Martin, 2013 Secada, 1992	Kitchen & Berk, 2016, 2017
34	Sociological Perspectives on Learning		Kilpatrick, Swafford, & Findell, 2001 Lampert, 2001	Whitacre & Nickerson, 2016 Hohensee, 2016 Kobiela & Lehrer, 2015
35	Psychological Studies & Replication		Melhuish, 2018 Makel & Plucker, 2014	Melhuish, 2018 Star, 2018 Jamil, 2018
36	Girls' Identity in Mathematics		Damarin, 2000 Mendick, 2005	Radovic, Black, & Salas, Williams, 2017 Darragh, 2018

Table 4 (cont.)

Bubble Number	Bubble Name	Location within the Foam (colored nodes)	Most Cited Article(s)	JRME Citing Article(s)
37	Undergraduate Mathematics		Bressoud, Mesa, & Rasmussen, 2015 Seymour & Hewitt, 1997	Rasmussen, Apkarian, Hagman, Johnson, Larsen, & Bressoud, 2019 Sadler & Sonnert, 2018

which comprise each bubble and the overall foam to develop an intuition about the research of the JRME 2010s.

Microanalysis: Bubbles

I proceed now by summarizing the 37 bubbles of research in the JRME 2010s: (1) Proof and Argument, (2) Professional Development, (3) Children's Learning, (4) Mathematical Discourse, (5) Schoenfeld, (6) Meaning of Equality, (7) Teaching's Influence on Learning, (8) Proof and Reform, (9) Mathematics Knowledge for Teaching, (10) Negative Numbers, (11) Limits and Calculus, (12) Culturally Relevant Mathematics African American & Indigenous, (13) Racial Identity & Success, (14) English Language Learner's Identity & Participation, (15) Achievement Gap, (16) Sociocultural Learning, (17) Children's Achievement, Intervention, & Trajectories, (18) Mathematics Curriculum, (19) Equity and Social Justice, (20) Math Achievement, (21) Mathematics Identity, (22) Proof in RUME, (23) Mathematics Teachers and Teaching, (24) Empirical Statistics, (25) Algebra, (26) Problem Posing and Multiple Solutions, (27) Racialized Mathematics Achievement Remediation, (28) Qualitative Metasynthesis, (29) Learning Disabilities, (30) Learning in Contexts, (31) Research on Research, (32) Gender and Achievement, (33) Urban Equity and Technology's Role, (34) Sociological Perspectives on Learning, (35) Psychological Studies & Replication, (36) Girls' Identities, and (37) Research in Undergraduate Mathematics Education. For each bubble (see Table 4), I provide the number used to indicate it on the map of the foam of the 2000s, its name, a mini map that shows the bubble's relative location within the foam of the field, the two to three most cited articles within that bubble, and two to three sample JRME articles that are located within that bubble.

In brief, the 2010s bubbles and the connections they make across time are:

- Bubble 1 (Proof and Argument) builds upon the Mathematical Proof bubble of the 2000s (14).
- Bubble 3 (Children's Learning) builds upon the Young Children's Learning and Development bubble of the 2000s (2).
- Bubble 4 (Mathematical Discourse) builds upon the Discourse & Language bubble of the 2000s (15).
- Bubble 5 (Schoenfeld) only has one JRME article: a commentary by Schoenfeld about his development as a mathematics education scholar across time. This article cites and connects to his Mathematical Thinking and Problem-Solving work of the 1990s (Bubble 12) and 1980s (Bubbles 7 & 11).
- Bubble 6 (Meaning of Equality) builds upon the Algebraic Equations and Errors bubble of the 2000s (8).
- Bubble 7 (Teaching's Influence on Learning) builds upon the Teaching and Learning bubbles of the 2000s (10 & 28).
- Bubble 8 (Proof and Reform) builds upon the Mathematical Proof bubble of the 2000s (14).
- Bubble 9 (Mathematics Knowledge for Teaching) builds upon the Mathematics Knowledge for Teaching bubble of the 2000s (5).
- Bubble 10 (Negative Numbers) builds upon the Number Sense bubble of the 1990s (3).
- Bubble 11 (Limits (and Calculus)) builds upon the Calculus and Function Concepts bubble of the 2000s (29).
- Bubble 12 (Culturally Relevant Mathematics (African American & Indigenous)) builds upon the Culturally Relevant Mathematics bubble of the 1990s (18).
- Bubble 15 (Achievement Gap) builds upon the Equitable Achievement bubble of the 2000s (17).
- Bubble 16 (Sociocultural Learning) builds upon the Mathematical Enculturation bubble of the 2000s (35).
- Bubble 18 (Mathematics Curriculum) builds upon the Standards-based Curriculum bubble of the 2000s (25).
- Bubble 19 (Equity and Social Justice) builds upon the Equity and Equitable Pedagogy bubble of the 2000s (27).
- Bubble 20 (Math Achievement) builds upon the Equitable Achievement bubble of the 2000s (17).
- Bubble 22 (Proof in RUME) builds upon the Mathematical Proof bubble of the 2000s (14).
- Bubble 23 (Mathematics Teachers and Teaching) builds upon the Pedagogy and Learning bubble of the 2000s (10).
- Bubble 24 (Empirical Statistics) builds upon the Data and Statistics bubble of the 2000s (21).
- Bubble 25 (Algebra) builds upon the Solving Algebraic Equations bubble of the 2000s (8).
- Bubble 27 (Racialized Mathematics Achievement Remediation) builds upon the Equitable Achievement: Class, Race, Sex bubble of the 2000s (17).
- Bubble 30 (Learning in Contexts) builds upon the Experience and Learning of Mathematics bubble of the 1990s (22).

- Bubble 32 (Gender and Achievement) builds upon the Gender Differences in Achievement bubble of the 2000s (34).
- Bubble 33 (Urban Equity (and Technology's Role)) builds upon the Equity and Equitable Pedagogy bubble of the 2000s (27).
- Bubble 34 (Sociological Perspectives on Learning) builds upon the Experience of Learning Mathematics bubble of the 1990s (22).
- Bubble 35 (Psychological Studies & Replication) builds upon the Scientific Research bubbles of the 2000s (3 & 4).

The remaining 11 bubbles that constitute new research foci that emerged in the 2010s include: (2) Professional Development, (13) Racial Identity & Success, (14) Identity & Participation, (17) Children's Achievement, Intervention, & Trajectories, (21) Mathematics Identity, (26) Problem Posing and Multiple Solutions, (28) Qualitative Metasynthesis, (29) Learning Disabilities, (31) Research on Research, (36) Girls' Identity, and (37) Research in Undergraduate Mathematics Education.

In Bubble 2 (Professional Development), research builds on work on teachers' knowledge (e.g., Ball, Thames, & Phelps, 2008) to consider the effects of professional development on teacher knowledge (Bell, Wilson, & Higgins, 2010) and teacher identity (Gresalfi, & Cobb, 2011).

Research clustered in Bubble 13 (Racial Identity & Success) builds on foundational work in critical race theory (Solórzano & Yosso, 2002) and stereotype management (McGee, & Martin, 2011) to provide anti-deficit counter narratives (Adiredja, 2019) and stories of mathematical persistence (Jett, 2019).

Bubble 14 (English Language Learner's Identity & Participation) research draws on positioning theory and the construction of identity in mathematics classrooms (Yamakawa, Forman, & Ansell, 2009), and other related areas, to interpret positioning, participation, and identity (Turner, Dominguez, Maldonado, & Empson, 2013) and the use of gesture (Shein, 2012) with English Language Learners.

Articles within Bubble 17 (Children's Achievement, Intervention, & Trajectories) build on research on preschool mathematics curriculum and early childhood intervention (Clements & Sarama, 2007, 2011) to provide a research-based critique of the Common Core (Clements, Fuson, & Sarama, 2019) and to provide intervention strategies for children (Cullen, Eames, Cullen, Barrett, Sarama, Clements, & Van Dine, 2018).

Research in Bubble 21 (Mathematics Identity) draws on discourse analysis (Johnstone, 2002) and the influence of student-student positioning in small groups on identity (Langer-Osuna, 2011) to unpack mathematics micro-identities (Wood, 2013), student participation (Esmonde, & Langer-Osuna, 2013), and fixed and shifting identities in mathematics classrooms (Bishop, 2012).

Bubble 26 (Problem Posing and Multiple Solutions) departs from findings from the TIMSS 1999 study on the importance of problem posing and solution strategies for student learning (Hiebert, Gallimore, Garnier, Givvin, Hollingsworth, Jacobs…Stigler, 2003) to understand the affordances and constraints of online teaching (Trenholm, Alcock, & Robinson, 2016) and to model student competency and autonomy on the basis of multiple solutions (Schukajlow & Krug, 2014).

JRME contributions in Bubble 28 (Qualitative Metasynthesis) draw on orienting work on qualitative metasyntheses (Berry & Thunder, 2012) and an exemplar metasynthesis on the mathematics experience of Black learners (Paterson, Thorne, Canam, & Jillings, 2001) to argue for the value of such qualitative metasyntheses for mathematics education research (Thunder & Berry, 2016) and to provide such a metasynthesis on the teaching mathematics for social justice literature (Harper, 2019).

Some researchers in Bubble 29 (Learning Disabilities) drew on research on the identification and intervention of mathematics learning disabilities (Gersten, Jordan, & Flojo, 2005; Swanson, 2007) to develop a number sense intervention for kindergarteners (Dyson, Jordan, Beliakoff, & Hassinger-Das, 2015). Another contribution in this bubble includes a literature review of 40-years of research on mathematical learning disabilities (Lewis & Fisher, 2016).

The research in Bubble 31 (Research on Research) was already discussed in the theoretical orientations chapter (Chapter 2) since it is within this bubble that the present study is situated. The research within this bubble includes research on mathematics education journal quality (Toerner & Arzarello, 2012; Nivens & Otten, 2017), quantification of researcher output (Hirsch, 2005), and the citation practices of mathematics education researchers (Leatham, 2015).

Related to Bubble 21 on mathematics identity, Bubble 36 specifically considers Girls' Identities in mathematics spaces. Early work on the gendering of mathematics ability (Damarin, 2000; Mendick, 2005) serve as a foundation for studies on the mathematics identities of girl mathematicians (Radovic, Black, Salas, & Williams, 2017) and the unpacking of the gendering of mathematical ability in young adult fiction (Darragh, 2018).

The research in Bubble 37 (Research in Undergraduate Mathematics Education) draws on the *MAA National Study of College Calculus* (Bressoud, Mesa, & Rasmussen, 2015) and research on undergraduates leaving the sciences (Seymour & Hewitt, 1997). Some research within this bubble includes two large-scale studies: the first on high-school factors that lead to college calculus success (Rasmussen, Apkarian, Hagman, Johnson, Larsen, & Bressoud, 2019) and the second on the characteristics of college precalculus through calculus 2 (Sadler & Sonnert, 2018).

Macroanalysis: Foam

Now that I have unpacked the 11 research foci that emerged in the JRME 2010s foam, I now transition to the macroanalysis. Here, I shift my gaze from the bubbles as individual research foci towards their positions relative within the foam and relative to each other to better understand the landscape of the field in the 2010s as presented within the JRME. Since my focus shifts now to the positions of the bubbles within the foam, to assist the reader in seeing their positions I refer them to Figure 42 which shows the collection of bubbles from the foam but does not include the dots that correspond to the articles within each bubble. In the following subsections I proceed through an analysis that first considers the centrality of the position of bubbles within the overall foam and second that considers the adjacency and overlap of various bubbles.

Central/Marginal Analysis

Among the topics that are central to the JRME 2010s foam are professional development of teachers' knowledge (Bubble 2), Schoenfeld's thinking and problem solving (Bubble 5), teaching's influence on learning (Bubble 7), proof and reform (Bubble 8 which includes NCTM's 2000 *Principles and Standards for School Mathematics*), mathematics curriculum (Bubble 18 which includes the *Common Core State Standards for Mathematics*), and problem posing and multiple solutions (Bubble

Figure 42. The bubbles of the 2010s JRME foam

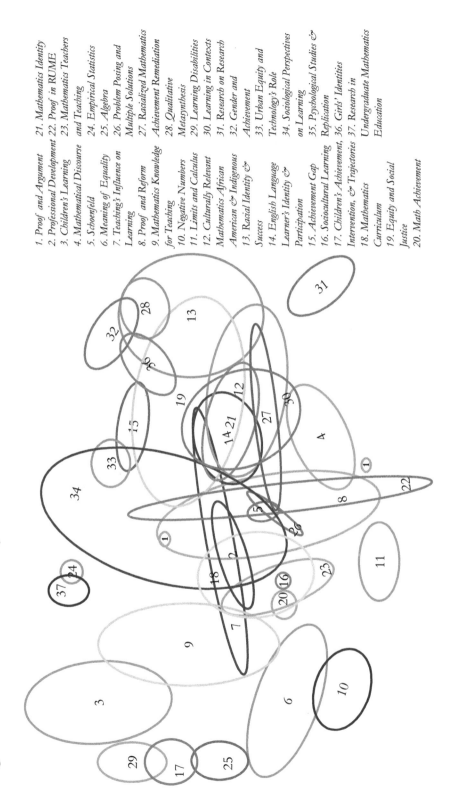

1. Proof and Argument
2. Professional Development
3. Children's Learning
4. Mathematical Discourse
5. Schoenfeld
6. Meaning of Equality
7. Teaching's Influence on Learning
8. Proof and Reform
9. Mathematics Knowledge for Teaching
10. Negative Numbers
11. Limits and Calculus
12. Culturally Relevant Mathematics African American & Indigenous
13. Racial Identity & Success
14. English Language Learner's Identity & Participation
15. Achievement Gap
16. Sociocultural Learning
17. Children's Achievement, Intervention, & Trajectories
18. Mathematics Curriculum
19. Equity and Social Justice
20. Math Achievement
21. Mathematics Identity
22. Proof in RUME
23. Mathematics Teachers and Teaching
24. Empirical Statistics
25. Algebra
26. Problem Posing and Multiple Solutions
27. Racialized Mathematics Achievement Remediation
28. Qualitative Metasynthesis
29. Learning Disabilities
30. Learning in Contexts
31. Research on Research
32. Gender and Achievement
33. Urban Equity and Technology's Role
34. Sociological Perspectives on Learning
35. Psychological Studies & Replication
36. Girls' Identities
37. Research in Undergraduate Mathematics Education

26). Among the topics that are more marginal to the JRME 2010s foam are, clockwise from the top left, children's learning (Bubble 3), research in undergraduate mathematics education (Bubble 37), empirical statistics (Bubble 24), gender and achievement (Bubble 32), girls' identity (Bubble 36), qualitative metasyntheses (Bubble 28), racial identity and success (Bubble 13), research on research (Bubble 31), calculus (Bubble 11), algebra (Bubble 25), children's achievement and intervention (Bubble 17), and learning disabilities (Bubble 29).

Nearness/Overlap Analysis

Here, I present an analysis which considers two sets of overlapping bubbles: teaching and learning research and equity research. The first set of overlapping bubbles on teaching and learning research (Figure 43, left) includes the following bubbles: (2) Professional Development, (5) Schoenfeld, (7) Teaching's Influence on Learning, (8) Proof and Reform, (16) Sociocultural Learning, (18) Mathematics Curriculum, (23) Mathematics Teachers and Teaching, and (26) Problem Posing and Multiple Solutions. Within this set, bubbles 5 (Schoenfeld's work) and 26 (problem posing and multiple solutions) overlap; this is expected given Schoenfeld's work on mathematical thinking and problem solving. Additionally, Bubble 16 (sociocultural learning) is contained within Bubble 23 (mathematics teachers and teaching) which suggests that sociocultural learning continues to be only a small part of teaching and learning. Since Bubble 8 (Proof and Reform) includes the NCTM *Principles and Standards for School Mathematics* and Bubble 18 (Mathematics Curriculum) includes the *Common Core State Standards for Mathematics*, there is little surprise that they overlap since they both include important policy documents in mathematics curriculum. Furthermore, the place where Bubble 7 (teachers' influence on learning) intersects with both bubbles 8 and 18 corresponds to the location of these curriculum documents. This is suggestive of the way that curriculum influences the ways in which teachers are able to influence the learning of students, or at least the way that such documents guide the research into teaching's influence on learning.

The second set of overlapping bubbles on equity research (Figure 43, right) includes the following bubbles: (12) Culturally Relevant Mathematics: African American & Indigenous, (13) Racial Identity & Success, (14) English Language Learners' Identity & Participation, (15) Achievement Gap, (19) Equity and Social Justice, (21) Mathematics Identity, (27) Racialized Mathematics Achievement Remediation, (28) Qualitative Metasynthesis, (32) Gender and Achievement, (33) Urban Equity and Technology's Role, and (36) Girls' Identities. First, bubble 28 (Qualitative Metasynthesis) is included here since the few metasyntheses that have been undertaken, discussed above, are on the experience of Black students and on the teaching of mathematics for social justice. Since teaching mathematics for social justice is often about racial justice (e.g., Gutstein, 2003), it is unsurprising that these both fall within the bubble on racial identity and success (Bubble 13). It is, however, remarkable that urban equity is distant from bubble 13 since urban is often used as a way to refer to students of color while simultaneously silencing explicit discussion about race (Paris, 2019). Another interesting distance is that while Bubbles 14 (English language learners' identity) and 21 (mathematics identity) share considerable overlap, the bubble on girls' identity (36) is disjoint. This may be partly accounted for by the conversation about gender being dominated by research on achievement gaps (Bubble 15) and gendered achievement gaps (32), thus pulling the conversation about gender towards those bubbles instead.

Figure 43. Image showing the two overlapping groups analyzed from the JRME 2010s foam: mathematics teaching (left) and equity research (right).

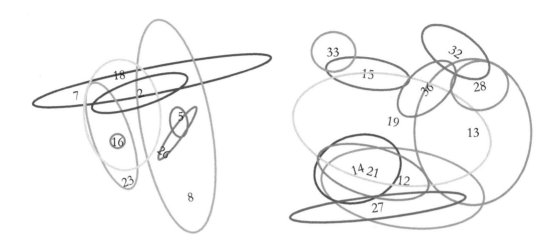

JRME: 1970-2019

Before I transition into the temporal analysis, an analysis which will consider both (1) the shifting bubbles and foams across time and (2) a composite foam which considers every article and citation together, I would like to revisit my aim. If I am able to look back, to see a story of what has been and show that what has been done in the name of mathematics education research has shifted across time, that what has been included, and therefore excluded, has neither been fixed nor progressive, what is included (and excluded) today is not the inevitable accomplishment of direct action by a cohesive collection of researchers; the research foci of our field of mathematics education research are "neither discovered truths nor preordained developments, but rather the products of conglomerations of blind forces" (Prado, 1995, p. 38). I am convinced, and you may or may not be, and to varying degrees depending on your context, perspective, and commitments, that the shifting number and foci of bubbles—some emerge, some pop, some merge, some split—suggests that the partage outlined by the JRME has been fluid across time: at least when considering each decade in isolation. Does the same hold when the decades are considered together? What happens when these foams are merged, when the 1970s, 1980s, 1990s, 2000s, and 2010s of the JRME are considered together? I turn now to that analysis.

Macroanalysis: A Foamy Field

In the preceding sections, each figure has used color to denote the bubble in which an article was placed by the Louvain modularity algorithm. I depart from that convention since my focus now shifts onto the composite JRME foam, the foam that considers every one of the 1,090 articles published in the JRME between 1970 and 2019 and the 33,273 citation relationships that they form. The JRME composite foam is shown in Figure 44.

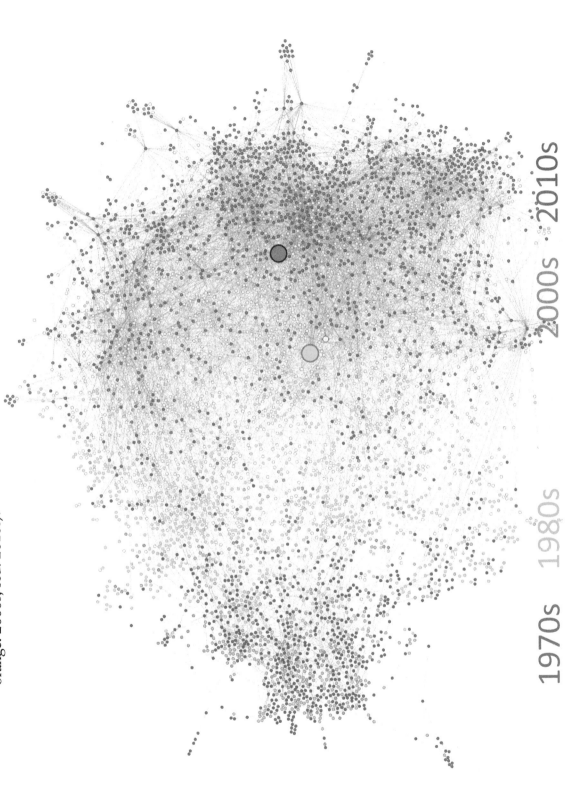

Figure 44. The JRME 1970–2019 foam—color denotes decade of publication (blue: 1970s; green: 1980s; yellow: 1990s; orange: 2000s; red: 2010s).

2010s

2000s

1970s   1980s

111

In Figure 44, and for the remainder of this chapter, the color of a node will denote the decade in which a JRME article was published and the decade in which a reference was first cited. The color-decade pairings are as follow: blue: 1970s, green: 1980s, yellow: 1990s, orange: 2000s, and red: 2010s. Figure 32 shows all 33,273 article-reference citation links from the five decades.

While it is true that what is shown in Figure 44 does not show the result of the Louvain modularity algorithm being applied (yet; see Figure 45 in the next section), the force-directed layout algorithm has been applied. This suggests that each of the citation links has been interpreted as a spring and the nodes have been interpreted as electrons and the system has been calculated until an equilibrium state is reached. That result is shown in Figure 44. Notice the generally chronological ordering from left to right. Also, however, notice that there are, for example, blue nodes, nodes from the 1970s, scattered across the composite foam.

The following is a truism: an article cannot cite an article that is published after it has been published (perhaps with the exception of *in preparation/in press* citations). For example, an article published in 1975 could not cite an article from 2005. It is also the case that the force-directed algorithm begins by placing each cited article adjacent to the very first article it cites. Therefore, a node that is blue either represents a JRME article that was published during the 1970s or a reference that was first cited during the 1970s. Then, articles that are blue but appear with the orange nodes of the 2000s, for example, has been cited a sufficient number of times in that decade that the spring forces of the citation links overcome the repulsion force between that node and its neighbors in its originating decade, and the repulsion force of every node between its starting point and ending point. This suggests that some ideas continue to be taken up across time and are denoted by blue nodes to the right of the blue dividing line (see Figure 45 to see these dividing lines), green nodes right of the green dividing line, and so on. Instead of listing every topic that has crossed its corresponding dividing line, I turn now to an analysis that uses the Louvain modularity algorithm to identify the densely connected subgroups of nodes.

Microanalysis: Volatile Bubbles

The bubbles that result from the Louvain modularity algorithm are shown in Figure 45. Superimposed onto the foam from Figure 44 are lines which show the approximate lines between decades: these lines are not clear cut as there is substantial travel of nodes around the turn of a decade (e.g., an article from January 1st, 1980 would necessarily, and almost exclusively, cite articles published in the 1970s) but serve as orienting lines for the foam as a whole. Additionally, superimposed on the foam are the bubbles, identified by a number (roughly left to right), and the colors of the bubbles are set to shift colors as they cross borders. For example, bubble 4 crosses the 1970s and 1980s and therefore is both blue and green. These circles indicate the location of the densest concentration of nodes from each bubble. That is to say, bubble 4 does not end in the 1980s; in fact, revisiting the previous section suggests that arithmetic is an area of focus across each of the 5 decades. What these circles show us, therefore, is the emergence of several macrobubbles, or macrofoci, of research published in the JRME between 1970 and 2019.

Across the five decades of research, 19 macrobubbles of research, or general foci of research, have emerged. Beginning in the 1970s and continuing through the 2010s, these foci are:

Figure 45. The JRME 1970–2019 Foam with Macrobubbles Superimposed.

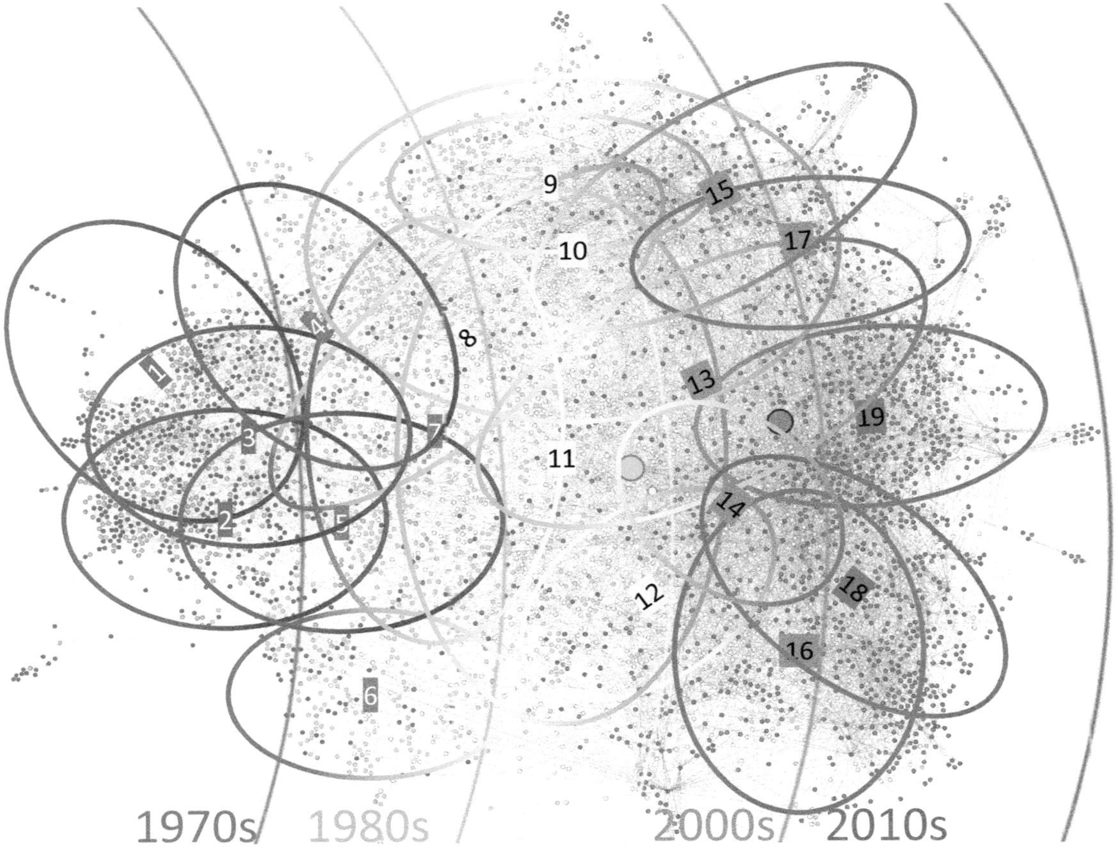

113

Figure 46. The JRME 1970–2019 Macrobubbles.

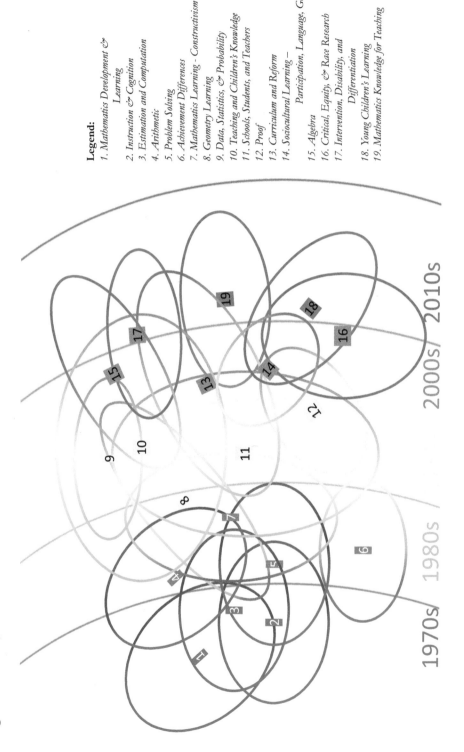

Legend:
1. Mathematics Development & Learning
2. Instruction & Cognition
3. Estimation and Computation
4. Arithmetic
5. Problem Solving
6. Achievement Differences
7. Mathematics Learning - Constructivism
8. Geometry Learning
9. Data, Statistics, & Probability
10. Teaching and Children's Knowledge
11. Schools, Students, and Teachers
12. Proof
13. Curriculum and Reform
14. Sociocultural Learning – Participation, Language, Gesture
15. Algebra
16. Critical, Equity, & Race Research
17. Intervention, Disability, and Differentiation
18. Young Children's Learning
19. Mathematics Knowledge for Teaching

(1) Mathematics Development & Learning, (2) Instruction & Cognition, (3) Estimation and Computation, (4) Arithmetic, (5) Problem Solving, (6) Achievement Differences, (7) Mathematics Learning - Constructivism, (8) Geometry Learning, (9) Data, Statistics, & Probability, (10) Teaching and Children's Knowledge, (11) Schools, Students, and Teachers, (12) Proof, (13) Curriculum and Reform, (14) Sociocultural Learning – Participation, Language, Gesture, (15) Algebra, (16) Critical, Equity, & Race Research, (17) Intervention, Disability, and Differentiation, (18) Young Children's Learning, and (19) Mathematics Knowledge for Teaching. The numbering is not strictly chronological (e.g., bubble 8 spans from the 1970s through the 2000s) but are more-or-less chronological in accordance with the left-to-right orientation imposed in Figure 45. As I had done in the decade analyses, I present Figure 45 without the individual nodes in Figure 46 to assist the reader in seeing the location, size, and orientation of each bubble.

The process of naming each bubble followed the process outlined in Chapter 2. The title of every article in the bubble was input into Wordle to generate a word cloud. These word clouds showed the most frequently occurring words within each bubble. I include each word cloud in Table 5 to illustrate the non-deterministic process of naming bubbles. The names that I have chosen to assign to each bubble are based on what words I noticed in each word cloud; the reader might see different keywords within each bubble and could compose a different set of names for these bubbles. Through such a process, the reader could compose a different narrative than the one I present next. Just as Foucault emphasized a plurality of knowledges (Fendler, 2010), I assert the plurality of interpretation and meaning that could be ascribed to this analysis. By choosing to enact Rancièrean equality (2004), I must accept that the reader is as capable of naming these bubbles as I am, and those names could be equally valid.

Table 5. Macrobubble of the JRME composite foam together with the word cloud and microbubble name.

Macrobubble Number	Word Cloud	Macrobubble Name
1		Mathematics Development and Learning
2		Instruction & Cognition

Table 5 (cont.)

Macrobubble Number	Word Cloud	Macrobubble Name
3		Estimation and Computation
4		Arithmetic
5		Problem Solving
6		Achievement Differences
7		Mathematics Learning - Constructivism
8		Geometry Learning

Table 5 (cont.)

Macrobubble Number	Word Cloud	Macrobubble Name
9		Data, Statistics, and Probability
10		Teaching and Children's Knowledge
11		Schools, Students, and Teachers
12		Proof
13		Curriculum and Reform
14		Sociocultural Learning – Participation, Language, Gesture
15		Algebra

Table 5 (cont.)

16	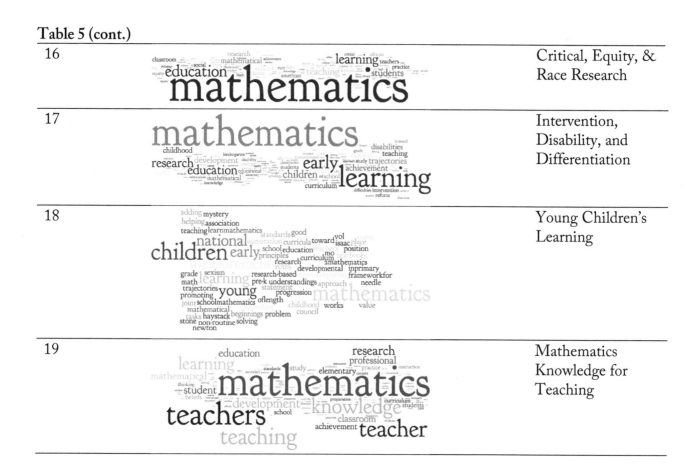	Critical, Equity, & Race Research
17		Intervention, Disability, and Differentiation
18		Young Children's Learning
19		Mathematics Knowledge for Teaching

Taking these macrobubble names together, I offer the following narrative for the development of the field of mathematics education research as published in the JRME between 1970 and 2019:

Mathematics education research began in the 1970s with a focus on mathematics teaching and learning of arithmetic, computation, and estimation, particularly from a cognitive perspective. In the 1980s, the field underwent a shift in focus from computation to problem solving and geometry. Under the specter of achievement differences, the field shifted towards mathematics teaching and learning from a constructivist perspective. A shifting curricular focus towards data, statistics, probability, and proof came with reform. In the 1990s, a social turn towards a holistic understanding of schools, students, and teachers yielded a non-cognitive approach to teaching and children's knowledge: sociocultural learning. In the 2000s and 2010s, critical, equity, and race scholars named non-instructional reasons for an achievement gap: systemic inequality. With the shifting curricular landscape and a push for measurable mathematics education, intervention emerged. Thankfully, with differentiation, naming mathematical disability, and the young children's need for intervention, the field was ready to respond by studying mathematics knowledge for teaching.

This narrative is illustrative of one reading of the development of the field of mathematics education across the past five decades. Looking back across the decades, from the microanalyses of the bubbles of each decade to each decade's foam, zooming out to the macrobubbles of the composite foam, I ask you: what is your reading?

Concluding Thoughts

Recalling the Sloterdijkian notion of bubbles (2011), the bubbles that I identified each constitute contingent groupings of related research clustered around particular research foci. The bubbles of each decade form a foam, or collection of co-fragile, codependent bubbles that together constitute a map of the foci that collectively outline the scope of mathematics education research during each decade. I compared and contrasted the bubbles and foams across time. First, I showed composite foams for each decade to identify the macro-foci of the field across time. Then, by sequentially presenting the decades sequentially, I was able to show those bubbles that pop, those that emerge, those that merge, etc. My presentation emphasized the shifting value that mathematics education researchers have placed on particular foci across time, suggesting that the research foci within the field of mathematics education researchers are neither the necessary nor inevitable destination of the field but rather are determined by researchers' shifting interests.

I conclude by revisiting the five aims of cartography discussed in chapter 3 as I applied them in this chapter:

(1) I documented something new, a citation network of the first five decades of articles published in the JRME;

(2) I attempted to make the network more understandable by presenting both decade and composite maps;

(3) I applied Louvain modularity and force-directed layout algorithms to reveal patterns in those citation patterns;

(4) I connected these network readings to my aims of showing the fluidity of what has constituted mathematics education research in the JRME across these five decades, and

(5) I set the stage for more exploration and ask you to interact with the maps at MathEdAtlas.org.

In the words of Rancière (1991):

What do you see?

What do you think about it?

What do you make of it?

5   PARTAGE II: *FOR THE LEARNING OF MATHEMATICS*

This chapter proceeds from an introduction to *For the Learning of Mathematics* (FLM) to an investigation into the bubbles of the 2010s and the foam that those bubbles constitute. The editors (past and present) of FLM themselves "believe the writing in FLM to be distinctive, in the sense of having unique style and purpose amongst journals in our field" (Barwell & Reid, 2019, p. 393). They continue "FLM is a journal for the learning, and the learners, of mathematics, rather than being of behavior or for didactics, research or teaching" (Barwell & Reid, 2019, p. 397. According to FLM's aims:

> The journal aims to stimulate reflection on mathematics education at all levels, and promote study of its practices and its theories: to generate productive discussion; to encourage enquiry and research; to promote criticism and evaluation of ideas and procedures current in the field. It is intended for the mathematics educator who is aware that the learning and teaching of mathematics are complex enterprises about which much remains to be revealed and understood. (FLM Aims)

Unpacking these aims, suggests to me that there are several proper ways to say, think, and do mathematics education research, including reflection, study, discussion, enquiry, research, criticism, evaluation of the teaching, learning, and researching of mathematics education and mathematics education research, its theories, ideas, and procedures. These aims paint one particular picture of what mathematics education research can be. And while this scope is quite broad, it is anchored to mathematics education and the ideas and procedures current in the field.

To understand what is current in the field, I perform a citation network analysis on the 187 articles published by FLM between 2010 and 2017. I end at 2017, instead of 2020, due to a moving wall limitation on the JSTOR database: there is a 3-year delay between article publication and its addition to the JSTOR repository. These 187 articles together included 3,595 citation relationships (for an average of 19 references per paper). Compared to JRME and ESM, FLM publishes considerably fewer articles per year. Nonetheless, as one of the major journals in mathematics education (Kaiser & Presmeg, 2019), the collection of articles published in FLM constitute a particular partage or distribution of what is sensible as mathematics education research.

FLM in the 2010s

Analysis, as outlined in chapter 2, of the articles published between 2010 and 2017 in FLM and their 3,595 references, yielded the map in Figure 47. The Louvain Modularity algorithm identified 14 modularity classes. These modularity classes, or bubbles, each constitute a particular research focus of the field of mathematics education research as published in FLM during this time. Connecting to the journal aims, these bubbles, since they come from the period 2010-2017, are the ideas current in the field. These ideas are (1) Perspectives on Mathematics Education, (2) Ethnomathematics and Critical Mathematics Education, (3) Mathematics Teaching, (4) Cultural Perspectives on Mathematics Learning: Semiosis, Enculturation, & Development, (5) Knowing in Mathematics, (6) Making Meaning in Mathematics: Language and Gesture, (7) Proof, (8) Mathematical Knowledge

Figure 47. Bubbles of research from FLM 2010-2017.

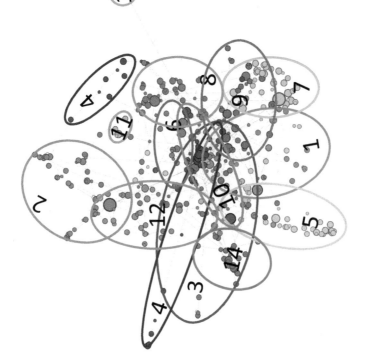

For the Learning of Mathematics
2010s

1. Perspectives on Mathematics Education
2. Ethnomathematics and Critical Mathematics Education
3. Mathematics Teaching
4. Cultural Perspectives on Mathematics Learning: Semiosis, Enculturation, & Development
5. Knowing in Mathematics
6. Making Meaning in Mathematics: Language and Gesture
7. Proof
8. Mathematical Knowledge for Teaching
9. Teacher Noticing and Attention
10. Philosophy of Mathematics Education
11. Discourses about Mathematics and Mathematical Discourse
12. Teaching Mathematics for Social Justice
13. Genre and Language
14. Embodied Mathematics

for Teaching, (9) Teacher Noticing and Attention, (10) Philosophy of Mathematics Education, (11) Discourses about Mathematics and Mathematical Discourse, (12) Teaching Mathematics for Social Justice, (13) Genre and Language, and (14) Embodied Mathematics. These fourteen bubbles together constitute the foam of mathematics education research in FLM during the 2010s. As shown in chapter 3 with the JRME, this foam across time is volatile: new bubbles emerge, distinct bubbles merge, bubbles burst. This foam does not constitute an eternal "Mathematics Education is..." but rather "mathematics education research (in the FLM) currently is...".

The remainder of this chapter is divided into two parts corresponding to two levels of analysis: microanalysis of the bubbles and macroanalysis of the foam. In the first part, I will discuss each bubble and their constituent articles in turn. In the second part, I will discuss the foam: the relative positions of bubbles within the foam (e.g., central and marginal bubbles) and the relative positions between bubbles within the foam (e.g., the overlap of bubbles #2 ethnomathematics and critical mathematics education and #12 teaching mathematics for social justice). After the orienting initial map (Figure 47) which shows the relative position of each of the fourteen bubbles in the foam, within each section a bubble map will show only the bubble of interest in color with the remainder of the nodes colored grey: this provides a snapshot of where each bubble is located within the foam at large.

Microanalysis: Bubbles in FLM

As shown in Figure 47, the 14 bubbles of research in the FLM during the period 2010-2017 are (1) Perspectives on Mathematics Education, (2) Ethnomathematics and Critical Mathematics Education, (3) Mathematics Teaching, (4) Cultural Perspectives on Mathematics Learning: Semiosis, Enculturation, & Development, (5) Knowing in Mathematics, (6) Making Meaning in Mathematics: Language and Gesture, (7) Proof, (8) Mathematical Knowledge for Teaching, (9) Teacher Noticing and Attention, (10) Philosophy of Mathematics Education, (11) Discourses about Mathematics and Mathematical Discourse, (12) Teaching Mathematics for Social Justice, (13) Genre and Language, and (14) Embodied Mathematics. What follows is a description of the most cited references in each bubble and which FLM articles cited those references. As a complete elaboration and review of each article is beyond the scope of this analysis, I instead provide the name and authors of several focal articles as evidence that the chosen bubble name is appropriate and to serve as an orientation to each bubble. These sections might serve as orienting texts and starting points for those interested in studying different research foci within the partage of mathematics education research outlined in the FLM.

Bubble 1: Perspectives on Mathematics Education

The first bubble of the 2010s FLM foam is named "Perspectives on Mathematics Education." Another possible name that I considered for this bubble was "mathematician's perspective on mathematics education" since the most cited references within this bubble are Burton's "Why is intuition so important to mathematicians but missing from mathematics education?" (1999) and *Mathematicians as Enquirers: Learning about Learning Mathematics* (2004). Relatedly commonly cited is Lockhart's "A Mathematician 's Lament: How School Cheats Us Out of Our Most Fascinating and Imaginative Art Form" (2009). Three other commonly cited articles, less connected to mathematician's perspectives are Zak & Reid's "Good-enough understanding: theorizing about the learning of complex ideas (Parts I & II)" (2003, 2004) and Fischbein's "Intuition and proof" (1982).

Among the FLM articles which cited and build on these works are Gadanadis' "Why Can't I Be a Mathematician?" (2012), Maciejewski & Barton's "Mathematical Foresight: Thinking in The Future to Work in The Present" (2016), Barabe & Proulx's "Revolutionizing the teaching of mathematics: The visionary Project of Seymour Papert" (2017), and Maheux's "Re-Counting Mathematics Education with Technology" (2014). These together are research elaborating different perspectives on the nature and future of mathematics education. Figure 48 shows the location of Bubble 1 within the foam of the FLM 2010s.

Figure 48. Location of the bubble "Perspectives on Mathematics Education" within the foam of the FLM 2010s.

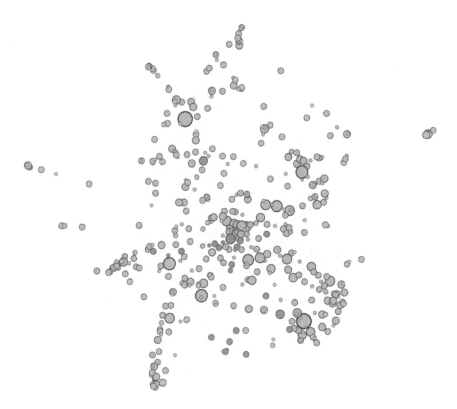

Bubble 2: Ethnomathematics and Critical Mathematics Education

The second bubble of the 2010s FLM foam is "Ethnomathematics and Critical Mathematics Education." The most cited article within this bubble is Skovsmose's "Towards a Philosophy of Critical Mathematics Education" (1994). Other frequently cited references within this bubble are Renert's "Mathematics for life: sustainable mathematics education" (2011), Vithal & Skovsmose's (1997) "The end of innocence: a critique of 'ethnomathematics'", Pais' "Criticisms and contradictions of ethnomathematics" (2011) and "A critical approach to equity in mathematics education" (2012), and Freire's *Cultural action for freedom* (1998).

Building on this breadth of critical work is work by Pais "Ethnomathematics and the Limits of Culture" (2013), Khan "Ethnomathematics As Mythopoetic Curriculum" (2011), Pais, Fernandes, & Matos "Recovering the Meaning of 'Critique' in Critical Mathematics Education" (2012), and

Appelbaum "Mathematical Practice as Sculpture of Utopia: Models, Ignorance, and the Emancipated Spectator" (2012). These articles interrogate the implicit meanings of ethnomathematics, critical mathematics education, and mathematical practice. Figure 49 shows the location of Bubble 2 within the foam of the FLM 2010s.

Figure 49. Location of the bubble "Ethnomathematics and Critical Mathematics Education" within the foam of the FLM 2010s.

Bubble 3: Mathematics Teaching

The third bubble of the 2010s FLM foam is "Mathematics Teaching." The most cited article is Davis' "Listening for differences: an evolving conception of mathematics teaching" (1997). Other frequently cited references are Lampert's "When the problem is not the question and the solution is not the answer: mathematical knowing and teaching" (1990) and Gattegno's What We Owe Children: The Subordination of Teaching to Learning (1970) and "The Common Sense of Teaching Mathematics" (1974). Also frequently cited was Arcavi's "Developing and Using Symbol Sense in Mathematics" (2005), which unlike his earlier "Symbol Sense" (1994) focuses on how 'experts' develop symbol sense in learners.

Among the FLM articles which cited these articles are Tabach's "The dual role of researcher and teacher: a case study" (2011), Coles' "Transitional Devices" on the images and analogies teachers can use to support students in connecting concrete examples to abstract concepts (2014), and Coles' and Brown's "Being mathematics teacher educators in the praxis of living" (2015). Together, then, these articles constitue research with a focus on the teacher and the teacher's role. Figure 50 shows the location of Bubble 3 within the foam of the FLM 2010s.

Figure 50. Location of the bubble "Mathematics Teaching" within the foam of the FLM 2010s.

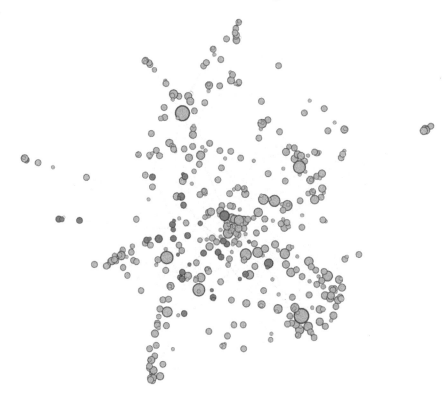

Bubble 4: Cultural Perspectives on Mathematics Learning: Semiosis, Enculturation, & Development

The fourth bubble of the 2010s FLM foam is "Cultural Perspectives on Mathematics Learning: Semiotic, Enculturation, & Development." The three nouns in the subtitle correspond to the three components of this bubble: semiosis (central), enculturation (top), and student development (left). See Figure 51 to see the location of Bubble 4 within the foam of the FLM 2010s and the positions of each component of the bubble: a large cluster towards the center of the foam, some articles towards the top side of the foam, and a few article towards the left side of the foam.

Cultural Perspectives on Mathematics Learning: Semiosis. The most cited articles within this portion of the bubble are Radford's "The seen, the spoken and the written: a semiotic approach to the problem of objectification of mathematical knowledge" (2002), "The anthropology of meaning, Culture and cognition: towards an anthropology of mathematical thinking" (2006), and "The ethics of being and knowing: towards a cultural theory of learning" (2008). Cited frequently, in addition to Radford's work is McNeill's *Hand and Mind: What Gestures Reveal About Thought* (1992).

Among the FLM articles citing these works are Samson & Schäfer's "Enactivism, Figural Apprehension and Knowledge Objectification: An Exploration of Figural Pattern Generalisation" (2001), Andrà's "How Do Students Understand Mathematical Lectures? Note-Taking As Retelling

Figure 51. Location of the bubble "Cultural Perspectives on Mathematics Learning: Semiosis, Enculturation, & Development" within the foam of the FLM 2010s.

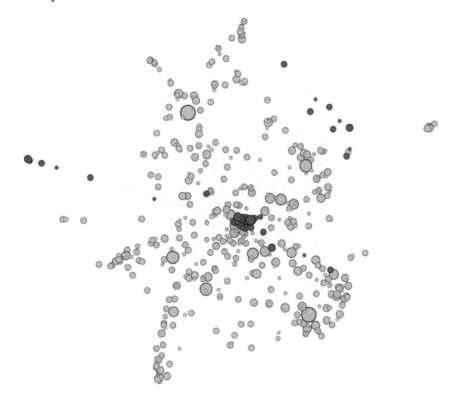

of the Teacher's Story" (2013), and Radford's "The Eye as a Theoretician: Seeing Structures in Generalizing Activities" (2012). Taken together, these articles are focused around the ways that students make sense of mathematics, whether it be through engaging in mathematical activities or taking notes or reading and listening to written and spoken language.

Cultural Perspectives on Mathematics Learning: Enculturation. The most cited references within this portion of the bubble are Bishop's "Mathematical Enculturation a Cultural Perspective on Mathematics Education" (1988) and Barton's *The Language of Mathematics: Telling Mathematical Tales* (2008). Among the FLM articles citing these articles are Davis' "A Three-Tier Teaching Model for Teaching Mathematics in Context" (2017) and Seah, Andersson, & Bishop's "What Would The Mathematics Curriculum Look Like if Values Were the Focus?" (2016), both of which situate mathematics education within culture. These articles move beyond mathematics as an external body of knowledge and interpret it as a social practice, with its own cultural norms, that individuals come to know and engage with.

Cultural Perspectives on Mathematics Learning: Development. The most cited articles within this portion of the bubble are Goos, Gailbraith, & Renshaw's "Socially mediated metacognition: creating collaborative zones of proximal development in small group problem solving" (2002) and Graven & Lerman's "Counting in threes: Lila's amazing discovery" (2014). Among the FLM articles which cite these works are Rood's "Geometrical Visualisation - Epistemic and Emotional"

(2010) and Abtahi's "Who/What Is the More Knowledgeable Other?" (2014) and "The 'More Knowledgeable Other': A Necessity in the Zone of Proximal Development?" (2017). Unifying these articles is a focus on how students develop in their mathematical thinking, whether in a group context or at an individual level.

Bubble 5: Knowing in Mathematics

The fifth bubble of the 2010s FLM foam is "Knowing in Mathematics." These articles form a constellation on perspectives on knowing, understanding, and what it means to know or understand different mathematical concepts. The most cited references within this bubble are Fischbein's *Intuition in Science and Mathematics: An Educational Approach* (1987), Piaget's *Genetic Epistemology* (1970), and Lamon's "Teaching Fractions and Ratios for Understanding: Essential Content Knowledge and Instructional Strategies for Teachers" (2012). More content specific are Steffe's "Schemes of action and operation involving composite units" (1992) and Lamon's "Rational numbers and proportional reasoning: toward a theoretical framework for research" (2007).

Among the articles citing these articles are the works by Tillema and colleagues: "Functions of Symbolizing Activity: A Discussion" (Tillema, 2010), "Developing Systems of Notation as a Trace of Reasoning" (Tillema & Hackenberg, 2011), and "A Quantitative and Combinatorial Approach to Non-Linear Meanings of Multiplication" (Tillema & Gatza, 2016). Further citing these articles is the work by Ulrich, in a two-part article, "Stages in Constructing and Coordinating Units Additively and Multiplicatively" (2016) which each elaborate what it means to know and understand in a mathematics context. Figure 52 shows the location of Bubble 5 within the foam of the FLM 2010s.

Figure 52. Location of the bubble "Knowing in Mathematics" within the foam of the FLM 2010s.

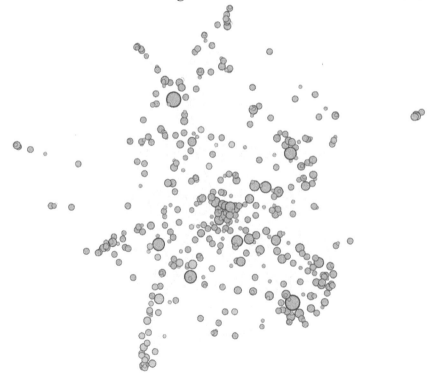

Bubble 6: Making Meaning in Mathematics: Language and Gesture

The sixth bubble of the 2010s FLM foam is "Making Meaning in Mathematics: Language and Gesture." The most cited reference within this bubble is Pimm's *Speaking mathematically: communication in mathematics classrooms* (1987). Other frequently cited references within this bubble are Hewitt's "Arbitrary and necessary: a way of viewing the mathematics curriculum" (1999), Arzarello, Paola, Robutti, & Sabena's "Gestures as semiotic resources in the mathematics classroom" (2009), Hughes' *Children and Number: Difficulties in Learning Mathematics* (1986), and Bussi & Mariotti's "Semiotic mediation in the mathematics classroom: artifacts and signs after a Vygotskian perspective" (2008).

Among the FLM articles citing these works are additional works by Pimm: "'The Likeness of Unlike Things': Insight, Enlightenment and The Metaphoric Way" (2010) and "Unthought Knowns" (2014). Additionally, Long's "Labelling Angles: Care, Indifference and Mathematical Symbols" (2011) and Frarugia's "On Semiotics and Jumping Frogs: The Role of Gesture in the Teaching of Subtraction" (2017) are among the FLM articles citing these works. From Pimm's *Speaking mathematically* to Frarugia's study on the role of gesture, each of these articles' studies aspects of language and gesture in the meaning making process of mathematics learning. See Figure 53 to see the relative position of the bubble within the foam of the FLM 2010s.

Figure 53. Location of the bubble "Making Meaning in Mathematics: Language and Gesture" within the foam of the FLM 2010s.

Bubble 7: Proof

The seventh bubble of the 2010s FLM foam is "Proof." The most cited work within this bubble is Lakatos' *Proofs and Refutations: The Logic of Mathematical Discovery* (1976). Together with Lakatos' text in the research bubble on proof is Balacheff's *Processus de preuve et situations de validation* [*Proving Processes and Situations for Validation*] (1987) and Leron's "Structuring mathematical proofs" (1983) and "A direct approach to indirect proofs" (1985).

Among the FLM articles to cite these references on proof are Leron & Zaslavsky's "Generic Proving: Reflections On Scope And Method" (2013), Weber & Mejia-Ramos' "On Relative And Absolute Conviction In Mathematics" (2015), Tanguary & Grenier's "Experimentation and Proof in a Solid Geometry Teaching Situation" (2010), and Dawkins' "When Proofs Reflect More on Assumptions than Conclusions" (2014). Figure 54 shows the position of Bubble 7 within the foam of the FLM 2010s.

Figure 54. Location of the bubble "Proof" within the foam of the FLM 2010s.

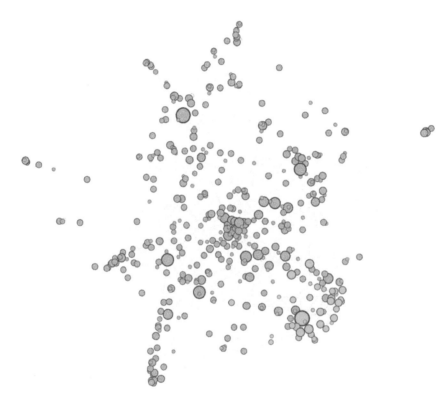

Bubble 8: Mathematical Knowledge for Teaching

The eighth bubble of the 2010s FLM foam is "Mathematical Knowledge for Teaching." In addition to Shulman's "Those who understand: Knowledge growth in teaching" (1986), the most cited articles within this bubble are Ball and colleagues' works "Content knowledge for teaching: What makes it special?" (Ball, Thames, & Phelps, 2008), "With an eye on the mathematical horizon: Knowing mathematics for teaching to learners' mathematical futures" (Ball & Bass, 2009), and "The mathematical understandings that prospective teachers bring to teacher education" (Ball, 1990).

Another frequently cited article is Davis & Simmt's "Mathematics-for-teaching: an ongoing investigation of the mathematics that teachers (need to) know" (2006).

Among the FLM articles to cite these references include Zazkis & Leikin's "Advanced Mathematical Knowledge in Teaching Practice: Perceptions of Secondary Mathematics Teachers" (2010), Creager & Jacobson's "Can Pedagogical Concerns Eclipse Mathematical Knowledge?" (2016), Zazkis & Mamolo's "Reconceptualizing Knowledge at the Mathematical Horizon" (2011), and Ribeiro & Mellone's "Interpreting Students' Non-Standard Reasoning: Insights for Mathematics Teacher Education" (2016). See Figure 55 for the location of Bubble 8 within the foam of the FLM 2010s.

Figure 55. Location of the bubble "Mathematical Knowledge for Teaching" within the foam of the FLM 2010s.

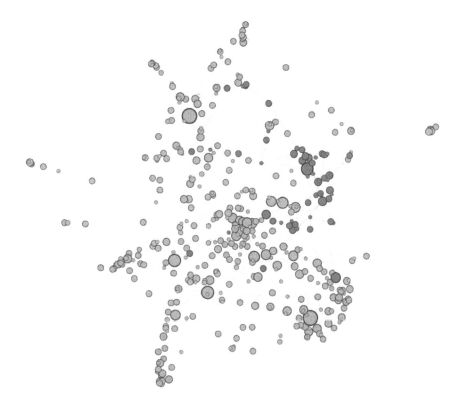

Bubble 9: Teacher Noticing and Attention

The ninth bubble of the 2010s FLM foam is "Teacher Noticing." The most cited references within this bubble are Mason's *Researching Your Own Practice: The Discipline of Noticing* (2002), "Attention and intention in learning about teaching through teaching" (2010), and "Mathematical abstraction as the result of a delicate shift of attention" (1989). Among the FLM articles citing these works are Palatinik & Koichu "Exploring Insight: Focus on Shifts of Attention" (2015), Chazan &

Herbst's "Challenges of Particularity and Generality in Depicting and Discussing Teaching" (2011), and Asghari's "Specularity In Algebra" (2012). Figure 56 shows the position of Bubble 9 within the foam of the FLM 2010s.

Figure 56. Location of the bubble "Teacher Noticing and Attention" within the foam of the FLM 2010s.

Bubble 10: Philosophy of Mathematics Education

The tenth bubble of the 2010s FLM foam is "Philosophy of Mathematics Education." The most cited references include Rowland's *The Pragmatics of Mathematics Education: Vagueness in Mathematical Discourse* (2000), Polyà's *How to Solve It: A New Aspect of Mathematical Method* (1945), D'Ambrosio & Kastberg's "Giving reason to prospective mathematics teachers" (2012), and von Glasersfeld's *Radical Constructivism: A Way of Knowing and Learning* (1995).

One of the FLM texts that cites some of these articles is Hackenberg's "Holding Together" (2013). This text is on the "theme of holding together what is seemingly disparate or even conflicting" (emphasis original, p. 16), a fitting theme since this category draws on articles that, at first, might not suggest a research focus of philosophy of mathematics education. Nonetheless, the way that some other FLM citing articles have taken them up in philosophical ways: Ernest's "What is our first philosophy in mathematics education?" (2012), McCloskey's "Caring in Professional Development Projects for Mathematics Teachers: An Example of Stimulation and Harmonizing" (2012) which considers the value of mathematics education and the role that caring plays in it, and Tatsis & Dekker's "Combining Approaches for the Analysis of Collaborative Mathematics Learning" (2010) which

132

unpacks the meaning of collaborative mathematics learning. See Figure 57 for the location of Bubble 10 within the foam of the FLM 2010s.

Figure 57. Location of the bubble "Philosophy of Mathematics Education" within the foam of the FLM 2010s.

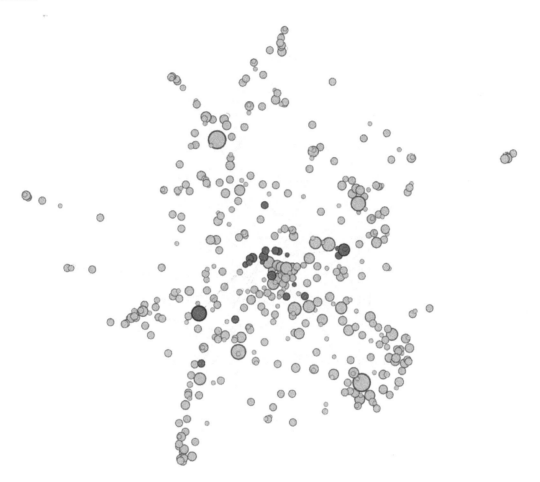

Bubble 11: Discourses about Mathematics and Mathematical Discourse

The eleventh bubble of the 2010s FLM foam is "Discourses about Mathematics and Mathematical Discourse." Similar to Bubble 4, this bubble has two components. See Figure 58 for the location of Bubble 11, and its two components, in the FLM 2010s foam. The first component is more centrally located and its most cited articles are Morgan's *Writing mathematically: The discourse of investigation* (1998) and Gerofsky's "Ancestral genres of mathematical graphs" (2011). Among the FLM articles citing these references are Beisiegel & Simmt's "Formation of Mathematics Graduate Students' Mathematician-as-Teacher Identity" (2012).

The second component of Bubble 11, located towards the top of the FLM 2010s foam, has Sfard's *Thinking as Communicating: Human Development, the Growth of Discourses, and Mathematizing* (2008) and Lappan, Fey, Fitzgerald, Friel, & Phillips' textbook *Thinking with Mathematical Models* among its most cited articles. Within this component, Temple's "Lexical density and the mathematics register" (2014) and Herbel-Eisenmann & Pimm's "The one and the many: Transcripts and the art of interpretation" (2014). Bridging these two components is Temple's article which cites Morgan (1998), Sfard (2008), and Lappan and colleague's textbook (2014).

Figure 58. Location of the bubble "Discourses about Mathematics and Mathematical Discourse" within the foam of the FLM 2010s.

Bubble 12: Teaching Mathematics for Social Justice

The twelfth bubble of the 2010s FLM foam is "Teaching Mathematics for Social Justice." The most cited references of this bubble are Gutstein's *Reading and Writing the World with Mathematics: Toward a Pedagogy of Social Justice* (2006), Frankenstein's "Critical mathematics education: an application of Paulo Freire's epistemology" (1983), Freire's *Pedagogy of the Oppressed* (2000). Other frequently cited articles include Walshaw's "Who can know mathematics?" (2014) and Appelbaum's "Embracing Mathematics: On Becoming a Teacher and Changing with Mathematics" (2008).

Among the FLM articles with social justice themes and citing these references are Harouni's "Reframing the Discussion on Word Problems: A Political Economy" (2015), Appelbaum's "Nomadic Ethics and Regimes of Truth" (2014), and Neumayer-Depipier's "Teacher Identity Work In Mathematics Teacher Education" (2013). These articles, while related to ethnomathematics and critical mathematics education, draw on a sufficiently distinct research base that Teaching Mathematics for Social Justice is separated into a distinct research bubble by the Louvain Modularity algorithm. See Figure 59 for the location of Bubble 12 within the foam of the FLM 2010s.

Figure 59. Location of the bubble "Teaching Mathematics for Social Justice" within the foam of the FLM 2010s.

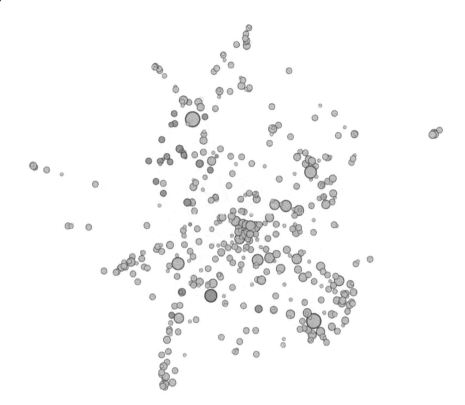

Bubble 13: Genre and Language

The thirteenth bubble of the 2010s FLM foam is "Genre and Language." This bubble is at the far right of the FLM 2010s foam (see Figure 60). This bubble largely discusses genre and language in mathematics education, both in classrooms and in research. Most cited within this bubble are Geiger & Straesser's "The challenge of publication for English non-dominant-language authors in mathematics education" (2015), Bakhtin's The Dialogic Imagination: Four Essays (1981), and Barwell's "Centripetal and centrifugal language forces in one elementary school second language mathematics classroom" (2014). Unlike most bubbles, Geiger & Straesser is also an FLM article which cites both Bakhtin and Barwell. Other FLM citing articles are Caron's "Challenges and opportunities for publishing in mathematics education: the personal viewpoint of a francophone researcher" (2017) and Fellus & Glanfield's "Reflections on the FLM pre-conference" (2017).

Bubble 14: Embodied Mathematics

The fourteenth, and final, bubble of the FLM 2010s foam is "Embodied Mathematics" (see Figure 61). Most cited references of this bubble include: Henry's *Incarnation: une philosophie de la chair* [*Incarnation: A Philosophy of Flesh*] (2000), Fasheh's "Over 68 years with mathematics: My story of healing from modern superstitions and reclaiming my sense of being and well-being" (2015),

Figure 60. Location of the bubble "Genre and Language" within the foam of the FLM 2010s.

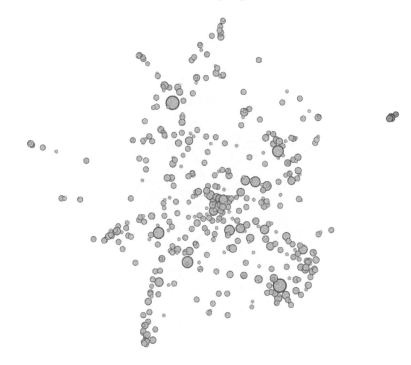

Figure 61. Location of the bubble "Embodied Mathematics" within the foam of the FLM 2010s.

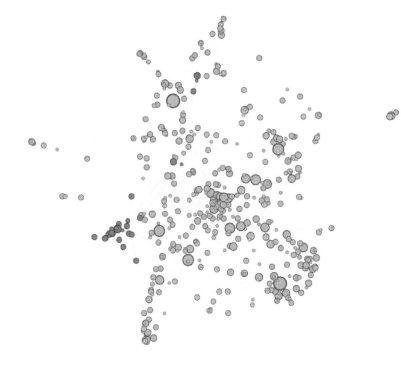

and Ingold's *Being Alive: Essays on Movement, Knowledge and Description* (2011). Among the FLM citing articles are Roth's "Incarnation: radicalizing the embodiment of mathematics" (2010), "excess of graphical thinking: movement, mathematics and flow" (2012), and "mathematical learning, the unseen and the unforeseen" (2015). Another citing article includes Proulx & Maheux's "Èpistémologie et didactique des mathématiques: questions anciennes, nouvelles questions [Epistemology and Didactics of Mathematics: Ancient Questions, New Questions]" (2012) showing the connection between Embodied Mathematics and what it means to know.

Macroanalysis: Foam of FLM

Having unpacked each of the 14 bubbles in turn, I now transition to the macroanalysis. Here, I shift my gaze from the bubbles as individual research foci towards their position relative within the foam and relative to each other to better understand the landscape of the field in the 2010s as presented within FLM.

The ForceAtlas2 algorithm encodes meaning in the spatial layout of the nodes; those highly connected nodes have more edges pulling them towards the center. For those less connected, the repulsion force from the other nodes exceeds the contraction force and they settle towards the margins. Given the spatial significance from the algorithm, then, the location of the bubble corresponds to that bubble's centrality/marginality within the foam and to that bubble's research focus' centrality/marginality within the field. Since my focus shifts now to the positions of the bubbles within the foam, to assist the reader in seeing their positions I refer them to Figure 62 which shows the collection of bubbles from the foam but does not include the dots that correspond to the articles within each bubble. In the following subsections I proceed through an analysis that first considers the centrality of the position of bubbles within the overall foam and second that considers the adjacency and overlap of various bubbles.

Central and Marginal Bubbles

Anchoring the center of the FLM 2010s foam are bubbles 10 (philosophy of mathematics education), 3 (mathematics teaching), 1 (perspectives on mathematics education), 6 (meaning making in mathematics), 8 (mathematical knowledge for teaching), and 9 (teacher noticing and attention). In fact, the center of the map occurs near the intersection of 1, 3, 4, and 10 (see Figure 62). The bubbles which are marginal to the FLM 2010s foam are the enculturation component of Bubble 4 (top right), Ethnomathematics and Critical Mathematics Education (Bubble 2), Genre and Language (Bubble 13), Embodied Mathematics (14), and Discourses about Mathematics and Mathematical discourse (Bubble 11). These bubbles are distinct in their relation to the field since they have little to no overlap with the more central bubbles.

Some bubbles, however, are neither central nor marginal. For example, Bubble 12 (Teaching Mathematics for Social Justice) has purposefully cited articles which are more central. This is evidenced by the overlap of Bubble 12 with Bubbles 3, 4, and 10. Likewise, Bubble 9 (Teacher Noticing and Attention) overlaps significantly with Bubbles 1, 3, 4, and 10. Rhetorically, then, other quasimarginal articles, such as Proof share citations with articles in Teacher Noticing and Attention which works to draw them towards the center of the foam. Another example, Bubble 5 (Knowing in Mathematics) has a significant portion at the margin yet shares common citations with Bubbles 3 and 10, serving to pull it more centrally.

Figure 62. The Bubbles of the 2010s FLM foam

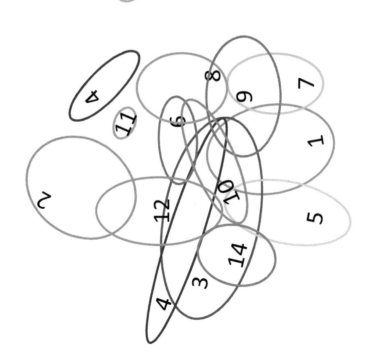

For the Learning of Mathematics

2010s

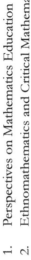

1. Perspectives on Mathematics Education
2. Ethnomathematics and Critical Mathematics Education
3. Mathematics Teaching
4. Cultural Perspectives on Mathematics Learning: Semiosis, Enculturation, & Development
5. Knowing in Mathematics
6. Making Meaning in Mathematics: Language and Gesture
7. Proof
8. Mathematical Knowledge for Teaching
9. Teacher Noticing and Attention
10. Philosophy of Mathematics Education
11. Discourses about Mathematics and Mathematical Discourse
12. Teaching Mathematics for Social Justice
13. Genre and Language
14. Embodied Mathematics

Relationships between Bubbles

Beyond describing the location of the bubbles within the foam, we can glean meaning from the position of one bubble relative to the position of other bubbles. Since there 91 pairwise comparisons that can be made with 14 bubbles (14 choose 2) and 364 ways to make three-way comparisons from 14 bubbles, I will not exhaustively make all comparisons. I offer a few comparisons that are striking to me, for one reason or another, but invite the reader, in an enactment of Rancièrean equality, to make their own noticings and draw their own comparisons. This act also goes back to the fifth purpose of cartography, the spirit of expansion, and I offer this as one path for further exploration.

First, it is interesting to me that Critical Mathematics Education (Bubble 2) and Teaching Mathematics for Social Justice (Bubble 12), while they overlap, are distinct bubbles. Given these both are foundationally with identifying and dismantling systems of power and oppression through mathematics, I would expect them to have similar research bases. Nevertheless, these two bubbles have distinct bases with the critical perspective of Skovsmose and colleagues in Bubble 2 is more marginal than the work of Gutstein, Frankenstein, and Freire in Bubble 12.

Second, while Mathematics Teaching (Bubble 3) and Mathematics Knowledge for Teaching (Bubble 9) both overlap in the center of the map, they share relatively little overlap. From this, it suggests to me that there is a substantial portion of the art of teaching mathematics which exceeds the pedagogical content knowledge of the teacher; part of this excess is captured by the intersection of mathematics teaching with Bubble 4 (cultural perspectives on mathematics learning), Bubble 14 (embodied mathematics), and Bubble 12 (teaching mathematics for social justice). Similarly, since Bubble 12 (teaching mathematics for social justice) is not fully contained by Bubble 3 (mathematics teaching), it suggests that there is more to teaching mathematics for social justice than just teaching mathematics.

Third, while embodied mathematics (Bubble 14) has significant overlap with teaching mathematics (Bubble 3), knowing in mathematics (Bubble 5) has considerably less overlap Bubble 3. This seems to suggest that researchers within the more nascent area of embodied mathematics have made considerable effort in connecting their work to the teaching of mathematics while the epistemological focus of knowing in mathematics has had significantly less penetration. This is not necessarily for lack of trying, but if more authors drew on these two bubbles, they would slowly move closer together over time.

Fourth, I find it interesting that Proof (Bubble 7) is marginal in the FLM foam, yet where it overlaps with more central bubbles is with Teacher Noticing and Attention (Bubble 9). This leads me to wonder if study of proof focuses significantly on teachers' noticing of student proof and proving or on what aspects of proof that teachers attend. Likewise, since Bubble 7 just touches Bubble 8 (Mathematics Knowledge for Teaching), I wonder how much attention has been paid to teachers' knowledge of proof and proving techniques.

The closeness is not the only meaningful relationship between bubbles. For example, the fact that Bubble 7 (Proof) and Bubble 2 (Ethnomathematics and Critical Mathematics Education) are nearly opposite each other in the foam, suggests that there is little to no interaction between that research. Yet, I would venture that ethnomathematics and critical mathematics researchers would be interested in the privilege afforded to the logico-deductive proof at sake of marginalizing indigenous ways of knowing. Indeed, such researchers might be interested in introducing indigenous proving techniques, offering a (potentially) radically different way to go about proof and argumentation in the mathematics classroom.

Concluding Thoughts

Recalling the Sloterdijkian notion of bubbles (2011), the bubbles here each constitute contingent groupings of related research clustered around particular research foci. The bubbles form a foam, or collection of co-fragile, codependent bubbles that together constitute a map of the foci that collectively outline the scope of mathematics education research published in FLM during the 2010s. I was able to identify the central and marginal bubbles and unpack the which bubbles overlapped and which were distant.

I conclude by revisiting the five aims of cartography discussed in chapter 3 as I applied them in this chapter:

(1) I documented something new, a citation network of research published during the 2010s in FLM;

(2) I attempted to make the network more understandable by applying the force-directed and Louvain modularity algorithms to encode meaning in layout and color;

(3) I unpacked each bubble to provide clarity on their contents and the research foci they constitute;

(4) I abstracted these bubble into a foam to provide insight into the foam of research, the marginal and central ideas published in FLM, and

(5) I set the stage for more exploration and ask you to interact with the map at MathEdAtlas.org.

In the words of Rancière (1991):

What do you see?
What do you think about it?
What do you make of it?

140

This chapter proceeds from an introduction to *Educational Studies in Mathematics* (ESM) to an investigation into the bubbles of the 2010s and the foam that those bubbles constitute. ESM, "one of the leading journals in mathematics education" (Goos, 2019), together with JRME, is one of the "two most cited and respected journals in our field by a substantial margin" (Williams and Leatham, 2017). Given the position that ESM holds within the field, it is important then to consider what types of mathematics education research its editors choose to publish. According to its aims:

> *Educational Studies in Mathematics* presents new ideas and developments of major importance to those working in the field of mathematical education. It seeks to reflect both the variety of research concerns within this field and the range of methods used to study them…The emphasis is on high-level articles which are of more than local or national interest. (ESM Aims).

Then, it seems, that the journal seeks new ideas and developments on a variety of topics from a variety of research approaches. Emphasizing the value placed on variety of research approaches, the editors emphasize that authors "should show critical awareness of other possible approaches" (ESM Editors, 2012, p. vii). Yet, within the same passage, assert that "authors will be expected to be familiar with work already published in the journal…[and that] reference is made to appropriate published sources that offer an authoritative overview of the area under consideration" (p. vii). Which suggests that, like FLM, research must be anchored to the research which has already been published in ESM.

For one history of ESM through its first 50 volumes, though "its history could be recounted in different ways, each placing the emphasis on a different aspect" (Hanna & Sidoli, 2002), I refer the reader to Hanna and Sidoli's "The Story of ESM." There, Hanna and Sidoli provide a history of the editorship, a narrative of the journal, and statistical summaries of the mathematical content (p. 142), topic (p. 145), level of schooling (p. 146), and research method (p. 147). One addition to this history is made by Goos (2019), and my present analysis constitutes another.

Here, I seek to understand what is current in the field, I proceed through performing a citation network analysis on the 445 articles published by ESM between 2010 and 2016. I end at 2016, instead of 2020, due to a moving wall limitation on the JSTOR database: there is a 3-year delay between article publication and its addition to the JSTOR repository. These 445 articles together included 18,628 citation relationships (for an average of about 41 references per paper). These articles and their citations together they constitute a particular partage or distribution of what is sensible as mathematics education research.

ESM in the 2010s

Analysis, as outlined in chapter 2, of the articles published between 2010 and 2016 in ESM and their 18,628 references, yielded the map in Figure 63. The Louvain Modularity algorithm identified 8 modularity classes. These modularity classes, or bubbles, each constitute a particular research focus of the field of mathematics education research as published in ESM during this time. Connecting to the journal aims, these bubbles, since they come from the period 2010-2016, are the ideas current in the field. These ideas are (1) Critical Theories and Philosophy of Mathematics Education, (2) Students' Learning of Concepts, (3) Students' Understanding of Concepts, (4) Teachers' Knowledge and the Teaching of Mathematics, (5) Proof and Argumentation, (6) Embodied

Figure 63. Bubbles of research from ESM 2010–2016.

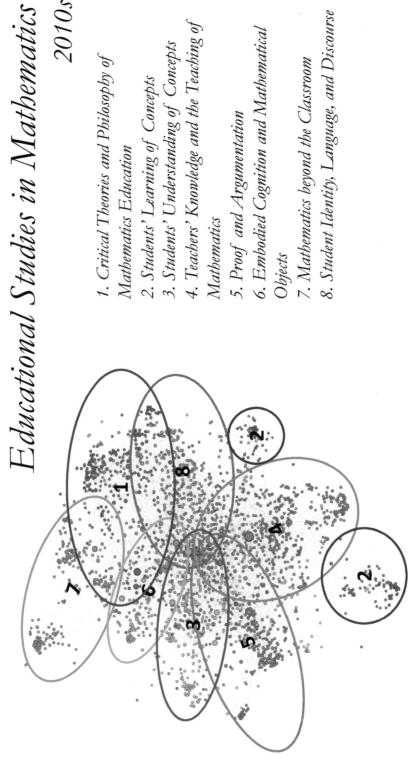

Educational Studies in Mathematics

2010s

1. Critical Theories and Philosophy of Mathematics Education
2. Students' Learning of Concepts
3. Students' Understanding of Concepts
4. Teachers' Knowledge and the Teaching of Mathematics
5. Proof and Argumentation
6. Embodied Cognition and Mathematical Objects
7. Mathematics beyond the Classroom
8. Student Identity, Language, and Discourse

Cognition and Mathematical Objects, (7) Mathematics beyond the Classroom, (8) Student Identity, Language, and Discourse. These eight bubbles together constitute the foam of mathematics education research in ESM during the 2010s. As shown in chapter 3 with the JRME, this foam across time is volatile: new bubbles emerge, distinct bubbles merge, bubbles burst. This foam does not constitute an eternal "Mathematics Education is..." but rather "mathematics education research (in the ESM) currently is...".

The remainder of this chapter is divided into two parts corresponding to two levels of analysis: microanalysis of the bubbles and macroanalysis of the foam. In the first part, I will discuss each bubble and their constituent articles in turn. In the second part, I will discuss the foam: the relative positions of bubbles within the foam (e.g., central and marginal bubbles) and the relative positions between bubbles within the foam. After the orienting initial map (Figure 63) which shows the relative position of each of the eight bubbles in the foam, within each section a bubble map will show only the bubble of interest in color with the remainder of the nodes colored grey: this provides a snapshot of where each bubble is located within the foam at large.

Microanalysis: Bubbles in ESM

As shown in Figure 63, the eight bubbles of research in the ESM during the period 2010-2017 are (1) Critical Theories and Philosophy of Mathematics Education, (2) Students' Learning of Concepts, (3) Students' Understanding of Concepts, (4) Teachers' Knowledge and the Teaching of Mathematics, (5) Proof and Argumentation, (6) Embodied Cognition and Mathematical Objects, (7) Mathematics beyond the Classroom, (8) Student Identity, Language, and Discourse. What follows is a description of the most cited references in each bubble and which ESM articles cited those references. As a complete elaboration and review of each article is beyond the scope of this analysis, instead, I provide the title and authors of several articles to serve as an orientation to each bubble. These sections might serve as orienting texts and starting points for those interested in studying different research foci within the partage of mathematics education research outlined in the ESM.

Bubble 1: Critical Theories and Philosophy of Mathematics Education

The first bubble discussed of the ESM 2010s is named Critical Theory and Philosophy of Mathematics Education. Some of the works in this bubble fall under Lerman's "The social turn in mathematics education research" (2000). For example, Brown's *Mathematics education and subjectivity: Cultures and cultural renewal* (2011), Dowling's *The sociology of mathematics education: Mathematical myths, pedagogic texts* (1998), and Boaler's *Experiencing school mathematics: Teaching styles, sex and setting* (1997) fall under this umbrella. Other most cited articles show the criticality of the work within this bubble: Foucault's *Power/knowledge: Selected interviews and other writings 1972-1977* (1980), Valero's "Socio-political perspectives on mathematics education" (2004), and Brown's "Lacan, subjectivity, and the task of mathematics education research, Signifying 'Students', 'Teachers' and 'Mathematics': A Reading of a Special Issue". Others yet, lean more solidly towards the philosophy of mathematics education and its intersection with critical theories: Skovsmose's (1994) "Towards a philosophy of critical mathematics education" and Radford's "The ethics of being and knowing: Towards a cultural theory of learning" (2008).

Among the ESM articles citing these references include some theoretical elaborations: Stinson and Bullock's "Critical postmodern theory in mathematics education research: a praxis of uncertainty"

143

(2012), Kollosche's "Criticising with Foucault: towards a guiding framework for socio-political studies in mathematics education" (2016), and Pais' "At the intersection between the subject and the political: a contribution to an ongoing discussion" (2016). Others bring critical theories to bear on mathematics, mathematics education, and mathematics education research: Pais & Valero's "Researching Research: Mathematics Education in the Political" (2012), Pais' "An ideology critique of the use-value of mathematics" (2013), Llewellyn's "Problematising the pursuit of progress in mathematics education" (2016). Others, still, trouble for-granted ideas within the field: Hossain, Mendick, & Adler's "Troubling 'understanding mathematics in-depth': Its role in the identity work of student-teachers in England" (2013), Nolan's "Dispositions in the field: Viewing mathematics teacher education through the lens of Bourdieu's social field theory" (2012), Radford's "On the role of representations and artefacts in knowing and learning" (2016), and Brown's "Rationality and belief in learning mathematics" (2016). Figure 64 shows the location of Bubble 1 within the foam of the ESM 2010s.

Figure 64. Location of the "Critical Theories and Philosophy of Mathematics Education" bubble within the ESM 2010s foam.

Bubble 2: Students' Learning of Concepts

The second bubble discussed of the ESM 2010s is named Students' Learning of Concepts. Figure 65 shows the location of Bubble 2 within the foam of the ESM 2010s. The articles in this bubble cluster around students learning and development of mathematical concepts. For example, some of the most cited references focus on the learning of number and operations: Fuson's *Children's counting and concepts of number* (1988), Fuson's "Research on whole number addition and subtraction"

Figure 65. Location of the "Students' Learning of Concepts" bubble within the ESM 2010s foam.

(1992), and Baroody's "The development of adaptive expertise and flexibility: The integration of conceptual and procedural knowledge" (with an introductory analysis on division; 2003). Other highly cited references included Vershaffel & Bryant's (2012) "Introduction" to a special issues on mathematical inversion (e.g., additive and multiplicative inverses), and Hiebert & Lefevre's (1986) "Conceptual and procedural knowledge in mathematics: An introduction analysis", the introductory chapter to Hiebert's edited text *Conceptual and Procedural Knowledge: The Case of Mathematics* that included analyses on counting, number concepts, and arithmetic. Even Ball's "The mathematical understanding that prospective teachers bring to teacher education; Prospective elementary and secondary teachers' understanding of division" (1990) considered teachers as learners.

Among the related ESM articles that cited some subset of these or related articles are Peters, De Smedt, Torbeyns, & Ghesquière's "Children's use of subtraction by addition on large single-digit subtractions" (2012) and Selter, Prediger, & Nürenbörger's "Taking away and determining the difference—longitudinal perspective on two models of subtraction and the inverse relation to addition" (2012).

Schoenfeld's "Mathematical problem solving" (1985), together with the ESM articles Voutsina's "Procedural and conceptual changes in young children's problem solving" (2012) and Schukajlow, Krug, & Rakoczy's "Effects of prompting multiple solutions for modelling problems on students' performance" (2015) constitute a part of the bubble focusing on learning problem solving.

In addition to the above topics, some articles within this bubble, such as Francisco's "Learning in collaborative settings: students building on each other's ideas to promote their mathematical understanding" (2013), consider collaborative learning. Two highly cited articles within this bubble are Yackel & Cobb's 2nd grade analysis "Sociomathematical norms, argumentation, and autonomy in mathematics" (1996) and Evans, Morgan, & Tsatsaroni's "Discursive positioning and emotion in school mathematics practices" (2006) analysis of three 8th-grade boys collaborative geometric learning.

Bubble 3: Students' Understanding of Concepts

The third bubble discussed of the ESM 2010s is named Students' Understanding of Concepts. Figure 66 shows the location of Bubble 3 within the foam of the ESM 2010s. This bubble, unlike the second bubble which focused on the learning of mathematical concepts, focuses on the definition, cognitive images, and understandings of concepts themselves. Among the most cited references within this bubble are: Sfard's "On the dual nature of mathematical conceptions: Reflections on processes and objects as different sides of the same coin" (1991) and "Thinking as communicating: Human development, the growth of discourses, and mathematizing" (2008); Tall & Vinner's "Concept image and concept definition in mathematics, with special reference to limits and continuity" (1981); Dubinsky's "Reflective abstraction in advanced mathematical thinking" (1991), Thompson's "Images of rate and operational understanding of the fundamental theorem of calculus" (1994), and Radford's "Signs and meanings in students' emergent algebraic thinking: A semiotic analysis" (2000).

Figure 66. Location of the "Students' Understanding of Concepts" bubble within the ESM 2010s foam.

Among those ESM articles within this bubble are Leung & Baccaglini-Frank's "Discernment of invariants in dynamic geometry environments" (2013), Kidron & Tall's "The roles of visualization and symbolism in the potential and actual infinity of the limit process" (2015); Kolar & Čadež's "Analysis of factors influencing the understanding of the concept of infinity" (2012), Leung and Lee's

"Students' geometrical perception on a task-based dynamic geometry platform" (2013), Simon, Kara, & Placa's "Categorizing and promoting reversibility of mathematical concepts" (2016), and Bråting & Peljare's "On the relations between historical epistemology and students' conceptual developments in mathematics" (2015).

Bubble 4: Teachers' Knowledge and the Teaching of Mathematics

The fourth bubble discussed of the ESM 2010s is named Teachers' Knowledge and the Teaching of Mathematics. Figure 67 shows the location of Bubble 4 within the foam of the ESM 2010s. This bubble includes the seminal articles on pedagogical content knowledge, Shulman's "Those who understand: Knowledge growth in teaching" (1986) and "Knowledge and teaching: Foundations of the new reform" (1987), and Ball and colleagues' work on mathematics knowledge for teaching: Ball, Thames, & Phelps' "Content knowledge for teaching: What makes it special?" (2000) and Ball & Bass' "Interweaving content and pedagogy in teaching and learning to teach: Knowing and using mathematics" (2008). Similarly, Ma's comparative *Knowing and teaching elementary mathematics: Teachers' understanding of fundamental mathematics in China and the United States* (1999) is included in this bubble. Among those frequently cited references, references more broadly relevant to the teaching of mathematics, are the National Council of Teachers of Mathematics' *Principles and Standards for School Mathematics* (2000); Brousseau's *Theory of didactical situations in mathematics* (1997), von Glasersfeld's *Radical constructivism: A way of knowing and learning* (1995), Silver's "On mathematical problem posing" (1994), and Freudenthal's *Mathematics as an educational task* (1973).

Figure 67. Location of the "Teacher's Knowledge and the Teaching of Mathematics" bubble within the ESM 2010s foam.

Among the ESM articles on the teaching of mathematics—including problem posing, analysis of student work, and developing student understanding—include: Wasserman's "Unpacking teachers' moves in the classroom: navigating micro- and macro-levels of mathematical complexity" (2015), Singer & Ellerton's "Problem-posing research in mathematics education: new questions and directions" (2013), Van Harpen & Sriraman's "Creativity and mathematical problem posing: an analysis of high school students' mathematical problem posing in China and the USA" (2013), Chernoff & Zazkis' "From personal to conventional probabilities: from sample set to sample space" (2011), and Gal & Lindchevski's "To see or not to see: analyzing difficulties in geometry from the perspective of visual perception" (2010).

Bubble 5: Proof and Argumentation

The fifth bubble discussed of the ESM 2010s is named Proof and Argumentation (see Figure 68). Within this bubble, some of the most-cited articles consider proofs and their purpose: Hanna & Barbeau's "Proofs as bearers of mathematical knowledge" (2008) and Rav's "Why do we prove theorems?" (1999). Other articles within this bubble consider argumentation: Krummheuer's "The ethnography of argumentation" (1995) and Inglis, Mejia-Ramos, & Simposon's "Modelling mathematical argumentation: The importance of qualification" (2007).

Figure 68. Location of the "Proof and Argumentation" bubble within the ESM 2010s foam.

Some of the highly cited references bring proof and augmentation together to consider (1) the relationship between proof and argumentation (Pedemonte's "How can the relationship between argumentation and proof be analysed?," 2007); (2) the role of examples (Watson & Mason's

Mathematics as a constructive activity: Learners generating examples, 2005); (3) investigate the role of intuition in proof and argumentation (Fischbein's *Intuition in science and mathematics: An educational approach*, 1987); or (4) the teaching of proof (Weber's "Traditional instruction in advanced mathematics classrooms: A case study of one professor's lectures and proofs in an introductory real analysis course," 2004).

Among the ESM articles that build upon the knowledge base are: Kidron & Dreyfus' "Justification enlightenment and combining constructions of knowledge" (2010), Moore-Russo & Connor's "Can slope be negative in 3-space? Studying concept image of slope through collective definition construction" (2011), Prusak & Hershkowitz's "From visual reasoning to logical necessity through argumentative design" (2012), Kidron & Dreyfus' "Proof image" (2014), Mejia-Ramos & Weber's "Why and how mathematicians read proofs: further evidence from a survey study" (2014), Krummheuer's "The relationship between diagrammatic argumentation and narrative argumentation in the context of the development of mathematical thinking in the early years" (2016), and Zazkis & Weber's "Bridging the gap between graphical arguments and verbal-symbolic proofs in a real analysis context" (2016).

Bubble 6: Embodied Cognition and Mathematical Objects

The sixth bubble discussed of the ESM 2010s is named Embodied Cognition and Mathematical Objects. See Figure 69 for the location of this bubble with the ESM 2010s foam. The most cited references within this bubble focus on embodied cognition and gesture, the digital-cognitive interface, or the nature of mathematical objects.

Figure 69. Location of the "Embodied Cognition and Mathematical Objects" bubble within the ESM 2010s foam.

Within embodied cognition and gesture, some of the most cited works are Radford's "Body, tool, and symbol: Semiotic reflections on cognition" (2006) and "Why do gestures matter? Sensuous cognition and the palpability of mathematical meanings" (2009), Lakoff & Núñez's *Where mathematics comes from: How the embodied mind brings mathematics into being* (2000), and McNeill's *Hand and mind: What gesture reveals about thought* (1992). Some of the ESM articles building upon this work include Arzarello & Robutti's "Growth point and gestures: looking inside mathematical meanings" (2015), Kynigos & Lagrange's "Cross-analysis as a tool to forge connections amongst theoretical frames in using digital technologies in mathematical learning" (2016), and Yoon & Thomas' "Grounded blends and mathematical gesture spaces: developing mathematical understandings via gestures" (2011).

Among the cited works on the digital-cognitive interface include Artigue's "Learning mathematics in a CAS environment: The genesis of a reflection about instrumentation and the dialectics between technical and conceptual work." (2002). Among the ESM articles building upon this work are Drijvers, Godino & Font's "One episode, two lenses A reflective analysis of student learning with computer algebra from instrumental and onto-semiotic perspectives" (2013) and Morgan & Kynigos' "Digital artefacts as representations: forging connections between a constructionist and a social semiotic perspective" (2016).

Lastly, some ESM articles that discuss the nature of mathematical objects are Font & Godino's "The emergence of objects from mathematical practices" (2013) and Godino, Font, & Willhelmi "Why is the learning of elementary arithmetic concepts difficult? Semiotic tools for understanding the nature of mathematical objects" (2011).

Bubble 7: Mathematics beyond the Classroom

The seventh bubble discussed of the ESM 2010s is named Mathematics beyond the Classroom. This bubble, building upon the work of Lave's *Cognition in practice: Mind, mathematics and culture in everyday life* (1988) has a significant emphasis on the use of mathematics outside of mathematics classrooms. This includes not only direct applications of mathematics, including statistics and use in skilled trades, but also how mathematics is communicated. Some other highly cited works within this bubble includes Vygotsky's *Thought and Language* (1986), Duval's *Sémiosis et pensée humaine* [*Semiosis and human thinking*] (1995), Sfard's "There is more to discourse than meets the ears: Looking at thinking as communicating to learn more about mathematical learning" (2001), Williams & Wake's "Black boxes in workplace mathematics" and "Metaphors and models in translation between college and workplace mathematics" (both published in 2007).

Among the ESM articles to study mathematics in the workplace are Roth's "Rules of bending, bending the rules: the geometry of electrical conduit bending in college and workplace" (2016), LaCroix's "Learning to see pipes mathematically: preapprentices' mathematical activity in pipe trades training" (2016), and Bakker & Akkerman's "A boundary-crossing approach to support students' integration of statistical and work-related knowledge" (2016).

Among the ESM articles which explore communication in mathematics are Nilsson & Ryve's "Focal event, contextualization, and effective communication in the mathematics classroom" (2010) and Ryve & Nilsson's "Analyzing effective communication in mathematics group work: The role of visual mediators and technical terms" (2012). Further, Bautista & Roth build upon Sfard's communication as thinking in "Conceptualizing sound as a form of incarnate mathematical consciousness" (2012).

Some of the most cited articles considering statistics education explicitly are Bakker's "Reasoning about shape as a pattern in variability" and "Design research in statistics education: On symbolizing and computer tools" (both from 2004). Statistics education has had uptake within ESM by Noll & Hancock "Proper and paradigmatic metonymy as a lens for characterizing student conceptions of distributions and sampling" (2016), Ben-Zvi & Bakker's "Learning to reason from samples" (2016), and Pfannkuch & Arnold's "What I see is not quite the way it really is: students' emergent reasoning about sampling variability" (2016). See Figure 70 for the location of bubble 7 within the ESM 2010s foam.

Figure 70. Location of the "Mathematics beyond the Classroom" bubble within the ESM 2010s foam.

Bubble 8: Student Identity, Language, and Discourse
The eighth, and last, bubble discussed of the ESM 2010s is named Student Identity, Language, and Discourse. This bubble focuses largely on the ways of being and doing mathematics, the identity affordances and constraints available to students, and the ways that discourse and language structure mathematical engagement. Among the most cited texts in this bubble are Vygotsky's *Mind in Society: The development of higher psychological processes* (1978), Schoenfeld's *Mathematical problem solving* (1985), Pimm's *Speaking mathematically: Communication in mathematics classrooms* (1987), Engeström's *Learning by expanding: An activity-theoretical approach to developmental research* (1987), Wenger's *Communities of practice: Learning, meaning and identity* (1988), Bernstein's *Pedagogy, symbolic control and identity: Theory, research and critique* (2000), and Boaler & Greeno's "Identity, agency and knowing in mathematics worlds" (2000).

Among the ESM articles in this bubble that build on identities and mathematics include Solomon & Radovic's "'I can actually be very feminine here': contradiction and hybridity in becoming a female mathematician" (2016), Braathe & Solomon's "Choosing mathematics: the narrative of the self as a site of agency" (2015), Darragh's "Identity research in mathematics education" (2016), and Andersson & Valero's "'I am [not always] a maths hater': Shifting students' identity narratives in context" (2016).

Other ESM articles which consider discourse in mathematics includes Herbel-Eisenmann, Wagner, Johnson, & Suh's "Positioning in mathematics education: revelations on an imported theory" (2015) and Domínguez & LópezLeiva's "Relational engagement: Proportional reasoning with bilingual Latino/a students" (2014). See Figure 71 to see the position of bubble 8 within the ESM 2010s foam.

Figure 71. Location of the "Student Identity, Language, and Discourse" bubble within the ESM 2010s foam.

Macroanalysis: Foam

Having unpacked each of the bubbles in turn, I now zoom out and shift my gaze onto the ESM 2010s foam itself. To assist the reader, I refer them to Figure 72 which shows the collection of bubbles from the foam but does not include the dots that correspond to the articles within each bubble.

Figure 72. The Bubbles of the 2010s ESM foam.

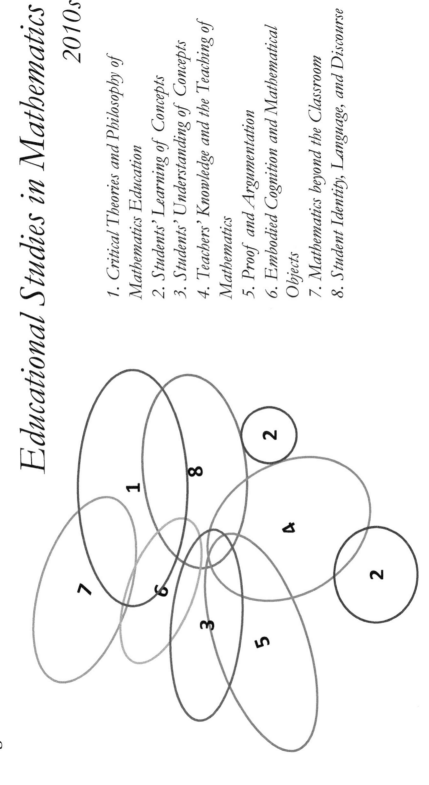

Educational Studies in Mathematics

2010s

1. Critical Theories and Philosophy of Mathematics Education
2. Students' Learning of Concepts
3. Students' Understanding of Concepts
4. Teachers' Knowledge and the Teaching of Mathematics
5. Proof and Argumentation
6. Embodied Cognition and Mathematical Objects
7. Mathematics beyond the Classroom
8. Student Identity, Language, and Discourse

Characteristics of the Bubbles

In contrast to those bubbles in the FLM 2010s foam, the bubbles in the ESM 2010s foam are considerably larger. There are a couple reasons for this. First, ESM published significantly more articles than FLM during the nearly the same length period: between 2010-2016, ESM published 445 articles (one issue each month) while FLM published 187 articles (quarterly issues) between 2010-2017. Second, ESM articles, on average, included more references than FLM articles: 41 vs. 19. This second characteristic, more references, might be account for by each journals word count: 5000 in FLM and 7000 in ESM (40% longer).

There are also, as a result of there being fewer, larger bubbles, a few conclusions that can be drawn about the foam of articles published by ESM. First, the articles published in ESM situate their work more broadly across the field of mathematics education research; in other words, the articles in FLM connect to and draw from very specialized literature bases within and outside mathematics education research while those in ESM, even when drawing on specialized literature bases, have more connections across the field (part of this may be a result of the Editors' mandate that they "connect to articles in ESM"). An intuitive sense of this can be developed by revisiting Figure 63 and seeing the way that different colored nodes pepper the bubbles of which they are not a part.

Additionally, there is significantly less overlap of the bubbles in the ESM compared to the bubbles in the FLM. To elaborate, each of the bubbles 3, 4, 5, 6, and 8 overlap slightly near the center of the map (near the location of NCTM's PSSM), the bubbles are largely disjoint. This suggests that, while the bubbles are oriented around a central concern, they are largely distinct in the topics they address.

Central and Marginal Bubbles

Unlike the analysis of the FLM foam, the ESM foam has less of a central/marginal orientation. The center of the foam is near the overlap of Bubbles 1, 3, 4, 5, 6, and 8; all but Bubbles 2 and 7 are situated near this center. Bubble 7, Mathematics beyond the classroom, and Bubble 2, Students' Learning of Concepts, are the most marginal. Given much of the field, as evidenced by the elaboration of each bubble, focuses on mathematics teaching and learning within mathematics classrooms, perhaps it is expected that Bubble 7 would be marginal. In contrast, unpacking the location of Bubble 2 might be worthwhile.

Looking back at some of the most-cited articles from bubble 2 (i.e., Fuson, 1988, 1992; Baroody, 2003; and Verschaffel & Bryant's special issue, 2010) shows a large emphasis on children's mathematical learning. As was the case in the JRME 1980s (Bubble 10 – Arithmetic), JRME 2000s (Bubble 2 – Young Children's Learning and Development), and JRME 2010s (Bubble 3 – Children's Learning), the study of young children, their mathematical brilliance, and elementary mathematics are often marginal in the field of mathematics education research. Indeed, the portion of Bubble 2 which is at the extreme bottom of the foam contains those articles mentioned here on children's mathematics.

Relationships between Bubbles

Since there are 28 different pairwise comparisons that could be made between the eight bubbles (8 choose 2) and 56 ways to choose 3 different bubbles for comparison, I will offer only a few here. However, in the spirit of expansion (Chapter 2), I hope that the reader, and other researchers, will undertake additional comparisons to emphasize other findings and relationships.

Of the bubbles, Bubble 1 (Critical Theories & Philosophy of Mathematics Education) and Bubble 8 (Student Identity, Language, and Discourse) have the largest overlap of any two bubbles in the 2010s ESM foam. This suggests topical overlap and reference overlap between these two research areas. Part of this overlap can be explained by the critical heritage of discourse analysis, positioning theory, and much identity work (Darragh's review elaborates this connection; 2016, p. 26). Likewise, Darragh makes connections to the post-structuralist work of Walshaw and Llewellyn (e.g., Walshaw, 2007 & Llewellyn, 2016), both of whose work is located in Bubble 1. Furthermore, Walshaw's *Working with Foucault in Education* (2007) has clear connections to the philosophy of mathematics education and is cited a number of times in Bubble 1.

Second, Bubbles 7 (Mathematics beyond the classroom) and 8 (Student Identity, Language, and Discourse), while at first glance may seem to be significantly different, share discourse as their intersection. The work by Ryve and Sfard on discourse in Bubble 7 and critical discursive theories (e.g., some work by Foucault) share a similar heritage. Furthermore, some of the work in Bubble 7 (e.g, Roth, 2016; LaCroix, 2016; and Bakker & Akkerman, 2016) focuses on the working identities (e.g, pipefitters) of their learners of mathematics. I wonder what might be gained if additional work in Mathematics beyond the Classroom might consider 'who teaches and who learns', thereby making a connection to Bubble 4, or how the mathematics of carpenters might have embodied elements (thereby connecting to Bubble 6).

Third, Bubble 4 (Teachers' Knowledge and the Teaching of Mathematics) overlaps every bubble but Bubble 1 (Critical Theories and Philosophy of Mathematics Education), Bubble 6 (Embodied Cognition and Mathematical Objects), and Bubble 7 (Mathematics beyond the Classroom). I would like to emphasize the distance between Bubbles 4 and 6 here, whereas the bubbles on teaching and embodied mathematics in the FLM foam were overlapping. Likewise, the bubbles for teaching and philosophy of mathematics education (Bubbles 4 & 1) intersect in FLM but do not intersect here. This suggests that in FLM these two areas are much more 'in conversation' than in ESM, yet that same overlap in FLM suggests that the distance between them here is not insurmountable. More attention is spent on cross-journal comparison in the next chapter.

Concluding Thoughts

Recalling the Sloterdijkian notion of bubbles (2011), the bubbles here each constitute contingent groupings of related research clustered around particular research foci. The bubbles form a foam, or collection of co-fragile, codependent bubbles that together constitute a map of the foci that collectively outline the scope of mathematics education research published in ESM during the 2010s. I was able to identify the central and marginal bubbles and unpack the which bubbles overlapped and which were distant.

I conclude by revisiting the five aims of cartography discussed in chapter 3 as I applied them in this chapter:

(1) I documented something new, a citation network of research published during the 2010s in ESM;

(2) I attempted to make the network more understandable by applying the force-directed and Louvain modularity algorithms to encode meaning in layout and color;

(3) I unpacked each bubble to provide clarity on their contents and the research foci they constitute;

(4) I abstracted these bubble into a foam to provide insight into the foam of research, the marginal and central ideas published in ESM, and

(5) I set the stage for more exploration and ask you to interact with the map at MathEdAtlas.org.

In the words of Rancière (1991):

What do you see?

What do you think about it?

What do you make of it?

7   DISCUSSION AND IMPLICATIONS

Since this is the final chapter of this book, there are a few loose ends to bring together and some final thoughts to share. Up to this point, I provided an orientation to the theories that influence the reading that I bring to this analysis and an elaboration of the specific methods of analysis that I employed. In chapter 4, I traced the emergence of bubbles across five decades of research published in the JRME. In chapters 5 and 6, I identified the research foci of FLM and ESM during the 2010s, respectively. Next, I bring the bubbles from the 2010s of the JRME, FLM, and ESM together. Afterwards, I revisit the findings for the JRME in the light of a similar study to understand the research foci of the JRME across the past five decades. The differences in our findings will emphasize the mixture/product chemical metaphor used to introduce Foucault's power-knowledge. I will also revisit the theories from chapter 2 to elaborate not only the connections between those theories and the analysis but also the implications for the field.

Comparisons between Journals

Recall from my section on mirror and levers, that my goal was twofold. First, if I am able to look back, to see a story of what has been and show that what has been done in the name of mathematics education research has shifted across time, I can show that what counts as mathematics education research has not been fixed across time. Second, if I am able to look across different journals and show that there is no consensus on what mathematics education research is today, I can show that mathematics education research is dependent upon the particular context in which it is produced and what counts today is not fixed. By accomplishing these two goals, it is easier to think of mathematics education research as a volatile foam of bubbles, where bubbles emerge, burst, merge, and split, behaving more like chance than an ordered system. The first of these goals was the objective of Chapter 4, I take on the second objective here.

In the JRME of the 2010s, my analysis yielded 37 distinct research foci (Chapter 4). In contrast, the corresponding analysis for FLM yielded thirteen research foci (Chapter 5) and the corresponding analysis for ESM yielded eight (Chapter 6). I include the names of each bubble in Table 6 and show the connections across the journals in Figure 73 (two bubbles in different journals are connected whenever they share a similar focus). It is clear that there are some commonalities, that there are topics that are discussed in all three of the journals: language use in mathematics, proof and argumentation, mathematics knowledge for teaching, thinking mathematically, constructivism, and politics and critical mathematics education.

There are also, however, topics in each journal that do not have directly comparable bubbles in the other journals. First, in JRME there are bubbles, for example, around professional development; racial identity and success; English language learner's identity and participation; children's achievement, intervention, and trajectories; learning disabilities; gender and achievement, psychological studies and replication; and research in undergraduate mathematics education. Second, in FLM there are bubbles around making meaning of mathematics and mathematics teacher education. Last, in ESM there is a bubble around mathematics beyond the classroom. Therefore, there is no consensus as to what constitutes mathematics education research.

Table 6. List of Bubble Number and Names for the 2010s of Each Journal.

Journal	Bubble Number and Names	
JRME	1. Proof and Argument	21. Mathematics Identity
	2. Professional Development	22. Proof in RUME
	3. Children's Learning	23. Mathematics Teachers and Teaching
	4. Mathematical Discourse	24. Empirical Statistics
	5. Schoenfeld	25. Algebra
	6. Meaning of Equality	26. Problem Posing and Multiple Solutions
	7. Teaching's Influence on Learning	27. Racialized Mathematics Achievement Remediation
	8. Proof and Reform	
	9. Mathematics Knowledge for Teaching	28. Qualitative Metasynthesis
	10. Negative Numbers	29. Learning Disabilities
	11. Limits and Calculus	30. Learning in Contexts
	12. Culturally Relevant Mathematics African American & Indigenous	31. Research on Research
	13. Racial Identity & Success	32. Gender and Achievement
	14. English Language Learner's Identity & Participation	33. Urban Equity and Technology's Role
		34. Sociological Perspectives on Learning
	15. Achievement Gap	35. Psychological Studies & Replication
	16. Sociocultural Learning	36. Girls' Identities
	17. Children's Achievement, Intervention, & Trajectories	37. Research in Undergraduate Mathematics Education
FLM	1. Language of Mathematics/ Mathematicians	8. Mathematics Knowledge for Teaching
	2. Social Nature of Mathematics Classrooms	9. Thinking Mathematically
		10. Mathematics Teacher Education
	3. Children's Mathematical Identities	11. Constructivism
	4. Proof	12. Phenomenology & Embodied Mathematics
	5. Philosophy of Mathematics & Ethnomathematics	13. Politics & Critical Mathematics
	6. Mathematical Concepts	
	7. Making Meaning of Mathematics	
ESM	1. Critical Theories and Philosophy of Mathematics Education	5. Proof and Argumentation
	2. Students' Learning of Concepts	6. Embodied Cognition and Mathematical Objects
	3. Students' Understanding of Concepts	7. Mathematics beyond the Classroom
	4. Teachers' Knowledge and the Teaching of Mathematics	8. Student Identity, Language, and Discourse

Figure 73. Connections between the Bubbles of the 2010s in Each Journal. Bubble number corresponds to the number and name in Table 6.

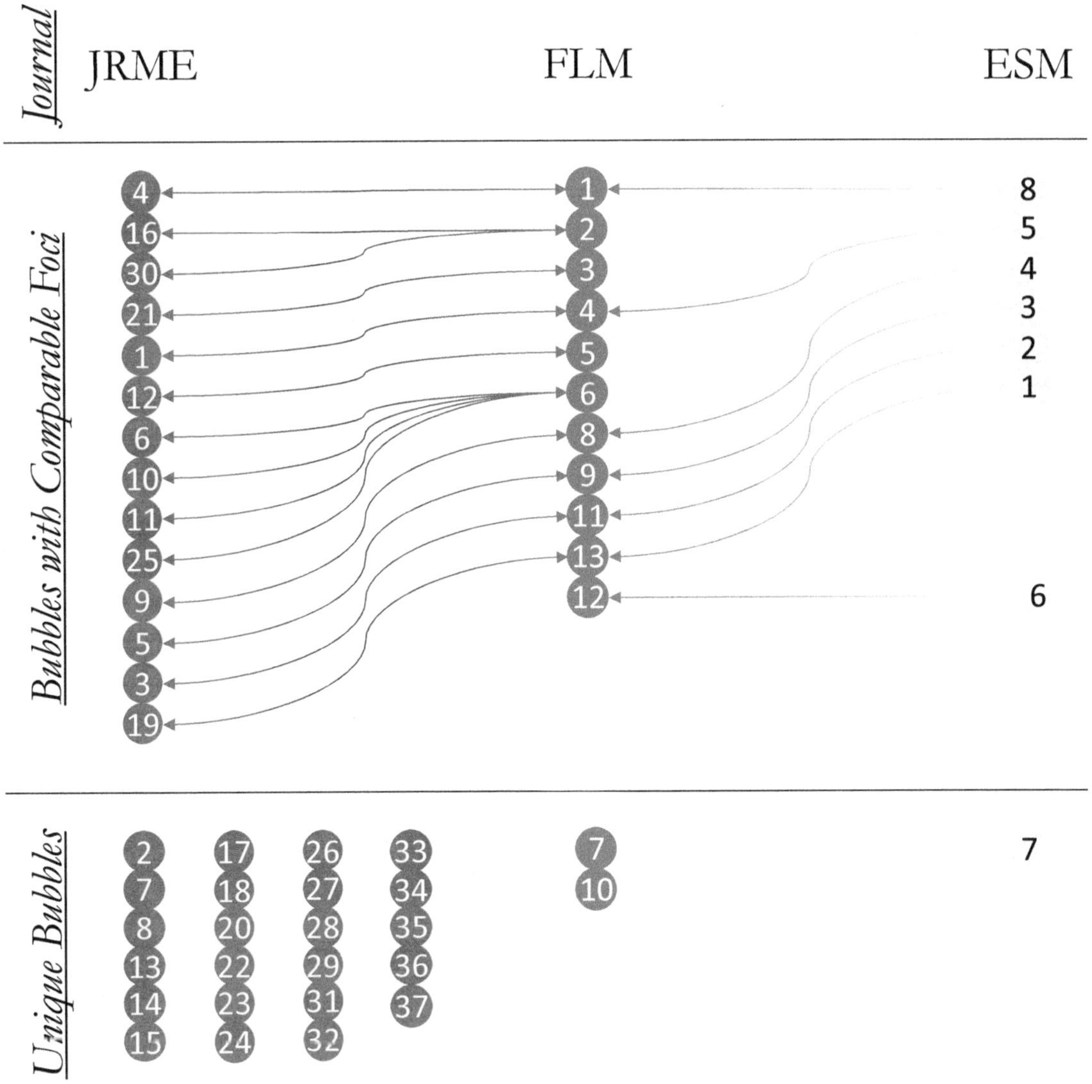

This is not, however, to suggest that there are no articles in FLM or ESM that consider, for example, professional development. In fact, McCloskey's "Caring in professional development projects for mathematics teachers: An example of stimulation and harmonizing" (FLM, 2012) is explicitly about professional development. McCloskey's article is classified within the philosophy of mathematics education bubble within FLM because of its numerous connections to references on an ethics of caring (e.g., Noddings, 1984) that draw it closer to other articles within the philosophy of mathematics education bubble. This suggests that there are not a sufficient number of articles within the FLM that cite literature explicitly about professional development for them to separate from the other bubbles.

Similarly, the lack of a corresponding bubble within JRME or ESM that are named "making meaning of mathematics" does not suggest that these topics are not addressed. Instead, there are bubbles such as the "meaning of equality" in the JRME which suggests that there has been sufficient work within the "making meaning" bubble that these more specialized foci have emerged.

As this comparison between journal shows, that while there is considerable overlap, there is no single grain size, topic, method, theory, or concept that unifies mathematics education research: each journal includes topics not discussed, or not discussed to the same extent, elsewhere. Recalling each journal's aims to be a "forum for disciplined inquiry into the teaching and learning of mathematics" (JRME), "to stimulate reflection on mathematics education at all levels" (FLM), and to "[present] new ideas and developments of major importance to those working in the field" (ESM), it is clear that each contribute to mathematics education yet each represent mathematics education research in a different way. Together with the analysis of Chapter 4 which showed that what constitutes mathematics education research has shifted across time, then, this discussion indicates that what currently constitutes mathematics education research is not fixed. This begins to restore the role of chance in our field, our field's focus has shifted as the interests of many researchers shifted across time. I discuss the implications of this after comparing these results to another analysis which attempted to characterize the past five decades of the JRME and ESM, but from a linguistic perspective.

Comparison to Other Research

In 2018, Inglis and Foster published "Five Decades of Mathematics Education Research" in the JRME. In their analysis, Inglis and Foster conducted a topic modelling analysis (e.g., Grimmer & Stewart, 2013) on the full text of every article published in the JRME and ESM since their inception. A topic modelling analysis considers which words co-occur within a text and extracts patterns of co-occurrence to find topics: lists of frequently co-occurring words that suggest some collection of research is related. To implement topic modelling, there is a certain reductionist assumption about language: the "so-called 'bag of words' model of text, which dramatically simplifies language" (Inglis & Foster, 2018, p. 469). This 'bag of words' model for natural language processing can be characterized thus:

> there is a finite number of words that we can use in our writing and since words have particular meanings, the use of certain words in some contexts is more likely than in others. For example, the word triangle is more likely to occur in a geometry paper than an algebra paper. Therefore, we can look at all the words that are used in an article, and since articles that are topically similar will use similar words in similar frequencies, articles with similar 'bags of words' can be clustered into a 'topic'.

This is the essence of Inglis and Foster's analysis.

For each topic, the authors include a list of the top 20 characteristic words (from the bag of words) and one single article that the highest proportion of topic words (when compared to the total number of words in the article). For example, Inglis and Foster's first topic (alphabetically) is "Addition and Subtraction." This topic's top 20 characteristic words include children, number, children's, addition, counting, subtraction, strategies, child, numbers, strategy, arithmetic, problems, mental, task, count, facts, instruction, development, tasks, & ten (p. 473) and the single article with the highest proportion of these words is Baroody's JRME article "The development of counting strategies for single-digit addition" (1987). My own JRME analysis in chapter 4 places Baroody's article into a bubble that I have named Arithmetic. This suggests some level of agreement between the two methods; next, I further compare the topics identified by Inglis and Foster to the bubbles I identified.

The 28 topics identified by Inglis & Foster's analysis include: (1) Addition and subtraction, (2) Analysis, (3) Constructivism, (4) Curriculum (especially reform), (5) Didactical Theories, (6) Discussions, Reflections, and essays, (7) Dynamic geometry and visualization, (8) Equity, (9) Euclidean Geometry, (10) Experimental designs, (11) Formal Analyses, (12) Gender, (13) History and Obituaries, (14) Mathematics education around the world, (15) Multilingual learners, (16) Novel assessment, (17) Observations of classroom discussion, (18) Problem solving, (19) Proof and argumentation, (20) Quantitative assessment of reasoning, (21) Rational numbers, (22) School algebra, (23) Semiotics and embodied cognition, (24) Sociocultural theory, (25) Spatial Reasoning, (26) Statistics and probability, (27) Teachers' knowledge and beliefs, and (28) Teaching approaches. I present this list of topics, together with corresponding bubbles from my analysis in Table 7. When the connection is not direct from the language of the topic/bubble, I include some discussion of the reason for the association.

Table 7. Table Correlating Inglis & Foster's topics of mathematics education research (2018) with the Bubbles Identified in This Analysis.

Topic Identified by Inglis & Foster (2018)	*Corresponding Bubble from My Analysis*
Addition and subtraction	JRME 1980s 10 – Arithmetic
Analysis	JRME 2010s 11 – Limits & Calculus [function, limit, and calculus are among the top words of the 'analysis' topic]
Constructivism	JRME 2000s 28 - Constructivist Teaching and Learning
Curriculum (especially reform)	JRME 2010s 18 - Mathematics Curriculum
Didactical Theories	JRME 2010s 23 - Mathematics Teachers and Teaching and JRME 2000s 10 - Pedagogy and Learning
Discussions, Reflections, and essays	None.
Dynamic geometry and visualization	JRME 1980s 5 - Children's Geometry [includes articles using LOGO]
Equity	JRME 2010s 19 - Equity and Social Justice
Euclidean Geometry	JRME 1970s 13 – Geometry and Secondary Mathematics Learning
Experimental designs	JRME 1970s 10 - Quantitative Research Methods
Formal Analyses	None.
Gender	JRME 2010s 32 - Gender and Achievement
History and Obituaries	None.
Mathematics education around the world	JRME 2000s 11 - Social Context of Learning: International Perspectives, JRME 1980s 14 - International Policy and Responses
Multilingual learners	JRME 2010s 14 - English Language Learner's Identity & Participation
Novel assessment	None.

Table 7 (cont.)

Topic Identified by Inglis & Foster (2018)	Corresponding Bubble from My Analysis
Observations of classroom discussion	JRME 2010s 21 – Mathematics Identity [this bubble includes positioning, discourse, and group interaction which are characteristic words for this topic]
Problem solving	JRME 1990s 12 - Problem Solving
Proof and argumentation	JRME 2010s 1 – Proof and argumentation and ESM 2010s 5 – Proof and Argumentation
Quantitative assessment of reasoning	JRME 1970s 11 - Factors for Differences in Achievement
Rational numbers	JRME 1980s 13 - Proportional Reasoning [includes rational numbers]
School algebra	JRME 2010s 25 - Algebra
Semiotics and embodied cognition	JRME 2010s 4 - Mathematical Discourse and ESM 2010s 6 - Embodied Cognition and Mathematical Objects
Sociocultural theory	JRME 2010s 16 - Sociocultural Learning
Spatial Reasoning	JRME 1970s 2 - Piaget's Spatial Concepts
Statistics and probability	JRME 2000s 21 - Data & Statistics and 32 - Probability
Teachers' knowledge and beliefs	JRME 2010s 9 - Mathematics Knowledge for Teaching and JRME 1990s 13 - Teachers of Mathematics [1990s 13 includes work on teacher belief]
Teaching approaches	Among others: JRME 2010s 7 - Teaching's Influence on Learning, and JRME 1970s 8 - Effect of Activity-Oriented Instruction

Of the topics identified by Inglis & Foster, there are only four categories for which my analysis did not identify one (or more) corresponding categories: (1) Discussions, Reflections, and Essays; (2) Formal Analyses; (3) History and Obituaries; and (4) Novel Assessment. The first of these categories seems to be made up of letters to the editor and other such non-research commentaries that were excluded from my analysis. Indeed, the 'article' with the highest proportion of words from this topic in Inglis & Foster's study was Roberts' "Letter to the Editor" (JRME, 2001). Likewise, the third of these included obituaries which were also excluded from my analysis. The reference article that Inglis & Foster includes is a 1990 ESM article which is beyond the scope of my ESM analysis. Within the articles published in the JRME 1970-2019 or ESM 2010-2016, there were an insufficient number of articles, drawing from some shared research base on history of mathematics education, to establish its own research bubble. The final two, Formal Analyses and Novel Assessment, however, warrant further discussion.

These two bubbles, Formal Analyses and Novel Assessment, were both instances of language that is unfamiliar to me and did not share a clear connection to any of the bubbles identified by my analysis. The first topic, formal analysis, was identified by characteristic words such as set, concept, elements, structure, group, and relation suggesting that these articles are related to set theory and the grouping of elements into sets. The representative article indicated by Inglis and Foster's study was Steiner and Kauffman's ZDM article on some classroom games that the authors developed to introduce modern/abstract algebra concepts such as groups of elements and operations defined on those elements (1969). Within the articles published in the JRME 1970-2019 or ESM 2010-2016, there were an insufficient number of articles on abstract algebra to establish it as its own research bubble.

The second topic, novel assessment, was identified by characteristic words such as task, assessment, modelling, competence, quality, performance, etc. indicating this topic's focus on assessment writ large. The representative article is Frejd's ZDM review on the assessment of mathematical modelling (2013). Within my ZDM analysis, this article is located within the "mathematics beyond the classroom" bubble. This occurs because of Frejd's work citing, and being cited by, other studies on the use and development of mathematical models outside of the mathematics classroom. For example, Frejd and Bergsten (ZDM, 2016) conducted interviews with professional mathematical modelers to characterize the types of professional mathematical modelling tasks.

The existence of these two topics identified in Inglis and Foster's study emphasizes the complementarity of different research approaches. Just as they have two topics that I did not identify, my study identified research foci within the field that Inglis and Foster did not. For example, within the JRME 2010s, my citation network analysis in Chapter 4 also identified a bubble on Professional Development (JRME 2010s 2) and two on specific mathematical concepts: the meaning of equality (JRME 2010s 6) and negative numbers (JRME 2010s 10). Similarly, my analysis identified four bubbles on race and mathematics education, each with their own particular approach: culturally relevant mathematics (JRME 2010s 6), racial identity and success (JRME 2010s 13), racialized mathematics achievement remediation (JRME 2010s 13), and urban equity and technology (JRME 2010s 33). Likewise, my analysis identified two bubbles on identity—mathematics identity (JRME 2010s 21) and girls' identity (JRME 2010s, 36)—and three on achievement: achievement gap (JRME 2010s 15); children's achievement, intervention, and trajectories (JRME 2010s 17); and mathematics achievement (JRME 2010s 20). For the sake of brevity, I will restrict this discussion to the 2010s JRME bubbles only, but expanding this would further emphasize the advantages that a citation network analysis has over a purely linguistic analysis.

In addition to our divergence in method, these researchers also adopt a different theoretical frame on research and its evolution than I have. Inglis and Foster adopt Lakatos' concept of research programme (1978), which decomposes the social project of research into its (1) hard core, (2) protective belt, and (3) heuristic. The hard core of a research programme is "collection of key assumptions and beliefs accepted by those who work within the programme" (Inglis & Foster, 2018, p. 464). According to Inglis and Foster, Lakatos conceives of a collection of auxillary assumptions, beliefs, and hypotheses that protect the hard core from anomalous evidence and falsification, which he calls the protective belt. Lastly, the heuristic is "collection of methods and problem-solving techniques that researchers within the programme use to make progress" (Inglis & Foster, 2018, p. 465). Lakatos' research programme, in his view, was "a means by which to maintain Popper's belief that science is a rational process while retaining Kuhn's much greater fidelity to history" (p. 464) in their accounts of how academic disciplines make progress. As I mentioned in chapter 2, part of my hope of bringing Sloterdijk's metaphor of bubbles and foams to this research was to elevate the role of chance in the development of the field of mathematics education research.

As discussed in chapter 2, and as illustrated by Fendler's (2010) chemical metaphor for Foucault's power-knowledge, knowledges are produced by applying theories to observations within particular contexts. In this study, knowledges about mathematics education research as a field were produced by applying Foucaultian, Rancièrean, and Sloterdijkian theories to citation data within this particular mathematics education context and from my particular perspective. Similarly, Inglis and Foster produces knowledges by applying Lakatos' ideas on research programmes and topic modelling to article text within their particular context and from their particular perspective (see Figure 74).

Figure 74. Equations of Foucault's theory of power-knowledge showing my application of theories (top) and Inglis and Foster's application of theories (bottom).

$$\textbf{Foucault} \atop \textbf{Rancière} \atop \textbf{Sloterdijk} \frac{\text{citation data}}{\text{mathematics education research context}} \longrightarrow \text{knowledges}$$
$$\textbf{researcher context \& perpsectives}$$

$$\textbf{Lakatos} \atop \textbf{Topic Modelling} \frac{\text{article text}}{\text{mathematics education research context}} \longrightarrow \text{knowledges}$$
$$\textbf{researcher context \& perpsectives}$$

These knowledges are not competing but complementary: analyzing the language used in research articles yields one particular insight and set of knowledges about the focus of the field of mathematics education research while my citation network approach provided another. Inglis and Foster conclude with "we have argued that mathematics education would benefit from greater interaction between the experimental psychology and sociocultural research programmes" but my recommendation will be much loftier. My interest has been in the interrogation of what counts as mathematics education research; I turn to that next.

Politics of Mathematics Education Research

> The politics of literature thus means that literature as literature is involved in this partition [partage] of the visible and the sayable, in this intertwining of being, doing and saying that frames a polemical common world (Rancière, 2004, p. 11)

Recall from Chapter 2 that, for Rancière, politics is not the study of systems of governance of nation-states. Democracy is more nuanced than δῆμος+ κράτος (people+power), or the power of the people. When we refer to the people, or the demos, there is an assumption of who is included. In ancient Greece, the *demos* excluded women, foreigners, and slaves.

When we refer to mathematics education research, the output of a group of people called mathematics education researchers, there is embedded within that notion of mathematics education researcher a belonging. Who are those researchers that are included? Who are those people whose research is heard? Whose fantasy becomes part of the common world, the shared social activity of mathematics education research?

As he states in the epigraph, the politics of literature is literature's involvement in the partage of the sensible. When something is written and its author decrees it as literature, it contributes towards (re)defining what literature is. This is precisely the politics of mathematics education research that I enact here. What I have presented is mathematics education research. It is mathematics education research because I have called it such, and it, simultaneously, redefines what we can call mathematics education research. When the first author to write about the mental models for addition and subtraction published their work in the JRME, what constituted mathematics education research was perturbed: there was no such thing before, and then there was. When the first researchers introduced cognitively guided instruction and suggested (rather radically) that children had ideas worth exploring, and building upon, mathematics education was perturbed. When the first mathematics education researchers argued that an individual's identities were relevant to what was happening in the mathematics classroom, that those identities were relevant when talking about the mathematics they were learning, mathematics education research was perturbed again. And now, when I say that mathematics education research is whatever we make of it, mathematics education research is perturbed.

Whenever we call something mathematics education research, we either reify existing lines along which something is included or excluded from the foam of mathematics education research, or we perturb them. We can blow additional air into bubbles that exist, we can reach in with our fingers and pop them, or we can blow—and hope—that a new bubble will emerge. The beauty of it all is that we cannot be sure what will happen. We can, however, be sure that things can change. Mathematics education research has not, and does not currently, have a fixed definition. Mathematics education research does not have a fixed, and proper, object of study. And it should not:

> The main interest in life and work is to become someone else that you were not in the beginning…What is true for writing and for a love relationship is true also for life. The game is worthwhile insofar as we don't know what will be the end. (Foucault, 1988, p. 10).

The reader will be highly disappointed if they were hoping I would offer a final, totalizing, all-encompassing definition of mathematics education research. Mathematics education research, as a field, is worthwhile insofar as we continue to change. The instant we draw a line and say, "on this side is mathematics education research and on the other is something else entirely," we lose the game. As soon as we say, *this* is and *that* is not, we are making a claim about what we can see, say, do, and think in the name of mathematics education research.

I am not saying that mathematics education research in the 1970s was not mathematics education research. I am not saying that what we do today in the name of mathematics education research is not mathematics education research. What I am saying is that we need to think of mathematics education research in time. What we called mathematics education research then was limited. What we call mathematics education research today is limited. And what we call mathematics education research tomorrow will be limited. But it can be less limited, less restrictive, and freer:

> My role - and that is too emphatic a word - is to show people that they are much freer than they feel, that people accept as truth, as evidence, some themes which have been built up at a certain moment during history, and that this so-called evidence can be criticized and destroyed. To change something in the minds of people - that's the role of an intellectual. (Foucault, 1988, p. 10).

Now, my role, and that is not too emphatic of a word, is to perturb the partage of the sensible that outlines what we, as mathematics education researchers, can see, say, think, and do in the name of mathematics education research. My role is not to define mathematics education research, it is our role to redefine it, to perturb what we think mathematics education research can be. Together, or as individuals blowing our own bubbles, we can change the foam, we can change the field. The journal aims and goals have pointed to some specter of a field called mathematics education research and said "as mathematics education researchers, we do this. You can do that, but you won't be doing that here." Yes, I will. And, yes, you can, too.

But, "I don't want to become a prophet and say, 'Please sit down, what I have to say is very important.' I have come to discuss our common work" (Foucault, 1988, p. 9). And I have a lot to discuss. When we refer to the field of mathematics education research, we are referring to a common world. When I call myself a mathematics education researcher, I am not making noise nor am I discussing things located in my own fantasy. I am a mathematics education researcher and I will be heard.

Looking Back at This Text

It's hard to say whether a book has been understood or misunderstood. Because, after all, perhaps the person who wrote the book is the one who misunderstood it. Because the reader would not be the one who understood or misunderstood it. I don't think an author should lay down the law about his own book. (Foucault, 2011, p. 385)

In this study, I drew on multiple theories, I used non-tradidtional methods, I generated maps of the field, I gave bubbles in each foam a name, and I argued that what we call mathematics education research is volatile. I am not arguing that these are the only theories on which we can draw. I am not arguing that these methods are best. I am not arguing that these maps, these names given to the bubbles are perfect; that they could not be refined or that no alternative can presented. In fact, I hope they are refined, I hope mathematics education researcher do present alternatives. I am not laying down the law about what I present, I am merely showing you what I see, telling you what I think about it, and telling you what I make of it all. Foucault responded to his critics:

It was argued that I had not properly described Buffon or his work and that my handling of Marx was pitifully inadequate in terms of the totality of his thought. *Although these objections were obviously justified, they ignored the task I had set myself*. I had no intention of describing Buffon or Marx or of reproducing their statements or implicit meanings, but, simply stated, I wanted to locate the rules that formed a certain number of concepts and theoretical relationships in their works. In addition, it was argued that I had created monstrous families by bringing together names as disparate as Buffon and Linnaeus or in placing Cuvier next to Darwin in defiance of the most readily observable family resemblances and natural ties. This objection also seems inappropriate since I had never tried to establish a genealogical table of exceptional individuals, nor was I concerned in forming an intellectual daguerreotype of the scholar or naturalist of the seventeenth and eighteenth century. In fact, I had no intention of forming any family, whether holy or perverse. On the contrary, I wanted to determine—a much more modest task—the functional conditions of specific discursive practices. (Foucault, 1969, p. 299, emphasis added)

166

And it may be argued that I have not adequately described the research within each bubble, or adequately unpacked each of the foams. The disturbed reader (Wheatley, 2005), the disoriented reader (Butler, 2000) might say that I created profane collections of articles, that I brought together totally unrelated ideas and put them together in a single bubble: a bubble that does not, *cannot*, make sense. But, to do so misses the point. My point is not to say that those bubbles and foams *were*, that these bubbles and foams *are*. My point is to say that what we can do in the name of mathematics education research need not be the rational culmination, the inevitable conclusion of what came before. What we can do is up to us.

Parting Thoughts

> If you knew when you began a book what you would say at the end, do you think that you would have the courage to write it? (Foucault, 1988, p. 9).

I know I would not have had the courage to begin. But, I did. I started on this exploratory study, on this cartographic expedition to see what *was*. Along the way I begin to notice things, that things were not as neat as they might want us to think they are. Mathematics education research *has* changed. And I surely hope that it continues to change. But how things change is not only up to me—though I hope some part of it is. It is up to *us*. What have been Rancière's words, are now my own:

What do you see?

What do you think about it?

What do you make of it?

References

Anzaldúa, G. (2012). *Borderlands: The New Mestiza*. Aunt Lute Books.

Aria, M., & Cuccurullo, C. (2017). bibliometrix: An R-tool for comprehensive science mapping analysis. *Journal of Informetrics*, 11(4), 959-975. https://doi.org/10.1016/j.joi.2017.08.007

Ausubel, D. P. (1960). The use of advance organizers in the learning and retention of meaningful verbal learning. *Journal of Educational Psychology*, (51)5, 367-72. https://doi.org/10.1037/h0046669

Barwell, R., & Reid, D. A. (2019). *For the Learning of Mathematics*: An Introduction to the Journal and the Writing within It. In Kaiser & Presmeg [Eds.], *Compendium for Early Career Researchers in Mathematics Education* (pp. 393-405). Springer.

Bastian, M., Heymann, S., & Jacomy, M. (2009, March). Gephi: an open source software for exploring and manipulating networks. In *Proceedings of the Third International Association for the Advancement of Artificial Intelligence Conference on Weblogs and Social Media*. AAAI.

Blondel, V. D., Guillaume, J. L., Lambiotte, R., & Lefebvre, E. (2008). Fast unfolding of communities in large networks. *Journal of Statistical Mechanics: Theory and Experiment*, 2008(10), 10008. https://doi.org/10.1088/1742-5468/2008/10/P10008

Bondy, A. & Murty, U. S. R. (2008). *Graph Theory*. Springer.

Borch, C. (2010). Organizational Atmospheres: Foam, Affect and Architecture. *Organization*, 17(2), 223–241. https://doi.org/10.1177/1350508409337168

Bourdieu, P. (2001). *Science of science and reflexivity*. University of Chicago Press.

Bruce, C.D., Davis, B., Sinclair, N., McGarvey, L., Hallowell, D., Drefs, M., Francis, K., Hawes, Z., Moss, J., Mulligan, J., Okamoto, Y., Whiteley, W., & Woolcott, G. (2017). Understanding gaps in research networks: using 'spatial reasoning' as a window into the importance of networked educational research. *Educational Studies in Mathematics* 95, 143–16. https://doi.org/10.1007/s10649-016-9743-2

Butler, J. (2000). The value of being disturbed. *Theory & Event*, 4(1). https://www.muse.jhu.edu/article/32568

Cai, J., Hwang, S., & Robison, V. (2019). *Journal for Research in Mathematics Education*: Practical Guides for Promoting and Disseminating Significant Research in Mathematics Education. In Kaiser & Presmeg [Eds.], Compendium for Early Career Researchers in Mathematics Education (pp. 425-42). Springer.

Chen, C. (2003). *Mapping scientific frontiers*. Springer.

Chen, C. (2006). CiteSpace II: Detecting and visualizing emerging trends and transient patterns in scientific literature. *Journal of the American Society for information Science and Technology*, 57(3), 359-377. https://doi.org/10.1002/asi.20317

Clarivate. (2019). HistCite: No longer in active development or officially supported. Retrieved from https://support.clarivate.com/ScientificandAcademicResearch/s/article/HistCite-No-longer-in-active-development-or-officially-supported

Cobo, M. J., López-Herrera, A. G., Herrera-Viedma, E., & Herrera, F. (2011). An approach for detecting, quantifying, and visualizing the evolution of a research field: A practical application to the fuzzy sets theory field. *Journal of Informetrics*, 5(1), 146-166. https://doi.org/10.1016/j.joi.2010.10.002

Ding, Y., Chowdhury, G. G., & Foo, S. (2001). Bibliometric cartography of information retrieval research by using co-word analysis. *Information Processing & Management*, 37(6), 817-842. https://doi.org/10.1016/S0306-4573(00)00051-0

Doll, W. E., Jr. (1989). Foundations for a post-modern curriculum. *Journal of Curriculum Studies*, 21(3), 243-53. https://doi.org/10.1080/0022027890210304

Dubbs, C. (2016). A Queer Turn in Mathematics Education Research: Centering the Experience of Marginalized Queer Students. In *Proceedings of the 38th Conference of the North-American Chapter of the International Group for the Psychology of Mathematics Education* (PME-NA). PME-NA.

ESM Editors. (2012). Advice to Prospective Authors. *Educational Studies in Mathematics*, 81(1), vii-viii. Retrieved from www.jstor.org/stable/23257769

Euler, L. (1741). Solutio problematis ad geometriam situs pertinentis. *Commentarii Academiae Scientiarum Petropolitanae*, 128-140.

Feinberg, J. (2014). Wordle [Computer software]. Retrieved from www.wordle.net

Fendler, L. (2014). *Michel Foucault*. Bloomsbury Publishing.

Foucault, M. (1969). What is an Author?. In J. Marsh, J.D. Caputo & M. Westphal (Eds.) (1992), *Modernity and its discontents*. 299-314. Fordham University Press.

Foucault, M. (1988). Truth, power, self: An interview with Michel Foucault. In *Technologies of the self: A seminar with Michel Foucault* (1988). 9-15. University of Massachusetts Press.

Foucault, M. (2011). The gay science. *Critical Inquiry*, 37(3), 385-403. https://doi.org/10.1086/659351

Garfield, E. (1955). Citation indexes for science: A new dimension in documentation through association of ideas. *Science*, 122(3159), 108–111. https://doi.org/10.1126/science.122.3159.108

Garfield, E. (2009). From the science of science to Scientometrics visualizing the history of science with *HistCite* software. *Journal of Informetrics*, 3(3), 173-9. https://doi.org/10.1016/j.joi.2009.03.009

Goos, M. (2019). *Educational Studies in Mathematics*: Shaping the Field. In Kaiser & Presmeg [Eds.], Compendium for Early Career Researchers in Mathematics Education (pp. 377-91). Springer.

Grimmer, J., & Stewart, B. M. (2013). Text as data: The promise and pitfalls of automatic content analysis methods for political texts. *Political Analysis*, 21(3), 267–297. https://doi.org/10.1093/pan/mps028

Groves, K. S., & Vance, C. M. (2015). Linear and nonlinear thinking: A multidimensional model and measure. *The Journal of Creative Behavior*, 49(2), 111-136. https://doi.org/10.1002/jocb.60

Hanna, G., & Sidoli, N. (2002). The story of ESM. *Educational Studies in Mathematics*, 50(2), 123-156. https://doi.org/10.1023/A:1021162617070

Hinze, S. (1994). Bibliographical cartography of an emerging interdisciplinary discipline: The case of bioelectronics. *Scientometrics*, 29(3), 353-376. https://doi.org/10.1007/BF02033445

Inglis, M., & Foster, C. (2018). Five decades of mathematics education research. *Journal for Research in Mathematics Education*, 49(4), 462-500. https://doi.org/10.5951/jresematheduc.49.4.0462

Garfield, E. (1981). *ISI Atlas of Science: Biochemistry and molecular biology*. Institute for Scientific Information, Philadelphia.

Jacomy, M., Venturini, T., Heymann, S., & Bastian, M. (2014). ForceAtlas2, a continuous graph layout algorithm for handy network visualization designed for the Gephi software. *PloS one*, 9(6). https://doi.org/10.1371/journal.pone.0098679

Kaiser, G., & Presmeg, N. (Eds.). (2019). *Compendium for Early Career Researchers in Mathematics Education*. Springer.

Lakatos, I. (1978). The methodology of scientific research programmes. *Philosophical Papers Volume 1*. Cambridge University Press. https://doi.org/10.1017/CBO9780511621123

Leatham, K. R. (2015). Observations on citation practices in mathematics education research. *Journal for Research in Mathematics Education*, 46(3), 253-269. https://doi.org/10.5951/jresematheduc.46.3.0253

Lima, M. (2013). *Visual Complexity: Mapping Patterns of Information*. Princeton Architectural Press.

Taylor, D. F. (2013). *Visualization in Modern Cartography*. Elsevier Science.

Machi, L. A., McEvoy, B. T. (2016). *The Literature Review: Six Steps to Success*. SAGE Publications.

Mauthner, M. (2000). Snippets and silences: Ethics and reflexivity in narratives of sistering. *International Journal of Social Research Methodology*, 3(4), 287-306. https://doi.org/10.1080/13645570050178585

Mercator, G. (1595) *Atlas sive Cosmographicae meditationes de fabrica mvndi et fabricati figvra*. Dvisbvrgi Clivorvm. Retrieved from the Library of Congress, https://www.loc.gov/item/map55000728/

Narin, F., Carpenter, M., & Berlt, N. C. (1972). Interrelationships of scientific journals. *Journal of the American Society for Information Science*, 23(5), 323-331. https://doi.org/10.1002/asi.4630230508

Newman, M. E. (2006). Modularity and community structure in networks. *Proceedings of the national academy of sciences*, 103(23), 8577-8582. https://doi.org/10.1073/pnas.0601602103

Nivens, R. A., & Otten, S. (2017). Assessing journal quality in mathematics education. *Journal for Research in Mathematics Education*, 48(4), 348-368. https://doi.org/10.5951/jresematheduc.48.4.0348

Noddings, N. (1984). *Caring: A Relational Approach to Ethics and Moral Education*. University of California Press.

Noyons, E., & Van Raan, A. (1994). Bibliometric cartography of scientific and technological developments of an R & D field: The case of optomechatronics. *Scientometrics*, 30(1), 157-173. https://doi.org/10.1007/BF02017220

Nylander, E., Österlund, L., & Fejes, A. (2018). Exploring the adult learning research field by analysing who cites whom. *Vocations and learning*, 11(1), 113-131. https://doi.org/10.1007/s12186-017-9181-z

Özkaya, A. (2018). Bibliometric Analysis of the Studies in the Field of Mathematics Education. *Educational Research and Reviews*, 13(22), 723-734. https://doi.org/10.5897/ERR2018.3603

Pais, A., & Valero, P. (2012). Researching research: Mathematics education in the political. Educational Studies in Mathematics, 80(1-2), 9-24. https://doi.org/10.1007/s10649-012-9399-5

Pan, X., Yan, E., Cui, M., & Hua, W. (2018). Examining the usage, citation, and diffusion patterns of bibliometric mapping software: A comparative study of three tools. *Journal of Informetrics*, 12(2), 481-493. https://doi.org/10.1016/j.joi.2018.03.005

Parks, A. N., & Schmeichel, M. (2012). Obstacles to addressing race and ethnicity in the mathematics education literature. *Journal for Research in Mathematics Education*, 43(3), 238-252. https://doi.org/10.5951/jresematheduc.43.3.0238

Prado, C. G. (1995). *Starting with Foucault: An Introduction to Genealogy*. Taylor & Francis.

Price, D. J. D. S. (1965). Networks of scientific papers. Science, 510-515. https://doi.org/10.1126/science.149.3683.510

Rancière, J. (1991). *The Ignorant Schoolmaster: Five Lessons in Intellectual Emancipation*. Stanford University Press.

Rancière, J. (1999). *Disagreement: Politics and Philosophy*. University of Minnesota Press.

Rancière, J. (2000). History and the Art System (interview with Yan Ciret). *Art Press*, 258, 18-23.

Rancière, J. (2004/2009). *The Politics of Aesthetics: The Distribution of the Sensible*. Bloomsbury Publishing.

Ranciere, J. (2009). *The Emancipated Spectator*. Verso Books.

Rancière, J. (2011). Against an ebbing tide: An interview with Jacques Rancière. In Bowman & Stamp [Eds.], *Reading Rancière*, (p. 238-251). Continuum.

Fruchterman, T. M., & Reingold, E. M. (1991). Graph drawing by force-directed placement. *Software: Practice and experience*, 21(11), 1129-1164.

Riaz, F. & Ali, K. M. (2011). Applications of Graph Theory in Computer Science. In *Proceedings of the Third International Conference on Computational Intelligence, Communication Systems and Networks*, (pp. 142-145). https://doi.org/10.1109/CICSyN.2011.40

Scott, J. (2017). *Social Network Analysis*. SAGE Publications.

Sloterdijk, P. (2011). *Bubbles*. Semiotext(e).

Sloterdijk, P. (2015). *Globes*. Semiotext(e).

Sloterdijk, P. (2016). *Foams*. Semiotext(e).

Standards for Reporting on Empirical Social Science Research in AERA Publications: American Educational Research Association. (2006). *Educational Researcher*, 35(6), 33–40. https://doi.org/10.3102/0013189X035006033

Standards for Reporting on Humanities-Oriented Research in AERA Publications: American Educational Research Association. (2009). Educational Researcher, 38(6), 481–486. https://doi.org/10.3102/0013189X09341833

Van Eck, N. J., & Waltman, L. (2014). CitNetExplorer: A new software tool for analyzing and visualizing citation networks. *Journal of Informetrics*, 8(4), 802-823. https://doi.org/10.1016/j.joi.2014.07.006

Van Eck, N. J., & Waltman, L. (2017). Citation-based clustering of publications using CitNetExplorer and VOSviewer. *Scientometrics*, 111(2), 1053-1070. https://doi.org/10.1007/s11192-017-2300-7

Waltman, L., Van Eck, N. J., & Noyons, E. C. (2010). A unified approach to mapping and clustering of bibliometric networks. *Journal of Informetrics*, 4(4), 629-635. https://doi.org/10.1016/j.joi.2010.07.002

Wang, Y., & Bowers, A. J. (2016). Mapping the field of educational administration research: A journal citation network analysis. *Journal of Educational Administration*, 54(3), 242-269. https://doi.org/10.1108/JEA-02-2015-0013

Wheatley, M. J. (2005). *Finding Our Way: Leadership for an Uncertain Time*. Berrett-Koehler Publishers.

Williams, S. R., & Leatham, K. R. (2017). Journal quality in mathematics education. Journal for Research in Mathematics Education, 48(4), 369-396. https://doi.org./10.5951/jresematheduc.48.4.0369